# BEAUTIFUL
# UNIVERSAL
# DESIGN

# BEAUTIFUL UNIVERSAL DESIGN

## A VISUAL GUIDE

Cynthia A. Leibrock

James Evan Terry

John Wiley and Sons, Inc.

New York   Chichester   Weinheim   Brisbane   Singapore   Toronto

*Cover illustration:* Kohler Universal Bathroom, Kohler Design Center, Kohler, Wisconsin; Designed by Cynthia Leibrock, EASY ACCESS, Fort Collins, Colorado, and Mary Beth Rampolla, Architect and Senior Project Designer, Eva Maddox Associates, Inc.

This book is printed on acid-free paper. ∞

Published by John Wiley & Sons, Inc.
Published simultaneously in Canada.

**Library of Congress Cataloging-in-Publication Data**

Leibrock, Cynthia.
    Beautiful universal design : a visual guide / Cynthia Leibrock. —
2nd ed.
        p.    cm.
    Rev. ed. of : Beautiful barrier-free. c1993
    Includes bibliographical references and index.
    ISBN 0-471-29306-7 (cloth : alk. paper)
    1. Architecture and the handicapped—United States.    I. Leibrock,
Cynthia. Beautiful barrier-free. II. Title.
NA2545. A1L45    1998
720' .87—dc21                                                        98–36453

Printed in the United States of America.

10 9 8 7 6 5 4 3 2 1

# CONTENTS

## 10. CASE STUDIES                                          157

# PREFACE

*Make level paths for your feet, so that the lame will not be disabled, but rather healed.*

HEB. 12:12–13 NIV

Universal design implies "it could happen to me."[1] Special needs are for someone else, someone who needs an exception. Universal design is not a specialized design niche accommodating a special user group. It is simply good design, and good design provides maximum opportunity and choice for all users throughout their lives.

Universal design is an ideal that never completely accommodates diversity but moves in that direction. The accommodation is simple and invisible, never segregating by ability or economic means. Universal design is expansive, integrating users into larger groups, opening markets to more consumers, and exceeding code to eliminate disability by design.

## Simplicity

Elaine Ostroff describes universal design as intuitive, simple to use, easy to understand, and tolerant of error.[2] The strict parameters of a universal design may actually inspire simplicity and purity of form. As a minimalist approach, it focuses attention on the user rather than on the equipment or facility.

Universal design requires minimal physical and mental effort by the user. An adaptable, adjustable, or flexible design may not be universal if it requires complicated changes or high physical effort. A movable ramp placed over stairs is an adaptation; it is not a universal solution. Modification is needed before each use, requiring strength and mobility to put the ramp in place.

In an effort to meet differences in user needs, complicated modifications are frequently made to existing products. In many cases these modifications only serve to make the products more difficult to use. Rather than empowering the user by saving time and energy, these technological dreams become maintenance nightmares, consuming time that could be spent in more creative pursuits. These contraptions frequently intimidate rather than support, reinforcing a feeling of inadequacy. In the process, they become visual advertisements of disability and age.

## Invisibility

Universal design is silent and invisible. Although it must be accessible and barrier free, it must go further to quietly meet the needs of all users. A silent and invisible design isn't labeled by complicated signage or advertised as "for the elderly and disabled." It is not a design prescription for a specific disease but a panacea that "heals" many diseases and accommodates many users without singling out anyone.

## Maximum, Not Minimum Design

Universal design is not a new term for code compliance. Polly Welch maintains that universal design is an alternative to the prevailing paradigms of minimum standards and exceptions to the norm. She goes on to suggest that designers have historically tended to interpret minimum standards as maximums, particularly when solutions beyond the minimum might result in higher cost.[3]

Design standards like those adopted under the Americans with Disabilities Act (ADA) are minimum standards. They are a good start, but they still separate us into special user groups, placing people with disabilities in one toilet stall and the rest in another, people in wheelchairs on the ramp while others quickly use the stairs. The ADA does not mandate a gradual slope to an entrance used by all. An ADA-compliant ramp can be so long and steep that over two thirds of people in wheelchairs cannot use it.[4]

Within the next 20 years, most boomers will personally experience the need for accessibility. They will be appalled at these minimum standards, as appalled as we are today by the following piece of legislation:

> No person who is diseased, maimed, mutilated, or in any way deformed as to be a disgusting or unsightly object or an improper person is to be allowed in or on the public ways of this city or shall expose himself to view under penalty of not less than $1 nor more than $50 for each offense.

Known as "the ugly law," this municipal ordinance existed in some cities in the United States as late as 1973. At one point in our history, this was the norm, much as code is the norm today. Universal design does more than is expected by the norm, surpassing the minimum to truly meet human needs.

## Integration

Universal design does not segregate. It encourages the participation of many users, many abilities. It can bring us together as we address our differences. Redundant solutions, like a turnstile for one group and a gate for another, take a separate-but-equal approach. Well-meaning designers often create barrier-free oddities, visually segregating people with abilities varying from the norm.

Too many older people struggle up stairways rather than make a spectacle of themselves by using the open lift installed to meet their needs. Too many ramps are attached as makeshift accommodations to meet code, destroying the appearance of a building while attracting unwanted attention to users. Too many cumbersome aids become institutional clichés, and too many people are isolated by their use.

## Elimination of Disability

We all have physical and mental differences, but 40 percent of Americans with disabilities seldom leave their homes because of architectural barriers, primarily doors and rest rooms.[5] Many of us have difficulty living independently and are handicapped by problems created not by ability or age but by obstacles in buildings. The decisions of designers and architects can either disable us or offer us a different way of using the space, a way that provides freedom without the "for handicapped people only" stigma.

Universal design solutions transcend ability with innovation. The technology is in place, there is an enormous need, and with a little imagination designers and architects can literally free us from handicaps by design, providing a world without barriers.

## Affordability

If universal design is to offer a choice to all users, it must be affordable. Accessibility may add as little as 1 percent to the total project cost of new construction.[6] These low costs are expected in commercial facilities when accessibility is considered during the initial design. Affordability and accessibility need not be mutually exclusive.

For the purposes of the Internal Revenue Service (IRS), many accessible products and designs are legitimate medical expenses that can be deducted if they exceed 7½ percent of an individual's adjusted gross income.[7] Examples include grab bars, widened doorways, and ramps. Businesses may deduct up to $15,000 per year for cost associated with the removal of qualified architectural barriers. Small businesses may be eligible for an annual $5,000 tax credit to comply with ADA requirements. The tax credit may also be used for consulting fees incurred in removing architectural barriers.[8] On the other hand, the cost of not complying with ADA may be lost customers, missed sales, poor service, complaints, or even lawsuits.

Some universal design expenses are reimbursable through public and private insurance programs. In addition, some states offer aid and low-interest loans through community development block grants and similar programs. The

Paralyzed Veterans of America also offers grants to qualified applicants.

Universal design can also lead to cost reductions. Design intervention is less expensive than staff intervention. In health care facilities, universal design encourages patients to take responsibility for their own health. This do-it-yourself philosophy increases patient efficacy and saves staff time and expense in the process.

Universal design can also be used to save the expense and indignity of institutionalization by accommodating health care at home. Universal homes are accessible to wheelchairs and walkers as well as medical equipment. Insurance and tax incentives continue to encourage use of home health care, covering a wider variety of therapies offered at home. The movement toward service delivery to the home is resulting in an overall reduction in cost as well as a surprising reduction in medical malpractice litigation. As consumers make more of their own health care decisions, the liability of practitioners and the costs of litigation are reduced.

On the average, Americans are impoverished within 13 weeks of institutionalization.[9] A national American Association of Retired Persons (AARP) survey found that 85 percent of older adults never plan to be institutionalized. They plan to stay in their homes and never move. Unfortunately, the same survey found that fully 15 percent of Americans over age 85 had to move into nursing homes.[10]

The Scandinavians maintain that no one should have to live in a nursing home, that no one should have to move along the continuum of care from independent living to assisted living and eventually into skilled nursing. The Bergweg project in Rotterdam, the Netherlands, offers another choice. Bergweg returned 160 nursing home patients to apartments designed universally to accommodate gurneys as well as wheelchairs. Assistance with the activities of daily living is offered in the apartments. The complex was built over an outpatient subacute center offering residents the dignity of returning to their apartments after treatment. This complex is not a medical model with the stigma of "going to the home," not a continuing care retirement facility that becomes an emblem of age and disability. It is not a model that leads to segregation, where independent living does not dine with assisted living and both live with

the threat of being moved into skilled nursing. In this model, all of the residents can receive skilled nursing and no one lives in a nursing home.

This is just one example of the financial and social benefits of universal design. In addition, a universally designed workplace reduces injury, employee turnover, and forced retirement. By retaining older workers, companies can benefit from a trained and reliable workforce while saving the cost of duplicating the medical benefits provided by Medicare. Universal design can also help companies retain injured workers, saving retraining, disabilities payments, and workers' compensation costs. A universally designed workplace expands the labor pool while universally designed products expand the market share.

## Expansion of the Market

Universal design does not limit the market to older and disabled people. It opens the market, transcending age and ability to offer equitable use to all. It does not target a specific market but expands the market to include consumers with a wide range of abilities. According to the U.S. Census Bureau, one out of every five Americans (age 15 and over) needs help seeing, hearing, speaking, walking, using stairs, lifting, carrying objects, getting around, or simply getting out of bed. Most products entirely miss this market.

In addition to helping people with disabilities, universal design accommodates children, people of all sizes, and older people. In 1980, only 10 percent of the U.S. population was age 65 or over. By the year 2020, 22 percent will be in this age group. It is estimated that there will be over 65 million Americans over the age of 65 by the year 2030,[11] and over a million boomers will reach the age of 100. Much market potential remains unexplored.

The second home market is an interesting example of a growing need for universal design. Enlightened boomers are already building homes for future retirement—and using them today as recreational retreats. They realize that affordable, accessible housing will not be available for them unless they build it themselves before retirement. The second home market is heating up as baby-boom parents become empty nesters. Many of these affluent couples have money to spend on themselves. By the year 2000, over four million households will own a second home.

Many of these couples will have no children to care for them when they are older, and most don't want to be cared for by their children. They are more receptive to self-care ideas.

Sixty percent of all disabilities occur after age 60.[12] Eighty percent of older people suffer from chronic limitation of mobility.[13] Fifty percent have arthritis, 29 percent have hearing difficulties, 16 percent have orthopedic impairments, and 17 percent have cataracts.[14] Older people use mobility, hearing, and vision devices at more than four times the rate for the total population,[15] and the fastest-growing demand for universal design may well be found in the aging population. Although most live in denial of these facts, there is less resistance to universal design in a second home that could be used for retirement than in the primary residence. Most people want to age in place, using their second homes as an orthopedic, supporting their independence.

## Older People

Who are "the elderly"? Hal Linden jokes that an elderly person is always ten years older than you are. With medical science extending the life span, Gail Sheehy notes in *New Passages*[16] that a woman boomer who reaches age 50 without cancer or heart disease can expect to see her ninety-second birthday. Japan is aging more rapidly than any other country. It took Japan only 24 years to move from 7 percent to 14 percent of the population over the age of 65. It has taken the United States 70 years to make this same demographic shift. In Japan today, 16 percent of the population is 65 or older, but more than 50 percent of all health care dollars are spent on these older people.[17] For this reason, the Japanese government already offers preferential interest rates on universally designed homes.[18]

Older people value universal designs that are accessible, safe, adaptable, and simple to use, making activities easier and more enjoyable. Products that create activity may actually be preferred over products that save time.[19] Such confusing gadgets as answering machines, videocassette recorders, and automatic teller machines are examples of time-saving products often avoided by this generation of older people.

In the United States, older people already control much of the market. According to the National Research Center of the National Association of Home Builders, ten years ago, senior citizens were estimated to be an $800 billion market and are probably a trillion-dollar market today. Older people are working longer and earning for a longer period of time. Many have rejected retirement as a myth, the dropping out of life at age 65. Some keep working because their identity and the value of their existence is linked to work. Others simply are not able to afford retirement. Many of the boomers are not saving for retirement. Most plan to rely on Social Security and other government assistance, but they are marrying later and having fewer children. This means fewer families to support their elders, fewer working taxpayers to fund the government assistance. Positions grow harder to fill and employers more willing to hire older workers. Employers are evaluating applicants by level of ability rather than age; universal design can significantly increase performance levels.

Universal design can reduce the fear of aging with supportive goods and services that complement capabilities. Those who fear aging are generally afraid that they won't be able to do what they want to do or will be segregated in the process. When addressing this market, designers need to remember that seniors resist housing and products that make them feel different or isolated from the norm. In addition, designers may increase the psychological and social distance between the older population and the rest of society by using the "separate and different" design approach.[20]

## Accommodating a Variety of Abilities

### Arthritis

According to the U.S. Census Bureau, at over 37 million Americans have arthritis[21] and one out of every five Americans will have arthritis by the year 2020. Most people with arthritis are not in wheelchairs. Instead, they have a variance in mobility, including a slower walking speed, a forward center of gravity, a stooped posture, and reduced stamina. This population benefits from products that are ergonomically designed—for instance, chairs that allow the user to lean forward and push off. Building routes should be planned so that occupants are not required to walk long distances. Corridors and doorways must provide adequate space for mobility aids. Elevators should serve all levels, and stairs should have appropriately designed handrails, treads, and risers.

People with arthritis often experience reduced strength, reach, and coordination. Joints may be more rigid, arm extension reduced, and muscle strength diminished. To prevent these differences from disabling, building designers must make modifications. Cabinets and other storage spaces, for example, should be located within easy reach. Controls must be operable with a closed fist; levers must replace knobs, and raised push buttons should be used instead of dials. If furnishings, accessories, or appliances must be movable, lightweight models should be specified.

People with varying levels of strength, reach, and coordination need products that can prevent accidents and increase reaction time in emergencies. Grab bars and handrails should be placed strategically in rooms. Tables and other items should have rounded corners. To reduce accidental burns, appliances should be properly placed and fire-retardant materials employed.

Building systems should be planned to provide increased reaction time and to control fire, security breaches, and other emergency situations. Examples include smoke alarms, motion detectors that trigger exterior lighting, and call systems that can send help at the push of a button.

## Buildings that Enhance Hearing

An estimated 22 million people in the United States have hearing impairments.[22] Many have difficulty with high-frequency sounds and problems separating voices from background noise. Through appropriate building design, ambient and transmitted background noise can be reduced. Static, which interferes with hearing aids, can be controlled. Increased lighting and supportive furniture arrangements can facilitate lip reading and improve the ability to distinguish sign language. Redundant cuing (e.g., signals with lights and vibration as well as auditory cues) can improve communication for people with variances in hearing.

## Designing for Visual Acuity

Almost 16 million Americans with reduced vision also profit from redundant cuing.[23] For example, raised numerals on office doors encourage tactile use. Chimes in elevators provide auditory cues to supplement vision. Reduced vision becomes a handicap when insufficient contrast or illegible detail is specified. Visual acuity can be increased with the use of larger lettering on signs and controls, contrasting molding around doorways, and lighting systems with the flexibility to increase lighting quantity as needed. In providing for people with reduced vision, designers and architects should allow for an increased number of diffused lighting sources to reduce glare. Diffusing finishes should be specified on floor, wall, ceiling, and furniture surfaces. Lighting transitions should be planned between light and dark areas to prevent the dazzle experienced when walking outdoors from a dark interior. Elevated protruding objects like spiral staircases must also be eliminated or shielded. People who use canes cannot detect obstructions over 2 ft 3 in. above the finished floor (a.f.f.) and can easily walk into the sharp corner of each protruding stair.[24]

## Environments for Mental Health

It is known that 2.8 million Americans have schizophrenia at some point in their lives (about 1 in 100).[25] According to a Johns Hopkins study, forty percent of homeless men have a chronic mental illness, as do 50 percent of homeless women. It is also known that many people with mental illness have a diminished ability to process information and difficulty in relating to unfamiliar environments. In addition, they experience increased stress due to diminished function. Yet, like all of us, they have a strong desire for independence and security, as well as a strong need for social interaction.

Little design research has been conducted in the field of mental health. Environmental planning seems to increase stress management capabilities by offering a sense of control, access to social support, and positive distractions in the physical surroundings. Access to nature is an example of a positive distraction. In laboratory tests, visual exposure to nature produced significant recovery from stress within five minutes.[26]

Designers and architects can meet some mental health needs by controlling the amount of information and stimuli in the environment. Confusing signage, a noisy environment, and lack of planning for wayfinding and orientation all contribute to stress. Stress management and independence can be enhanced through design for efficacy, or the ability to control. In hospitals, provide separate thermostats in the patients' rooms and access to a patient's laundry room and kitchen. Patient-centered hospitals offer a choice of background music and artwork to return control to the individual.

Many people with mental illness take medications that may reduce strength, coordination, mobility, and stamina. For people on high doses of tranquilizers, for instance, each motion may seem as difficult as moving through a vat of molasses. Products should be specified that are inviting to use, require little physical energy, and are easy to maintain. A spa, for example, may be more inviting and easier to use than a bathtub or shower.

People with Alzheimer's disease and related dementias experience declining intellectual function, cognitive impairment, and loss of clear consciousness. Building designers can support both caregivers and people with Alzheimer's by providing reference points to the past and present, a homelike environment with safe and secure exterior and interior spaces, and a consistent and relatively uncomplicated space that is easy to negotiate. All of these design criteria offer the user a more independent lifestyle and more success in task accomplishment, leading to an enhanced self-image.

## Access by Wheelchair Users

Much has been written about accessible design for the approximately 1.5 to 2 million Americans in wheelchairs, but surprisingly little has been done, and even less has been done well. Stairs abound and slopes on ramps exceed requirements. Maneuvering spaces are inadequate, and narrow doorways still prevent access. Elaborate accessibility plans are substituted for good design; wheelchair users are forced into freight elevators where garbage is frequently transported. They are assigned remote locations for entrance and exit, making convenient, integrated use impossible. Much of the storage in most buildings is out of reach, and those items that can be accessed may

be difficult to use because of the angle of reach required from the wheelchair.

Good designers recognize the need to exceed code to meet the requirements of their clients. Many people in wheelchairs, for instance, require a $5 \times 5$ ft turnaround space in public bathroom stalls, even though that space is not always required by code. Others need the assistance of a spouse or aide, yet unisex bathrooms are seldom offered because they are not yet mandated. Door openings are often based on clearance of the wheelchair, not the elbow clearance needed by the user.[27]

## Adults of Shorter Stature and Children

There are over 50 thousand adults of shorter stature in the United States. Added to the number of children and people in wheelchairs who use our buildings, a substantial portion of the population needs storage, displays, seating, work surfaces, and controls at a lower height than the average person. Leverage is difficult on door hardware at standard height, especially panic hardware. Doorknobs are also difficult for use by people with small hands, and curbs are too high for those with short legs. Stairs treads are also too high, and often the handrails are unusable. For people with shorter legs, distances take more effort to traverse; resting places are needed on longer routes. Chairs are easier to use than booths, and chairs without arms can be approached from three sides. Most standard height faucets must be approached from the end of the counter to be within reach. Many people can only reach an inch or two over the top of an obstruction like a 34 in. high counter. Without obstruction, some can reach as high as 48 in. a.f.f. Higher bulletin boards cannot be read, but larger print helps. Low vision panels in doors also help to prevent accidents.

So there it is. When we design for the average user, we accommodate only a few people well. Our population is not a homogeneous mix of average people, yet that is how we have always designed. Wasn't it only 130 years ago that surgeons first realized that the standard practice of using unsterilized instruments was killing their patients? Our buildings seldom kill but frequently disable, and this is unnecessary because we have the ability to empower rather than disable by design.

For some design problems, one size fits all. For others, one size won't work, and the only solution is to offer choices. One building entrance should serve everyone, but one drinking fountain does not serve a range of users. Universal design recognizes the rich diversity of our population and serves us all.

There are more universal design solutions than there are designers. This book is our attempt to spark your interest in finding those solutions. We have collected a broad range of ideas, but our success will be measured by your success in applying these ideas to your work. Let us know how you do. As we continue collecting solutions, we will share them through the Internet and future publications.

# ACKNOWLEDGMENTS

In addition to those who have been acknowledged in the first edition, *Beautiful Universal Design* could not have been produced without the efforts of Gail Austin. The hundreds of designs and products that are illustrated in this book were culled by Gail from thousands of examples. We also gratefully acknowledge the work of Susan Behar, who selected the art for the first edition.

Over a period of many years, five people have offered limitless support of our mission: Deb Carlson from Dupont Flooring Systems, Wayne Ruga from The National Center on Health Design, Patricia Moore from Guynes Design, William Saunders from The Harvard Graduate School of Design, and Amanda Miller from John Wiley & Sons. Without their support, this book would not have been possible.

We also wish to acknowledge the support of Beth Harrison in editing, Michael Powell in photography, and Suzanne Thomas from the Nevada Governor's Committee on Employment of People with Disabilities for her project research on our behalf. Thanks for research support also goes to Jane Langmuir of the Rhode Island School of Design, Jennifer Ashley and Wallace Williams of Gresham, Smith and Partners. Judith Miley and Paul Grayson, AIA, were also very generous in sharing their resources. Thanks also to Becky Bradley of Bank of America, Kimberly Eckeart from Dupont Flooring Systems, Ann Reineking of Kohler, and Melissa Bayles for efforts "beyond the call of duty" to provide illustrations.

In Canada, Laurie Ringaert of The Canadian Institute of Barrier-Free Design also offered research support, and Betty Dion, by unselfishly sharing her time and wisdom, made significant contributions to the accuracy of the manuscript. In Japan, Hirko Machida, Dr. Kose Satoshi, and Yoshiaki Goto shared their research, and, in Holland, Filo Laken offered innovation in research on aging.

Cynthia Leibrock wishes to thank her husband for the hours of editing and rewriting that he contributed to this project. She also wishes to thank her brother, Eric Hildebrand, for all of his help. He has inspired many with his brave and faithful battle with mental illness. She would also like to acknowledge the support of her colleagues at Colorado State University. Through the encouragement of Antigone Kostiopolis, this book has become a reality.

James Evan Terry thanks the entire staff at Evan Terry Associates, who supported Gail Austin as she searched for the products and designs illustrated in this book, and especially to Missy Mauk, who helped get the whole process organized, and Brenda Moffett and Edwina Dees, who kept it organized and made thousands of calls to manufacturers, designers, and photographers. Also, Marvin Martin and Dan Woosley suggested countless products and projects, and Beth Santoro coordinated all of the electronic image scanning protocols. Finally, Laura Ludwig coordinated the details during the layout and publishing phase of the work. Jim also acknowledges a debt of gratitude to his wife Darcy and their four children, who went without his presence more often than they wished during the time he was working on the book, and to Jim's brother Joe, a head injury survivor, for the insights and motivation he provided.

This book, though credited on the cover to two people, was truly the work of dozens of people who were committed to its success. We acknowledge that, without their insights, efforts, and countless hours of hard work, we would have little to offer to you, our reader.

# BEAUTIFUL
# UNIVERSAL
# DESIGN

# EXTERIOR PLANNING, RAMPS, STAIRS, AND ELEVATORS

Universal design meets the needs of all users, not just the average or the exceptional. Universal design should be the standard rather than the exception. It should be expected that well-designed buildings provide the minimal amenities of a usable approach, a supportive site, landscaping that can be enjoyed by people of all abilities, and accessible routes throughout.

Universal design integrates; it does not segregate into user groups. Universal design is an elevator used by all, not an open lift separating the users from those who are able to negotiate the adjacent stairs. Universal design is a reinforced elevator shaft inside stacked closets so that a residential elevator can be added at a later date. It is not a temporary ramp ruining the appearance of the building, attached as an afterthought, and usable by only a few.

Universal design is invisible. Emblems of age and disability are often specified by well-meaning designers attempting to make a building accessible. Universal design does not advertise the physical differences of the user.

## EXTERIOR PLANNING

Universal design begins with a covered entry at each exterior doorway. (Fig. 1-1) This is appreciated by anyone who is looking for keys or waiting for a ride. Outdoor seating in this area is also helpful. Plan the entry with a slip-resistant surface that

1-1

drains away from the door. The entry should be protected from wind to allow the door to be easily opened. If a passenger loading zone is necessary, it should be visible from the front door. It must be slightly sloped for drainage, not to exceed 1:50. At a minimum, it must be 5 ft in width and 20 ft in length parallel to the vehicle space. In a passenger loading zone or garage, a minimum vertical clearance of 9 ft 6 in. is needed by some vans.[1] Well-lighted access aisles should be provided in all parking areas or garages for transfer to a car or van. People who transfer to a car equipped with hand controls require a 5 ft clear space to completely open the driver side car door and transfer. (Fig. 1-2) Those using a perpendicular side lift on a van require a wide access aisle (8 ft) on the passenger side of the 8 ft parking space.[2] The access aisle should be marked with diagonal striping. The space and access aisle must be level (not exceeding a slope of 1:50 in all directions).[3]

A universal parking space is 11 ft wide with a 5 ft wide access aisle. It provides space to transfer from either a car or a van. This extra width also allows users to park toward one side or the other depending on transfer needs. This is especially important in front-in-only parking (where users cannot back in to facilitate transfer). When universal spaces are provided, van-accessible spaces

| Total Parking in Lot | Required Minimum Number of Accessible Spaces |
|---|---|
| 1 to 25 | 1 |
| 26 to 50 | 2 |
| 51 to 75 | 3 |
| 76 to 100 | 4 |
| 101 to 150 | 5 |
| 151 to 200 | 6 |
| 201 to 300 | 7 |
| 301 to 400 | 8 |
| 401 to 500 | 9 |
| 501 to 1000 | 2 percent of total |
| 1001 and over | 20 plus 1 for each 100 over 1000 |

1-3

are not required. Special "van-accessible" signage is not required in universal spaces, but each space must be marked with the international symbol of accessibility.

Two accessible parking spaces may share a common access aisle, but diagonal spaces must have access aisles on both sides because vehicles cannot back in. Provide all accessible parking spaces in the lot closest to the accessible entrance, but calculate a minimum of one accessible parking space per lot. (Fig. 1-3)

From the access aisle or passenger loading zone, an accessible route should be provided to all buildings on the site. (Fig. 1-4) The route should

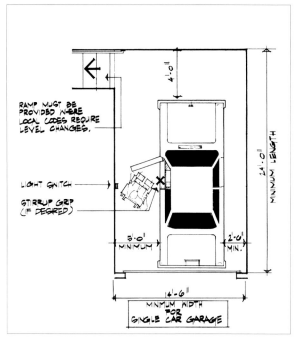

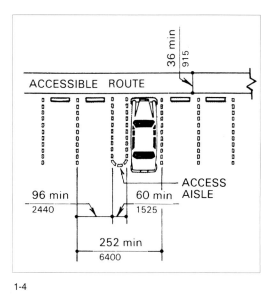

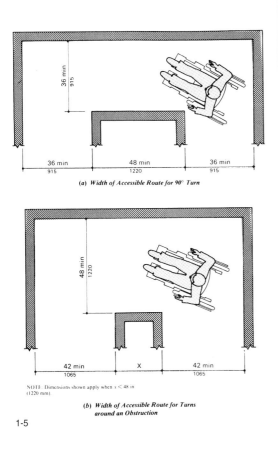

36 min
915

36 min
915

48 min
1220

36 min
915

*(a) Width of Accessible Route for 90° Turn*

48 min
1220

42 min
1065

X

42 min
1065

NOTE: Dimensions shown apply when x < 48 in
(1220 mm).

*(b) Width of Accessible Route for Turns around an Obstruction*

1-5

1-6

be free of auto traffic and protected from adverse weather elements. It should be well illuminated and maintained. The minimum clear width for a single wheelchair is 3 ft, but a universal route is 44 in. in width[4] (except at 48 in. turns) (Fig. 1-5) to accommodate the needs of both adults and children who need increased maneuvering space. When the route crosses a driveway, it must remain level or the slope can pull people in wheelchairs out into the street.

Provide seating and resting places on longer routes. Street furniture and equipment should be recessed in alcoves, and a companion seat must be provided next to each space planned for a person in a wheelchair. (Fig. 1-6) Water fountains, benches, waste receptacles, telephones, trees, and other objects that overhang the route are obstacles to everyone and should be contrasted from their surroundings. For blind adults, these objects must protrude no more than 4 in. between 27 in. above the finished floor (a.f.f.) and 80 in. a.f.f. Blind children may need protection from protruding objects as low as 1 ft a.f.f.

Maps of the parking area are always helpful, especially to people with differences in hearing or speech who may be hesitant to ask for directions. Install adequate lighting for map use and crime prevention. Maps with raised letters or Braille symbols are important, as are auditory cues such as talking signs, which deliver verbal information by remote control. (Fig. 1-7)

A quiet building site is necessary for people with differences in hearing as well as for people who rely more on their sense of hearing than on their vision. People with speech differences also need quiet spaces in which they can be heard easily, and people with mental, learning, and developmental differences profit from reduced noise levels. In new construction, select a site away from

1-7

1-8

major roads, airports, and railroads. Windows and doors should be oriented away from sources of noise adjacent to the site. (Fig. 1-8) In existing construction, earth berms and exterior plants can be placed in front of windows and doors to buffer noise. An earth berm can also be used as a ramp.

Elevated gardens are convenient for gardeners who get stiff while kneeling, for people using mobility aids, and those who have trouble reaching the ground. Pots and planters should be at least 2 ft in height and should be accessible from both sides if they exceed a 2 ft depth. They can be mounted on stands, walls, or racks. (Fig. 1-9) Specify nontoxic plants to protect children, pets, and people with allergies.

Flowerpots and baskets can be suspended by a pulley system that allows them to be lowered for pruning and watering. Choose watering products that do not become too hot to hold after sitting in the sun. An alternative method for watering is a drip irrigation system. In addition, carts and watering wands can be used with gardening activities. A vertical garden offers easy access to plants. One version, featured by the Chicago Botanical Gardens, consists of a coarse screen mounted loosely to a wall. The screen is lined with sphagnum, filled with potting soil, and planted through holes cut in the screen. (Fig. 1-10)

Patios offer sheltered gardening. An accessible cooking grill should be provided, and seating

1-9

1-10

1-11

should be at wheelchair seat height (17–19 in. for adults and 11–17 in. for children depending on age). Transfer walls at a lower height may be added to move from a wheelchair to the grass or sand. Patios and recreation areas should be covered and extend into an accessible escape route. (Fig. 1-11)

Attach the garage on the same level as the main building. Include a covered two-car garage to protect the user as well as an attendant or guest. In commercial spaces, plan a covered connection between buildings. (Fig. 1-12) A covered exterior route may be critical for emergency escape. Such

1-12

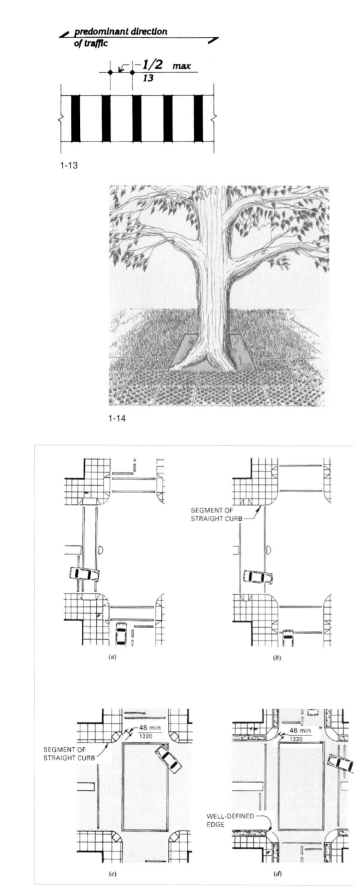

1-13

1-14

1-15

a route usually consists of a covered sidewalk around the perimeter of the building. For security and safety, the sidewalk should be well lighted. It must be adequately drained yet free of gratings with wide openings that could catch on wheels and crutches. Openings in gratings must be of a size that does not permit passage of a ½ in. diameter sphere, and elongated openings must be perpendicular to the route of travel. (Fig. 1-13)

Loose soil, brick, sand, and cobblestone surfaces are examples of textures that are unstable and difficult for many people. Soil stabilizers such as pine resin emulsion, fly ash, bentonite, ground seed hulls, latex polymers, and enzymers should be selected according to soil type.[5] A stabilizing mat can also be used over loose soil or sand. (Fig. 1-14)

Abrupt edges and drops in the sidewalk pose tripping hazards for everyone and a barrier for people using mobility aids. Specify adequate drainage and sidewalk subbase construction to prevent settling and the resulting changes in level. Ramp existing changes of level exceeding ¼ in. Bevel changes of level between ¼ in. and ½ in.[6]

Where an accessible route crosses a curb, provide a curb ramp with the least possible slope. A maximum slope of 1:12 is permitted in new construction. Curb ramps must not extend into the parking access aisle or the accessible route. When the accessible route crosses an island, provide a level space of at least 4 ft between the curb ramps. It is usually best to eliminate the curb ramps entirely by cutting the island down to ground level.

1-16

Specify flared sides on curb ramps (preferably with a maximum slope of 1:12), as steep sides can pose a tripping hazard to pedestrians. (Fig. 1-15) When using flared sides on a diagonal curb ramp at a marked crossing, at least 24 in. of straight curb is required within the crossing area. (Fig. 1-16) A minimum 48 in. landing at the bottom of the ramp must also be contained within the marked crossing to allow people with vision differences to stay oriented.

Curb ramps may be a hazard to people with differences in vision who use curb edges to signal the beginning of the street. Use a uniform textural cue to prevent this problem. (Fig. 1-17) Also, use color and texture on sidewalk intersections that lead directly into the street or parking lot and around the perimeter of reflecting pools.

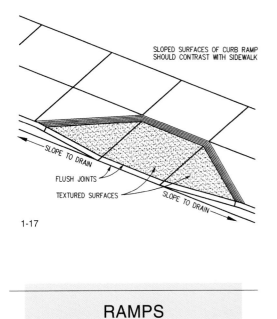

1-17

## RAMPS

Ramps are poor design. Older people often experience instability on ramps and prefer stairs. People using mobility aids are frequently segregated to the ramp while everyone else takes a separate path. Ten percent of people with ambulatory differences and over 20 percent of wheelchair users cannot use a 1:12 ramp. Over two thirds of wheelchair users cannot use a 1:12 ramp in a 30 ft length.[7] If possible, eliminate ramps through earthwork and site grading. If the approaches to the

1-18

building do not exceed a slope of 1:20, ramps are not necessary. If ramps are the only choice for access, try to keep the maximum slope at 1:20. This slope is also recommended for children.

Permanent ramps attached to a home may reduce the resale value and limit prospective buyers. Wood or metal ramps are easy to dismantle. Wood ramps are easier to build and can be modified if mistakes are made in construction. (Fig. 1-18) Use fire-retardant wood that has been pressure treated (or is decay resistant, like redwood). Hot-dip galvanized bolts and screws (with washers) should be used to resist corrosion.

Plan fire-retardant residential wood ramps with commercial nonskid surface finishes. Do not specify carpet for ramps, especially indoor/outdoor carpeting, which may become slippery when wet. Sheet vinyl and painted surfaces are also slippery when wet or dusty, but ribbed rubber matting works well. Install the ribs to run across the width of the ramp.

Permanent concrete ramps are usually more expensive than wood, but concrete ramps are easier to maintain and last longer. Specify a sand-float or broom finish brushed across the slope, not with it, to prevent slipping. A broom finish across the ramp is also easier for blind people to sweep with a cane. Avoid exterior ramps in climates with ice and snow, or cover them with a canopy. Built-in electric heating coils can also be considered.

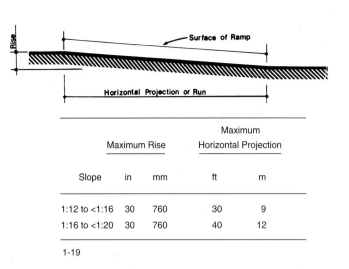

| | Maximum Rise | | Maximum Horizontal Projection | |
| Slope | in | mm | ft | m |
| --- | --- | --- | --- | --- |
| 1:12 to <1:16 | 30 | 760 | 30 | 9 |
| 1:16 to <1:20 | 30 | 760 | 40 | 12 |

1-19

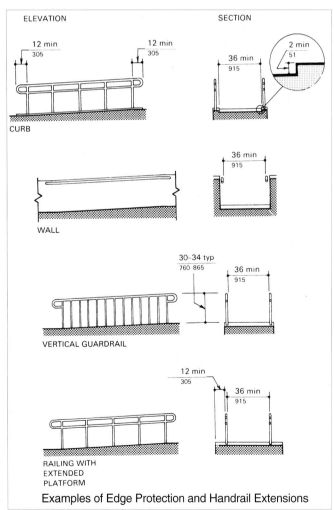

Examples of Edge Protection and Handrail Extensions

1-20

Portable ramps are the least expensive, but they can be too steep for many people to use. If the ramp is 3 ft in length and used on a 6 in. step, the user must negotiate a 1:6 slope. This is twice as steep as ramps built to most required standards; even a 1:10 slope is too steep for most wheelchair users and could cause the wheelchair to tip.[8]

To meet minimum standards, the slope of an interior or exterior ramp must not exceed 1 in. of rise for every 1 ft of length (1:12), and the cross slope must be no greater than 1:50. When a 1:12 ramp is not the least possible slope, it is not complying with ADA. If possible, use a shorter ramp with a more gradual slope. The ramp must never exceed 30 ft in length without a landing. (Fig. 1-19) A 20 ft length is a more nearly universal solution, especially for children.

Curbs with a minimum height of 2 in. must be installed on both sides of the ramp to serve as guardrails for wheels and crutch tips. (Fig. 1-20) Use low curbs instead of sidewalls to prevent scrapes and bumps. (Fig. 1-21)

Handrails must extend 12 in. beyond the top edge of the ramp, and the extension must be parallel to the floor. Handrails can be used by both pedestrians and people in wheelchairs who pull themselves up the ramp. Handrails must always be

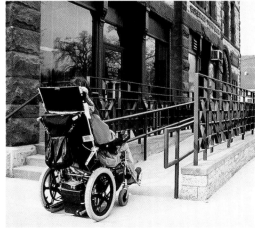

1-21

installed on both sides of the ramp if it has a rise greater than 6 in. (or a length greater than 6 ft). Install at a height of 34–38 in. for adults and another set at 20–28 in. for children depending on age. (Fig. 1-22) Handrails are not required by ADA on curb ramps or ramps adjacent to assembly seating areas. Shorter ramps without handrails must have flared sides to prevent tripping accidents.

The landings at the beginning and end of the ramp and at any turnaround point must be 5 ft in length and as wide as the ramp. The landings must be slightly sloped (not to exceed 1:50) for drainage.

When a door opens onto the ramp, the entrance platform must extend at least 18–24 in. on the side next to the latch so that the door can be opened without backing up a wheelchair or walker. The ramp should be directed toward the latch side of the door if the door swings open onto the ramp. If the door opens into the building, orient the ramp to the hinge side of the door. (Fig. 1-23)

The width of a ramp must be a minimum of 3 ft for one-way traffic including wheelchairs and walkers, 4 ft for two-way ambulatory traffic, and 5 ft for two wheelchairs to pass. (Fig. 1-24) Because the width is an almost insignificant factor in the total cost of the ramp, a 5 ft minimum width is desirable whenever possible.

1-22

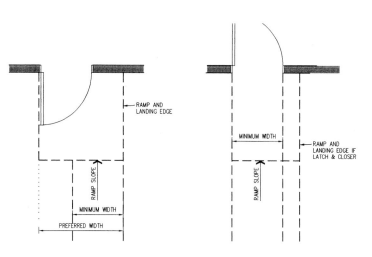

PREFERRED LOCATIONS OF RAMPS APPROACHING LANDINGS AT DOORS

1-23

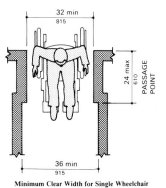

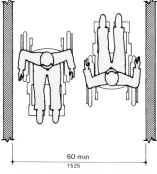

Minimum Clear Width for Single Wheelchair

Minimum Clear Width for Two Wheelchairs

1-24

1-25

1-27

A ramp into a swimming pool should not exceed a slope of 1 ft of rise per 10 ft of length.[9] It must be 3 ft wide with edging and handrails on each side, which can be used to guide a shower wheelchair during entry and exit. (Fig. 1-25) Shower wheelchair users become buoyant (and lose control of their wheelchairs) at a depth of 2 ft 10 in.[10] (2 ft 6 in. for children).[11] A portable lifting device can be used in place of a ramp where space or budget is limited.

A series of steps can also be used to access a pool, with the highest step planned at wheelchair seat height (between 17 and 19 in. for adults and between 11 and 17 in. for children).[12] In one creative installation, steps were replaced with a series of smooth rocks incorporated into the design. (Fig. 1-26)

1-26

An accessible 4 ft route should be planned around the pool. Both the ramp and the route must have a nonslip surface. (Fig. 1-27)

## LIFTS, ELEVATORS, STAIRS AND AREAS OF RESCUE ASSISTANCE

### Lifts and Elevators

Universal design of lifts and elevators involves more than code compliance. Ambient light levels should be increased in the interiors by the use of lighter finishes and diffuse light sources. Mirrors and confusing patterns may reduce stability in a space that is inherently unstable. Redundant cues (such as audible and visible floor notification) are particularly important to decrease reaction time and increase efficacy. Contrast around the edges of the floor covering is helpful to people with low vision.

1-28

1-29

In residential environments and unusual commercial circumstances, a wheelchair lift may be used in place of an elevator.[13] (Fig. 1-28) On a lift with a door, specify a locking device that prevents the lift from moving unless the door is locked. The lift should be designed to protect against entrapment under the platform and any failure that could cause the platform to drop. A slippery or jolting platform may cause users to lose their balance. For visual integration, the lift can store in the floor or ground when not in use. (Fig. 1-29.)

Two types of inclined lifts are available to lift a seated user up a stairway, both usually following the handrail. The first type works well for an ambulatory use, but wheelchair users must transfer onto a seat and then into a second wheelchair at the other end. (Fig. 1-30) This type is used when the lift serves one particular individual or where the stair width is limited. The lift seat stores at the bottom of the stairs to permit unobstructed use of the stairway. Folding seats are also available. The second type of inclined lift includes a fold-down platform that carries users in their wheelchair. If a lift requires a separate power unit, be sure it does not block the accessible route.

If any of the various types of lifts are chosen over an elevator, the designer should pay special attention to the controls. Keyed lifts should not be used in public areas unless some foolproof method is developed to prevent the keys from being lost. Use keyless lifts in easily supervised areas where children can be prevented from playing on them. A constant pressure switch stops the lift immediately when released, but it is more difficult to operate than a simple on/off switch.

1-30

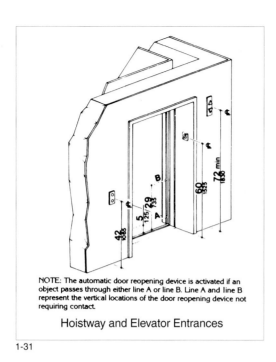

NOTE: The automatic door reopening device is activated if an object passes through either line A or line B. Line A and line B represent the vertical locations of the door reopening device not requiring contact.

Hoistway and Elevator Entrances

1-31

Freight elevators are not acceptable as the only vertical access for people who use wheelchairs, and most standards prohibit their use to meet accessibility requirements. For an accessible elevator, a minimum interior size of 4 ft 6 in. 5 ft 8 in. should be maintained, but an existing cab that is at least 4 x 4 ft clear may be acceptable in some situations. The door should be a minimum of 3 ft wide.

The elevator must be automatic and self-leveling (within a tolerance of ½ in.). Leveling should be tested with a full load as well as without a load.[14] The clearance between the car sill and the hoistway must not exceed 1¼ in. The elevator should start and stop smoothly, and a fold-down seat (for more than four stops)[15] and a stationary handrail should be provided to improve balance.

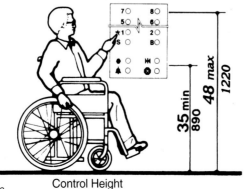

Control Height

1-32

A visual indicator on each elevator control button should light when touched and extinguish when the command is completed. All car controls, as well as the car platform, landing sill, and car threshold, should be illuminated to at least 5 foot-candles.[16] Position indicators must incorporate redundant cuing, offering both visual and audible cues. In the hall, an audible signal must sound once for the up direction and twice for the down (or use a spoken announcement of up or down).

Call buttons must be installed at a height of 3 ft 6 in. a.f.f., with the up button on top. Consider a second call button for adults of shorter stature or children installed at a height of 3 ft a.f.f.[17] Any object placed or installed beneath the call buttons must not project into the space more than 4 in.[18] A call button must be a minimum of ¾ in. in diameter. Hall lanterns, indicating which car is answering the call, must be a minimum of 2½ in. in the smallest dimension and must be centered over the door at 72 in. minimum a.f.f. In addition, a 2 in. high raised floor designation with Braille must be mounted on both jambs at 5 ft a.f.f. (Fig. 1-31) A second designation could be installed at 48 in. for children when appropriate.[19] A tactile star must be provided on both jambs at the main entry level.

Interior control panels must be installed within reach for adults of shorter stature, children, and people in wheelchairs. (Fig. 1-32) Controls for children should be installed no higher than 3 ft a.f.f.[20] Some panels are designed to be mounted horizontally to improve reach. Arrange the numbers in ascending order, reading from left to right. A floor number or other raised designation must be installed to the left of the button and must contrast with the background. (Fig. 1-33) Numerals above the door must illuminate, and a signal must sound as the car passes or stops at a floor. A spoken announcement at each floor is preferred by people who are blind, and this may be substituted for the signal.

Many people with mobility and vision differences take a little more time to find the elevator and enter the car. The elevator must have an audible and a visual signal to indicate arrival, and this signal must be adjusted to allow extra reaction time. ADA and Uniform Federal Accessibility Standards (UFAS) require a minimum of 5 seconds from noti-

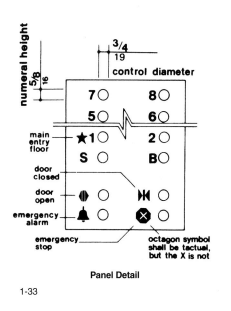

**Panel Detail**

1-33

fication until the door begins to close. The following formula is used to calculate the time (T) a door must remain open from notification: $T = D/(1.5 \text{ ft/s})$, where D equals the distance from the call button to the center of the elevator door. But earlier notification inconveniences no one because it does not increase the amount of time the door is actually open. According to ADA, the door can be open for as little as 3 seconds. If the door becomes obstructed, it must reopen without requiring contact and remain open for at least 20 seconds.[21] The reopening device must be activated without physical contact by sensing any obstructions between 5 in. a.f.f. and at least 29 in. a.f.f.

In addition, if an emergency two-way communication system is provided inside the car, it must comply with the accessibility requirements for height, hardware, and length of cord, if any. It must not require the user to speak or hear. A separate audio system (like a telephone or an intercom) may be incorporated in addition to an alarm system. Push-button intercoms are easier to use and tougher to vandalize than systems requiring the use of a handset. Only the nonverbal alarm system is required, however. Instructions for use should be both tactile and visual.

## Areas of Refuge

During an emergency evacuation, elevators in most buildings cannot be used as a required exit. Many people cannot use stairs for the evacuation, so the ADA requires construction of a safe place to wait for assistance.[22] The building should also be equipped with evacuation equipment. (Fig. 1-34)

These areas of rescue assistance or areas of refuge are required in the same number as required exits. They must be provided in all new buildings on accessible floors that depend solely on elevators (unless the building has a supervised automatic sprinkling system). The areas are usually placed adjacent to (or inside) stairways or in a pressurized elevator lobby, and each area must have clear floor space for two wheelchairs (unless reduced in size by a local authority). There are also requirements for instructional signage and two-way communication (both visible and audible) to request help and receive confirmation that help is on the way.

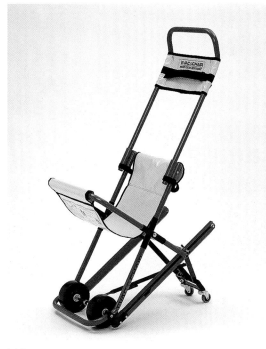

1-34

## Stairs and Handrails

Many people have difficulty negotiating spiral or curved staircases, which require balance and dependence on the handrails. Straight staircases should provide a safe stopping place midway between floor levels to help those who are prone to dizziness or those who need to conserve energy. A seat on the landing is also helpful to many. (Fig. 1-35)

At least 3 ft of clearance must be provided between the handrails on stairs (4 ft on stairs adjacent to an area of refuge). Handrails must be installed on both sides of the stair to accommodate people who are stronger on one side than the other. They must be continuous on the inner rail at switchbacks and doglegs, and the gripping surface must be uninterrupted. Mount the top of handrails at a height of 2 ft 10 in.–3 ft 2 in. above the stair nosing.[23] A lower

1-36

handrail can be installed at a height of 20–28 in. for use by children depending on age. It should have a diameter of 1–1¼ in. for maximum safety.[24]

Each handrail should have an outside diameter of 1½ in. for the strongest and most comfortable grip for both children and most adults. It must have rounded ends or return to the wall, floor, or post to minimize the chance that it will snag clothing and cause a fall. The handrail must not extend into the pedestrian pathway by more than 4 in.[25] A handrail must also clear the adjacent wall by exactly 1½ in. This is enough space to allow a panic grab during a fall, but not wide enough to be dangerous. Some people place their entire lower arm on the handrail to push up, and the arm could become wedged between the wall and the rail if a larger clearance is allowed. To prevent scraped knuckles, the wall surface behind the handrail must not be rough textured. Texture can be used on the handrail itself for improved grip and orientation. Notches or grooves can be cut in the rail to identify location. Braille and audible cues may also be added. (Fig. 1-36) Handrails must not rotate within their fittings.

A handrail can be recessed to a maximum of 3 in. if the recess extends at least 18 in. above the top of the rail.[26] The handrail must extend 12 in. beyond the top and 12 in. plus the width of one riser beyond the bottom of stairs, and the extension must be parallel to the floor. At the bottom, the

1-35

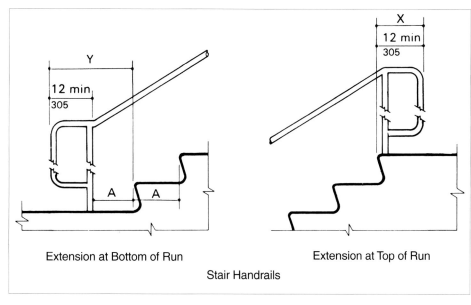

Extension at Bottom of Run          Extension at Top of Run

Stair Handrails

1-37

handrail must continue to slope for a distance of the width of one tread. The remaining 12 in. must be horizontal. (Fig. 1-37)

People who are a little unsteady on their feet may be able to manage steps more easily than ramps, but do not design steps with abrupt or square nosings that project more than 1½ in. It is easy to catch a toe on this overlap. Use wedge-shaped fillers on existing square nosings. Open risers are nearly impossible for people with canes or other mobility aids to use. Consider a clear filler for an open riser. (Fig. 1-38) Keep every riser constant at the same height (7 in. maximum preferred) and every tread constant at a minimum of 11 in. deep in any flight of stairs.[27] (Fig. 1-39) Tread width must also be con-

sistent within each flight, as varied widths can create optical illusions that affect the balance of users. Avoid confusing patterns on stairway floor coverings for the same reason.

To prevent people from walking into hanging stairways or other elevated protruding objects, install wing walls or curbs under them. Guardrails or planters could also be used. (Fig. 1-40)

(a) Flush Riser          (b) Angle Nosing          (c) Rounded Nosing

Usable Tread Width and Examples of Acceptable Nosings

1-39

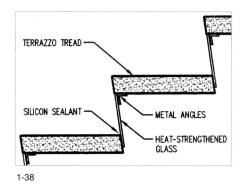

TERRAZZO TREAD

SILICON SEALANT

METAL ANGLES

HEAT-STRENGTHENED GLASS

1-38

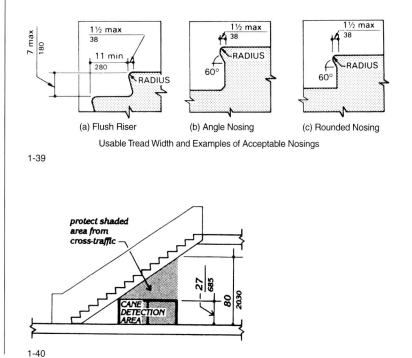

protect shaded area from cross-traffic

CANE DETECTION AREA

1-40

On stairs, color-contrast the edge of treads and risers so that the edges can be spotted more easily. This is especially important on the first and last steps. With self-illuminating strips, the edges can be seen in the dark. (Fig. 1-41) Also contrast the handrails with the wall so that they can be seen more quickly in an emergency. (Fig. 1-42)

1-42

1-41

Single stairs can be difficult to see and are dangerous when they are not expected or lighted properly. Many building codes do not allow them, but when use is permitted, a change in texture or color on the single stair helps. Texture should also be used to mark stairway landings and other areas that are hazardous to people with differences in vision. Landings at exterior stairway entrances may become slippery when wet, so they must be slightly sloped (not exceeding 1:50) for drainage.

# ELECTRICAL, MECHANICAL, AND ACOUSTICAL EQUIPMENT

2

Discriminating architecture does not discriminate. The challenge of the designer is to apply sophisticated technology to solve problems without drawing attention to individual differences. From door levers that double as night-lights to sophisticated "smart house" systems, technology can enable everyone to live more independently.

## SWITCHES

Lowered electrical switches are helpful for wheelchair users, children, adults of shorter stature, and people with a shorter reach. Locate light switches at the height of the door lever (3 ft above the finished floor [a.f.f.] for use by people in wheelchairs, most adults of shorter stature, and small children).[1] The thermostat should be at 4 ft a.f.f. to prevent access by small children.

Switches should be placed for convenience as well as for ease of access. At a minimum, plan switches at each entrance to a room. In lecture halls, plan light switches that can be controlled by the lecturer from the front of the room. To save unnecessary trips, plan a master switch at both the back door and at bedside to control all lights in a residence. Sound-

activated switches can be helpful to control fixtures that are out of reach. These switches engage with a clap of the hands and can be a great help for people who have trouble seeing the switch or those who just want to save steps. Timer switches are also convenient and are especially good choices for outside lighting.

2-1

17

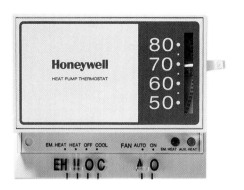

2-2

2-3

In bedrooms, consider a lighted switch that can act as a beacon in the dark. Visual acuity can often be improved by installing dimming rheostats on each switch to control the quantity of light in the room. A rheostat is also helpful for task lighting. (Fig. 2-1) For example, it may be necessary to increase lighting over the kitchen sink or in other areas where detailed work takes place.

Thermostats with large high-contrast numbers are helpful to all users in low lighting conditions. Some thermostats feature an audible click between settings. (Fig. 2-2) In the bedroom, heating, cooling, ventilation, and remote controls should be placed conveniently near the bed but should not be near a heat register, which could affect the temperature reading. Keep all controls at a uniform level except those that could be hazardous to young children; place the latter at a height of 4 ft a.f.f.

Make sure the main switch box is installed in an accessible area. If the switch box location is not well lighted, add a magnetic flashlight on the box. Replace old fuse panels with circuit breakers to accommodate everyone, but especially people with arthritis or prosthetic hands. Label all circuits, and keep the top of the box at a universally reachable height of 4 ft a.f.f.

2-4

Wall mount kitchen fan controls or use a fan mounted on the counter with controls within reach. (Fig. 2-3) Wall mount the switch for the bathroom light both inside and outside of a small bathroom. It is always helpful to have lighting before negotiating a confined space. Switches in two locations may be flashed as part of a warning system for people with hearing differences.

Wall guards may be necessary around some switches where dirt and stains are a problem. Specify palm toggle switches, which can be operated with the elbow or a closed fist. (Fig. 2-4) Pressure- and rocker-type switches are easier to operate than conventional toggle switches. Pull chains are easy to handle if a loop is attached to the end of the chain so that grasping is not necessary.

Projecting switch plates are easier to locate in areas with reduced lighting. Self-illuminated trim for switches and levers is also helpful and could be installed at bedroom, bathroom, and entry doors. (Fig. 2-5) It may be necessary to add night-lights as well. Low-voltage lighting on the floor surface can aid in wayfinding. (Fig. 2-6)

Color contrast between the plate and the wall makes the switch easier to see. (Fig. 2-7) Contrast between the switch and the plate is also helpful.

2-6

2-5

2-7

## ELECTRICAL OUTLETS

2-8

For small appliances, install an electrical outlet just above the surface of a countertop or table. Everyone has difficulty reaching outlets under counters and tables; it may be impossible for people with mobility differences. Many cannot reach an electric cord on the floor. Cup hooks next to an outlet can be a temporary solution to the problem, but a face plate that holds an unplugged cord would be better. (Fig. 2-8) For the hair dryer or shaver, add an electrical outlet on the side wall of the bathroom, with a ground-fault circuit interrupter to protect against shock. (Fig. 2-9)

2-9

15″
(38cm)

Floor level

Note:  ↓ Denotes maximum height permitted;  ↑ denotes minimum

2-10

Extension cords can pose a tripping hazard and can become entangled in wheelchairs, walkers, and crutches, not to mention feet. To eliminate cords, add receptacle outlets to the floor plan after considering furniture, appliance, and lamp placement. Determine if additional outlets are needed in the bedroom for such things as medical appliances, communication systems, text telephones, and alarms. A special outlet, for example, may be necessary to add a flashing alarm or for recharging a power wheelchair. Locate such an outlet in a well-ventilated area where noxious gases from charging will not build up. An outlet above an exterior door allows a call light or alarm to be added at a later date. Crucial call systems, ventilator outlets, and emergency fire alarms should all be supplied with emergency power.

Electrical outlets must be accessible; a height of 15 in. (Fig. 2-10) is preferable (16–20 in. for children in wheelchairs).[2] Make sure there is a receptacle outlet on the landing of all stairways for vacuuming. In rooms, outlets should be spaced within reach of most cords (no farther than 8 ft apart).

Flexibility is the key to accommodate a wide range of abilities. Plan additional phone jacks, raceway outlets (Fig. 2-11), and antenna hookups. In the kitchen, locate multiple outlets on the front of the counter for easier reach. Some appliances may even need an outlet under the counter. For example, a mixer could be stored under the counter on a pop-up shelf.

2-11

## LIGHTING

Keep wall fixtures within reach and consider ceiling fixtures that pull down for task lighting (and easy bulb replacement). (Fig. 2-12) Many people in wheelchairs, adults of shorter stature, and children can reach these fixtures using a grabber. Those that cannot be lowered should be installed with long-life bulbs. Extra lighting is helpful when taking a shower from a shower chair or seat. Recess a vapor-proof light fixture in the ceiling of all shower stalls. The light can be combined with an exhaust fan. (Fig. 2-13)

Keep lighting consistent from room to room. Install dimming rheostats to keep corridor lighting levels low at night.[3] Many people have trouble adjusting to sudden changes from light to dark areas. Create a transition zone, such as a well-lighted entryway or porch, between the outdoors and the interior. Put side lights at the entrance to a bright room. Side lights and other accent lighting (instead of flat fluorescent light) can help people to maintain orientation within the room. Use shades or diffusers on all sources to prevent glare. Glare increases the deterioration rate of the retina,[4] and unprotected bulbs have high temperature surfaces capable of carbonizing dust, a source of irritation to many people with allergies.[5]

2-13

Place lighting (and windows) to throw light toward, not down, staircases. (Fig. 2-14) Use a diffuse source to prevent glare, not a directed source like a spotlight. Even lighting also prevents disorientation and confusion created by highlight and shadow. Stairways and landings, especially the head and foot of the stairs, are potentially dangerous areas. If these spaces are dark, the pupils dilate and it is more difficult to focus on the stairs. Keep the quantity of light adjustable throughout the entire space.

2-12

2-14

2-15

Many older people require 4–5½ times more light to distinguish a figure from the background (at least 100 foot-candles for close work).[6] If lighting quantity increases, be careful to avoid excessive heat by using low-heat output luminaries.

Additional lighting is also important in areas where concentration is required, decisions are made, or danger is present. Decision areas, like a reception room and entryway, may require increased lighting. (Fig. 2-15) Many accidents occur in the kitchen and bathroom, so extra lighting becomes critical to accident prevention.

Glare is a problem for many people, including some older people and others with vision problems. Use diffusers on light fixtures, and provide several low-intensity light sources rather than one bright source. Keep lights high and well diffused over the task area. Use low-glare surfaces on counters, floors, furnishings, and walls. Control window glare with draperies.

Adequate lighting is particularly important for people with hearing differences to read facial expressions, body movements, and gestures. Avoid bright wall sconces, backlighting, and shadows where people gather to talk or listen to speakers and interpreters.

Several factors should be considered when using fluorescent lighting. First, specify fixtures with minimum flicker, which can trigger epileptic episodes in some people. Second, hyperactive children and some people with concentration differences may experience a shortened attention span and nutritional problems triggered by fluorescent lighting.[7] Third, studies have shown that people with Alzheimer's disease and emotionally disturbed adolescents become more agitated under fluorescent lighting.[8] Fourth, fluorescent ballasts may interfere with hearing aids. Finally, cool fluorescent light emphasizes the blue-green tones that are most difficult for people with cataracts to perceive.[9] When planning fluorescent lighting, keep in mind that a lighting spectrum as close as possible to daylight may reduce depression, fatigue, hyperactivity, and the incidence of some diseases. The daylight spectrum also may increase calcium absorption and reaction time to light and sound.[10] This, in turn, may increase productivity. The ultraviolet light in the spectrum is also helpful in sanitizing the space for people with allergies.[11]

Lighting design can help establish a feeling of intimacy and control. Efficacy is especially important to people previously disabled by design. Intimacy is created by lighting the perimeter walls of a room and keeping the center darker. People feel more comfortable and sit closer together without feeling as if they are invading each other's territory. (Fig. 2-16)

Track lighting allows the quality and quantity of light to be altered as the user's needs change. With track lighting, the angle of the beam, the light color, and the light fixture can all be easily adjusted. For a change, light can be directed away from the ceiling of the room, creating a more personal feeling in the space. (Fig. 2-17) For example, kitchen lighting fixtures can be directed at hanging cabinets to keep the light level below ceiling height without creating glare. Track lighting can be used to graze light over rough surfaces, to frame a painting in light (using a projector), or to change the location of a chandelier.

A less institutional appearance is achieved when only the light is seen, not the source of the light. Exposed lighting systems are often harsh and glaring and can visually dominate a space. With concealed lighting systems, the emphasis is placed on the beauty of the room and its occupants rather than on the light fixtures. Concealed fixtures are often less expensive than decorative fixtures. Concealed systems can be used to back

| Mood | Lighting |
|---|---|
| Gaiety | Higher levels of illumination with color and movement. Changing effects of color and changes in illumination should not be sudden, but should be smooth and stimulating. |
| Solemnity | Subdued patterns of light with emphasis at dramatic points. Color should be used sparingly and with atmospheric effect. Changes of illumination should be imperceptible. |
| Restfulness | Low brightness patterns, no visible light sources, subdued color, dark upper ceiling, and a low wall brightness, decreasing upward to the ceiling. |
| Activity | Higher levels of illumination, with proper local lighting for the more difficult visual tasks. |
| Warmth | Colors at the red end of spectrum: red, red-orange, orange, yellow, amber, gold, and pink. |
| Coolness | Colors at cool end of spectrum, such as blue, blue-green, green, magenta, and violet. These colors mixed with white produce various cool tints. |
| Human complexion | Light tints of red, such as pink and rose, improve human complexion and produce pleasant effects. Blue, blue-green, purple, and green detract from the human complexion, and produce ghastly effects. |
| Dramatic color of object | Spotlight by a beam of light of same color. |
| Prevent fatigue | Avoid use of intense red, blue, or purple light. |

NASA, *Habitability Data Handbook*, MSC-03909, pp. 3-18.

2-16

2-17

light wall accessories, to diffuse light on draperies, or to light the ceiling. (Fig. 2-18) Under-cabinet lighting can illuminate matte finish counters without glare.

Recessed lighting under stairs prevents accidents without creating glare. Low-voltage lighting strips can be added to stairway floor coverings as an alternative treatment. (Fig. 2-19)

2-18

2-19

## HEATING

The type of heating system specified is important in meeting the needs of people with a wide range of abilities and sensitivities. Passive solar heating, electric baseboard heaters, and hot water radiators offer even heating without drafts. Passive solar and fluid-filled electric radiant heating are often advantageous for people with allergies because the relatively low surface temperatures of these systems do not carbonize dust.[12] For people who cannot easily sense heat, warm radiators should be covered to prevent burns. This is especially important when users must lean across the heater from a wheelchair to operate window controls.

For people who take longer to react to emergencies, choose electric heat rather than gas or oil systems. Replace oil heating units with heat pumps, which offer both cooling and heating with energy efficiency.

Heat pumps, however, and other forced-air heating systems often cause drafts, which are uncomfortable for everyone and can be problematic for people with sensation differences. Sometimes an adjustment to the louvers or airflow velocity can help. With a forced-air system, make sure the floor registers have narrow slats (not greater than ½ in. wide)[13] and will not catch a crutch tip, walker, or wheelchair. If the register has elongated openings, place the long dimension perpendicular to the typical route of travel. (Fig. 2-20)

Ambient noise inconveniences everyone but disables people with hearing differences. Reduce background noise and vibrations by isolating forced-air heating, ventilating, and air-conditioning (HVAC) units in a separate room. Insulate heating and ventilation ducts to control fan noise. Replace or line metal ductwork with 1 in. insulated duct board. Silencers may also be installed near fans. Regulate airflow velocities to control turbulence-induced noise and select registers with low sound-production ratings. Avoid the noise of forced-air heating systems by using passive solar heat, elec-

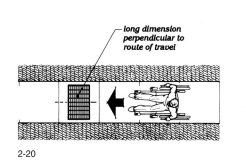

long dimension
perpendicular to
route of travel

2-20

tric baseboard heating, radiant ceiling heat, or a hot water radiator. Because static may affect hearing aid operation, provide increased humidity to minimize static. A humidifier, dehumidifier, or purifier can be added to a forced-air system or used as a separate unit. (Fig. 2-21) A dehumidifier that does not rely on the air conditioner may be helpful in minimizing mildew, mold, and dust mites. These common allergens are minimized when the relative humidity is below 50 percent.

A wall heater with a fan is used by some people with coordination differences to dry off after bathing, but the grill may become hot enough to cause a burn. Specify a well-protected model that can be programmed to automatically warm the space early in the morning before use. This is helpful to everyone but may be critical to people with reduced circulation. Consider a ventilating ceiling heater with a fan in the dressing area for extra warmth.

For people in chairs or wheelchairs, adults of shorter stature, and children, a ceiling fan moves warm air to a lower level. A fan can be reversed to cool in the summer. A remote-control switch should be provided to change speeds or dim the light on the fan without extreme requirements of reach and motion.

Radiant ceiling heat without a fan may not provide sufficient warmth at the height of adults of shorter stature, children, and people in wheelchairs. Most of the radiant heat remains close to the ceiling with this system. A ceiling fan helps to some extent, especially with high ceilings, but a wall-mounted radiant heater is more effective.

People with reduced circulation may prefer a general ambient temperature of 75°F or more, while others with allergies to mold and fungi need to keep the temperature between 65° and 70°F (with relative humidity at 45–55 percent).[14] People with multiple sclerosis, however, are often less tolerant of heat than others. Those with cardiovascular problems are at higher risk in extremes of hot and cold, while individuals with cystic fibrosis and spinal cord injuries have difficulty perspiring and are more prone to heat stress. Finally, people with hyperthyroid conditions may have thermal regulation problems. In meeting these individual needs, specify a programmable heating system that allows temperatures to change over time.[15] An electronic thermostat helps to conserve energy, which is even more important when higher ambient temperatures are required. (Fig. 2-22)

2-21

2-22

## VENTILATION AND CONDITIONING

A universally designed HVAC system accommodates a variety of needs without disabling anyone by design. People with respiratory problems may prefer buildings that are above grade on dry sites with protection from wind. For people with allergies, a dehumidifier and air purifier may be helpful, and some houseplants are also effective in purifying the air. (Fig. 2-23)

Even with air purity, hypoallergenic heating, and exceptional ventilation, it is virtually impossible to control all of the allergens in the interior. However, once allergies are identified, reactions can often be reduced with proper maintenance, a sensible selection of products, including an uncoated paper filter system, and well-designed ventilation allowing at least one air change per hour. Air-to-air heat exchangers can minimize energy waste as fresh air is brought in.

| Pollutant | Sources | Solutions |
|---|---|---|
| Formaldehyde | foam insulation | Philodendron |
| | plywood | Spider plant |
| | carpeting | Golden pothos |
| | furniture | Corn plant |
| | paper goods | Chrysanthemum |
| | household cleaner | Mother-in-law's tongue |
| Benzene | tobacco smoke | English ivy |
| | gasoline | Marginata |
| | synthetic fibers | Janet Craig |
| | plastics | Chrysanthemum |
| | inks | Gerbera daisy |
| | oils | Warneckei |
| | detergents | Peace lily |
| | rubber | |
| Trichloro-ethylene | dry cleaning | Gerbera |
| | inks | Chrysanthemum |
| | paints | Peace lily |
| | varnishes | Warneckei |
| | lacquers | Marginata |
| | adhesives | |

2-23

Petrochemicals, toxic finishes, adhesives, and phenols are but a few of the hundreds of irritants commonly found in building materials. In addition, common house dust, dust mites, mold spores, cigarette smoke, and animal dandruff frequently cause problems. Toxins typically build up in closets and storage areas, and good ventilation is critical in these spaces.

## ACOUSTICAL DESIGN

In health-care environments, noise has been shown to contribute to wandering by patients, fewer visits by family and friends, and staff turnover.[16] Staggered-stud construction is a simple idea that can be easily applied to reduce sound transmission. (Fig. 2-24) This construction technique opens an air space in the wall that can be filled with insulation. For people with allergies, avoid cellulose, fiberglass, and rock wool insulation; specify vermiculite and perlite, which are also resistant to moisture, mold, and mildew.[17] It is especially important to control sound transmission between the social and private spaces of the interior. For example, in a private residence noises from the bathroom and bedroom should be isolated from the living room.

A variety of wall, floor, and ceiling finishes is available to absorb sound generated within a room. A wall of drapery, for example, can absorb nearly half of the noise produced.[18] Sound baffles used across a hallway can be effective in absorbing ambient noise while visually reducing the length of the space.

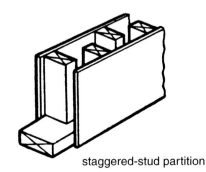

staggered-stud partition

2-24

Unwanted noise is known to be a stress producer. It is most annoying when its source is not evident and when it is not predictable. Even if the noise cannot be eliminated, the resulting stress can be reduced or eliminated by providing a means to control the stressor.[19] In a residence, specify a tambour window treatment to control street noise. In a commercial space, spring-mount transformers and isolate vibration from mechanical equipment.

White noise is a mixture of frequencies used to cover distracting sounds, but it is not universally beneficial. It has been used extensively to reduce stress but can be distracting, particularly when hearing and concentration are important. When white noise is broadcast throughout a space, it can reduce orientation because it makes the area appear uniform; this is especially difficult for people who are blind and use sound as an orientation cue.[20]

## SECURITY SYSTEMS

People who are disabled by design have a slower reaction time in responding to emergencies. Security systems offer an early warning and can increase reaction time. At least four types of systems are available: ultrasonic motion detectors, pressure mats, passive infrared photoelectric sensors, and switch sensors. Each type can be powered by batteries or direct wiring.

VOICE CONTROL

2-25

2-26a                2-26b

Ultra-high-frequency sound waves in motion detectors or other security systems can interfere with hearing aids. Use pressure mats, passive infrared photoelectric sensors, and switch sensors instead. (Infrared and radio-frequency technology is also used for sound amplification in theaters and auditoriums to support people with hearing differences.)

For a private residence, consider a home automation system with an electric locking device for the entry door coupled with an intercom system. When the doorbell is heard (or when a flashing light is activated by the system), the lock can be checked by remote control from anywhere in the interior. The doorbell can be answered and the door unlocked without having to move to the entry. (Fig. 2-25) This is important to people who cannot reach the door quickly and risk missing visitors or deliveries altogether. A video monitor can be added to the system, giving a clear picture of a visitor at the front door. (Fig. 2-26) Outdoor light controls are an essential part of this system. An entry light that comes on automatically at night is another good choice. With any electrical security system, plan a backup if power is lost.

If there is a medical emergency or security breach, proximity to the call system is a crucial issue. Many alarm devices are available to call for help with the push of a button. One type triggers an automatic telephone communication system, which calls an answering service and plays a recorded message stating the location of the emergency. It dials a second number if there is no answer at the first, and continues dialing both numbers until it gets a response. This system could be critical in the event of a fall or for people who have difficulty speaking or hearing, especially in an emergency.

It may also be important to include an emergency call system in the bathroom. Extend elastic cords through eyelets around the entire perimeter of the room at two levels, 4 in. above the floor and above the door lever at 3 ft 6 in. a.f.f. Attach the cord to toggle switches that activate the alarm. Alternately, a touch system could be installed on the baseboard so that a person could call for help anywhere in the building. (Fig. 2-27) A commercial call system may be as simple as a buzzer or as involved as a teleconferencing device. In less critical situations, a telephone or intercom in the bathroom may be sufficient. Most intercoms can be monitored in other rooms when the channel is left open, so a call for help can be heard throughout the building. (Fig. 2-28) In a residence with young children or with a family member with Alzheimer's disease, the intercom can be used to monitor the use of outside doors. When a door opens, the intercom begins to beep. A quieter system incorporates a computer chip into a wristband to delay or lock the door whenever the user approaches. (Fig. 2-29)

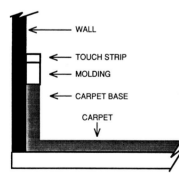

WALL

← TOUCH STRIP
← MOLDING
← CARPET BASE

CARPET
↓

DETAIL-SIDE ELEVATION OF
WALL MOUNTED TOUCH STRIP

2-27

An automatic garage door opener makes another essential contribution to security. The remote control allows people with strength, reach, and coordination differences to raise and lower the door. The garage door system should include an automatic light with a lengthy delay to allow time to drive into the garage, unload the vehicle, and go inside. (Fig. 2-30) Some systems are equipped with touch pads, smoke detectors, carbon monoxide detectors, and burglar alarms for added security.

2-29

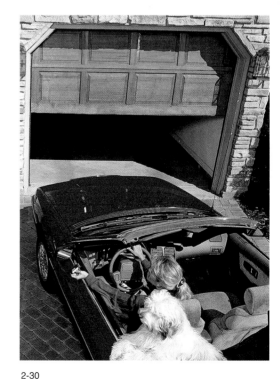

2-28

2-30

## ENVIRONMENTAL CONTROL SYSTEMS

Remote-control devices can be used to accommodate a wide variety of abilities. Almost any switch can be changed to a remote control with a transmitter and receiver. Some transmitters are sonic and do not require a battery; others are operated by touch. Remote-power door openers, for example, can be used in conjunction with bedside environmental controls to let pets in and out of the house and to control lighting. (Fig. 2-31)

Environmental control systems operate many devices, including aide alerts, tape recorders, page turners, televisions, electric beds, lights, and drapery controls. Computer-driven systems can run security checks and lower interior temperatures when a room is not in use. (Fig. 2-32) Some systems do not require manual control but can be operated simply by puffing into the switch or controlling the switch by inhaling or "sipping." When units are operated with a puff/sip switch, tongue switch, rocking lever, communication aid, or small computer, add separate manual controls for use by a guest or aide.

A series of tabletop rocker switches can serve as a less expensive version of an environmental control system. These units are often used to control a lamp, air conditioner, television, radio, and small intercom. The multiple cords associated with this system, however, are a tripping hazard for many people and difficult for people using mobility aids.

Specialized devices are available for people with differences in hearing or speech. Examples include text telephones and computers that communicate by telephone. Closed-captioned television provides

2-31

both aural and written cues, and earphones allow amplification without disturbing others. For people with reduced hearing, doorbells and alarms should be selected in frequencies under 10,000 Hz22 or wired to vary the level of light in the house.

2-32

## SMOKE DETECTORS AND ALARMS

In a residence, smoke detectors should be installed adjacent to each bedroom and at the top of the stairway. Another smoke detector should be installed in the living room if it is more than 15 ft away from a bedroom unit. A third should be installed in the basement, perhaps near the furnace room. Be sure to consider location in relation to air supply and air return registers. (Fig. 2-33) A gas leak detector may also be required. Select a model with photoelectric and ion chamber detection to warn of both smoke and heat. The detector should also sound a warning when the battery needs to be replaced. Some models provide a battery within reach of adults of shorter stature and wheelchair users.

Vibrating pagers and visual signals can be used to alert a deaf person to an emergency situation or to a crying child. At night, the alarm can be connected to an electrical solenoid bed vibrator used under the pillow. A variable-intensity fan should not be used as a nighttime fire alarm because it could blow smoke in the face of a sleeping individual.

Alarms must be provided in rest rooms and other general usage areas. (Fig. 2-34) Alarms must produce a visual warning and a sound that exceeds the prevailing equivalent sound level in the room or space by at least 15 dbA or exceeds any maximum sound level with a duration of 60 seconds by 5 dbA, whichever is louder.[21] A white strobe light is most easily seen as a visual warning; colored light (particularly red) is not effective[22] and seldom complies with the brightness requirements. The flash rate must not exceed 5 flashes per second, or it may trigger an episode for a person with epilepsy. An episode may also be triggered by a large num-

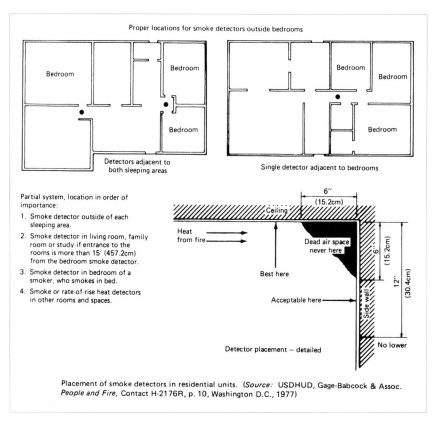

Placement of smoke detectors in residential units. (*Source:* USDHUD, Gage-Babcock & Assoc. *People and Fire,* Contact H-2176R, p. 10, Washington D.C., 1977)

2-33

ber of low-intensity lamps. Use a single lamp when it can provide the necessary brightness and intensity. Where multiple signals can be seen from any one location, install a synchronizer to reduce the chances of triggering seizures. The alarms must be placed 80 in. above the highest floor level within the space or 6 in. below the ceiling, whichever is lower, to reduce the potential of concealment by smoke. No place in any room or space can be more than 50 ft from the signal (measured in a horizontal plane). In large rooms and spaces exceeding 100 ft across (without obstructions 6 ft a.f.f.) alarms may be placed around the perimeter in lieu of suspending them from the ceiling.[23] For a more comprehensive alarm specification, consider exceeding the ADA Accessibility Standards by following the American National Standards Institute (ANSI) A117.1-1997.

2-34

# CEILING AND WALL FINISHES

# 3

From color prescriptions for healing environments to the use of contrast, hue, intensity, and texture, finishes can empower or disable. The power of design, color, and pattern can be used to turn confusion into visual organization, isolation into social integration, and monotony into stimulation.

Finishes can increase light reflectance and light quantity without increasing glare. As the lenses of the eyes yellow with age, up to 5 times more light quantity may be required for tasks.[1] As cataracts develop, glare from this extra lighting can be incapacitating unless light-absorbing finishes are specified.

Sound-absorbing finishes reduce ambient noise and improve hearing ability. Skillfully used contrasting finishes can define a doorway or room perimeter, supporting the wayfinding system and efficacy of the user. The enlightened designer can make a difference through the artistic and functional use of finishes.

## PATTERN AND COLOR

Blue and green tones come to focus in front of the retina and appear to recede, while orange and red tones come to focus behind the retina of the eye and cause the surface to visually advance or lower.[2] Many adults of shorter stature, children, and people in wheelchairs are more comfortable with a lower ceiling height, and pattern and color can be used to visually lower an existing ceiling. A lower ceiling also helps a room appear cozier and less institutional. (Fig. 3-1).

3-1

3-2

Yellow or blue color schemes may cause difficulties for people who have yellowing lenses. Yellow colors can become so intense that they may become annoying. Blue, blue-green, and violet color schemes may appear to be gray, especially in daylight or fluorescent light (in a blue color spectrum). Blue tones can be distinguished from other colors more easily at night when lighted by tungsten light (standard lightbulbs). Red tones appear to be the least affected by yellowing lenses.[3] Bright lighting intensifies color, while texture makes tones appear darker.[4]

Lighter color schemes that do not absorb light are important to improve visual acuity. (Fig. 3-2) Dark color schemes adjacent to bright windows can dazzle and make it difficult for people to distinguish objects located near the window.[5]

3-3

Contrast between the floor and wall color make it easier to identify the edges of a room. To evaluate this contrast, each color can be correlated to a shade of gray. If the color contrasts by more than two digits on the gray scale, the contrast is adequate to increase the imagery of objects.[6] (The gray scale consists of ten increments from black to white and can be found illustrated on the back of many printer's rules.)

A contrasting baseboard helps to define boundaries, and a door frame in a contrasting color draws attention to the doorway. (Fig. 3-3) As most doors are left open, contrasting the door frame is more important than contrasting the door itself. Window frames should not be contrasted to prevent them from being confused with doors.

There is some evidence that converging lines created by contrasting baseboard, wainscoting, valance, and handrails can be visually confusing to some people. This problem becomes most apparent at the end of a corridor.[7] On the other hand, when these elements are blended together into a monochromatic color scheme, a hallway appears wider and shorter. This technique can visually reduce the appearance of a long institutional corridor.

In spaces where people spend considerable time, a monochromatic color scheme may become monotonous and boring. Research has shown that this can contribute to sensory deprivation, a condition found in many institutions, which leads to disorganization of brain function, deterioration of intelligence, and an inability to concentrate.[8]

For specific diseases, consider color prescriptions for healing environments. For people with learning differences who experience a deficiency of perception, plan variety in color, pattern, and texture. Walls of mirror, however, should not be used to add variety and expand spaces.[9] Visually confusing mirrors are too distracting and can make concentration and orientation difficult. For people with mental illness who hallucinate or deal with distortion of perception, keep colors and textures as unambiguous and understated as possible.[10] An interior with few textures and colors is also helpful for people who are susceptible to sensory overload. Low-intensity colors, especially for background surfaces, are most

appropriate for this population.[11] People with dementia who become easily disoriented may identify with smaller spaces that are colored differently, are well defined, and are planned in human scale. Spatial definition can also help develop a sense of security. To offer a feeling of control, the perimeter walls and ceilings should be clearly defined and not extend into other spaces.

Disorientation also occurs when people are isolated from natural light and cannot differentiate between night and day. This phenomenon is referred to as *ICU psychosis* and occurs when circadian rhythms are disturbed. It can be cured using light therapy featuring periodic exposure to light representing daily cycles.[12] Light therapy can also be used to cure insomnia. According to the National Aeronautics and Space Administration (NASA), "light therapy regimen works better than sleeping pills in helping astronauts rest during the day and stay alert at night."[13]

Color can affect perceptions of time, size, weight, and volume. In a space where pleasant activities occur, such as a dining or recreation room, a warm color scheme makes the activities seem to last longer. In rooms where monotonous tasks are performed, a cool color scheme can make time seem to pass more quickly.

Warm color hues are often associated with extroverted responses and social contact. A quiet, relaxing, or contemplative atmosphere is created by cool hues. Cool colors can balance a warm space, whether the warmth is created with lighting, color selection, or actual temperature. Color contrast can be used to create varying moods.

Researchers in the field of anthroposophic medicine maintain that color can be used to help patients regain health. According to their studies, color should progress from hard tones to soft, luminescent tones as patients move from outside to inside. The most intimate and vulnerable spaces, like patient rooms, should have the softest colors. Patient rooms with warm colors are used to build up from a "cold" illness (defined as a *sclerosis*), and cool blue or violet tones are used to dissolve or break down inflammation.[14]

People who spend much of the day in bed may grow tired of facing a patterned or highly textured wall covering. Perforated and other ceiling patterns may also be visually confusing. Use strong patterns on walls adjacent to or in back of the bed only. Even in these locations, texture and pattern may produce a response of stimulation rather than relaxation. Control of the ceiling pattern can actually reduce stress. For example, a patient could be offered a choice of videotapes to project on the ceiling of a dentist's office or a choice of artwork to suspend on the ceiling of a hospital room.

Stripes on the wall can appear to be bars, and wavy patterns can appear to be in motion, affecting mobility.[15] Wall coverings in small patterns presented in limited amounts can be pleasing to the eye. (Fig. 3-4) Primary colors—red, yellow, and blue—and strong patterns are pleasing at first but may eventually become tiring. Also, the boundary between two intense colors eventually becomes visually unstable.[16] Use intense colors

for accents only or for contrast to improve visual organization. Brightly colored grab bars, door frames, levers, and switches, for instance, are easier to find than others.

## TEXTURE

People lean on walls occasionally for support; remember that a slick, glossy wall surface offers no friction for stability. Specify well-textured patterns. (Fig. 3-5) Semigloss finishes can be washed with little damage and are more resistant to soil than flat finishes, but the latter diffuse light, hide minor flaws, and appear less institutional. Flat finishes also reduce glare, which may be visually confusing.

Heavy plaster wall texture can be damaged by carts and mobility aids. It can also be abrasive when people rub against it. For people with allergies, a light gypsum plaster on metal lath may be the best choice. It should be left unpainted, but it

3-5

3-6

3-7

can be tinted with hypoallergenic, nontoxic dyes.[17] Vegetable dyes can be used in a casein and beeswax medium.[18]

In relaxation areas, use textured, sound-absorbing wall coverings that keep the space quiet. (Fig. 3-6) Control of ambient noise is important here to maximize concentration and hearing. Noise from mechanical equipment outside a room can be controlled with vibration isolators, duct insulation, and wall insulation. Low-frequency noise generated within the space can be absorbed by sound panels. (Fig. 3-7) Place the panels on at least two adjacent (not opposite) walls at the critical height for sound absorption (between 2 ft 6 in. and 6 ft 8 in. above the finished floor [a.f.f.]).[19] Be sure there are no acoustical leaks between the ceiling and the wall.

Hard surfaces are often used to meet fire codes, but echoes off these surfaces can create an institutional atmosphere and cause hearing and concentration difficulties. There is one exception to this rule: blind people may prefer hard, shiny surfaces and a relatively live sound-reflecting interior to help locate sound cues.[20] An open doorway, for

example, can be identified because it does not reflect sound like the adjacent surfaces. But in some areas, such as hallways, echoes may be confusing, making a conversation appear to be on one side of the corridor when it is really on the other.[21] Sound-absorbing finishes are a better choice in these areas.

## WALL PROTECTION

Protective corners, wall coverings, moldings, and baseboards are necessary to prevent damage of wall surfaces by carts and mobility aids. Use 9 in. high baseboards suitable for staining for additional wall protection. Use an oil stain finish that can be touched up if scratched. A carpet base matching the floor carpeting minimizes the institutional appearance of the high baseboard. (Fig. 3-8) Be sure that carpet base complies with local applicable fire codes.

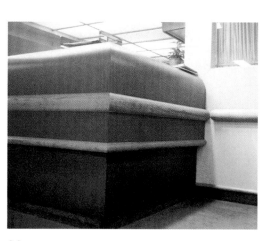

3-8

3-9

3-10

To protect corners from damage by carts and mobility aids, recess metal corner guards during construction or surface-mount metal or plastic guards after construction. Clear or colored plastic guards or wood moldings are not as institutional in appearance but not as durable as metal. Plastic and wood chair rails are also available. (Fig. 3-9)

Consider low-pile, fire-retardant coordinating carpet on the walls of high-traffic areas for acoustical control and protection from carts and mobility aids. (Fig. 3-10) End the wall carpet at 36–42 in. a.f.f., the height of the back of a wheelchair, and cap it with a chair molding. Again, always ensure that wall carpet complies with local fire code. Wall carpet and fabric significantly contribute to flame spread if inappropriately selected, but fire-retardant upholstery fabric can provide wall protection in low-traffic areas. Use a special adhesive designed for fabrics, as a regular adhesive may soak through to the surface.

With a properly sealed and insulated wall, fabric can be applied directly over textured wall surfaces like concrete or cinder block with minimal preparation. With fabric on the wall, the space can be personalized with wall hangings without visually harming the walls; nail holes will not show when wall hangings are changed. (Fig. 3-11) Some solution-dyed polyolefin can be cleaned with undiluted chlorine bleach with no effect on the color. Fabric can also be hung using a track system or draped over the ceiling. (Figs. 3-12, 3-13)

Ceiling moldings prevent wallpaper from peeling if they overlap the paper. They are especially necessary with heavy papers or fabrics that are used to protect walls from carts and mobility aids.

Vinyl wall covering weighing at least 13 oz per square yard can also offer abrasion resistance.[22] It is especially useful in areas where spills are a problem. Tedlar and Prefixx are both nonporous and prevent stains from migrating into the vinyl.[23] They are more expensive than some wall fabrics, show nail holes more easily, and do not offer the acoustical absorption qualities of fabric. Still, they can be lined to cushion a wall from carts and mobility aids while offering some acoustical control of low-frequency noise.

3-11

3-13

A chair rail is an important addition to dining or conference areas where chairs are used with delicate wall finishes. It can also protect the wall from carts and mobility aids. Wainscoting can serve the same purpose, but it visually reduces the size of a small room. (Fig. 3-14)

3-12

3-14

Textured tongue-and-groove planking in an oil finish is a good choice for walls exposed to abrasion. (Fig. 3-15) It should be glued and nailed to the wall before the finish is applied. An oil finish can be easily repaired if damaged by carts and mobility aids. Thin wood paneling has a higher flame spread rating than planking. Heat causes delamination and separation of the paneling, allowing the wood to burn more easily. Prefabricated scored paneling has an institutional appearance and cannot be easily touched up if scratched.

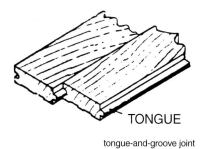

TONGUE

tongue-and-groove joint

3-15

Wood veneer rolls can be applied like wallpaper at a lower cost than solid wood. Veneers can also be wrapped around curved surfaces. Tambour wood sheets also serve this purpose and offer additional wall protection. In universal design curved corners are often specified to increase the view around the corner and to prevent accidents, but beware that carved walls are confusing to people who depend on touch for orientation. (Fig. 3-16)

Specify stains on frames and doors whenever possible; limit the use of paint and varnish, which are more difficult to touch up. With abrasion caused by carts and mobility aids, oil-based stains can be sanded and touched up in spots without major refinishing. When specifying resin or paint, use an epoxy surface wall paint with a water-resistant finish to prevent the paint from washing off. Urethane resin paints are so tough they are often used for floors, but they are not as resistant to fading as epoxy. (Fig. 3-17) Use low-luster paint to reduce reflection and glare.

Ceramic wall tile offers excellent protection from carts and mobility aids as well as water damage. It can be easily maintained if a colored latex cement grout is specified. Darker grouts are not as easily stained, and latex additives to portland cement make grout less absorptive. Silicone and urethane grouts also resist stains on walls.[24] Wall tile should be installed in portland cement when moisture and pressure are expected during use.

3-16

EVALUATION GUIDE: PAINTS

| | | | RESIN | | | |
|---|---|---|---|---|---|---|
| Property | Oil | Alkyd | Epoxy | Urethane | Vinyl | Acrylic |
| Abrasion Resistance | 2 | 3 | 4 | 5 | 3 | 4 |
| Hardness | 2 | 3 | 4 | 5 | 3 | 4 |
| Flexibility | 3 | 3 | 5 | 4 | 5 | 5 |
| Adhesion | 4 | 4 | 5 | 3 | 3 | 5 |
| RESISTANCE TO: | | | | | | |
| Acid | 1 | 2 | 5 | 5 | 3 | 3 |
| Alkali | 1 | 2 | 5 | 4 | 3 | 4 |
| Detergent | 2 | 2 | 5 | 4 | 3 | 3 |
| Fading | 3 | 4 | 3 | 2 | 5 | 5 |
| Heat | 2 | 3 | 3 | 3 | 3 | 4 |
| Moisture | 3 | 3 | 4 | 4 | 2 | 2 |
| Strong Solvents | 1 | 2 | 5 | 5 | 3 | 3 |

Legend: 5 = excellent, 4 = very good, 3 = good, 2 = fair, 1 = poor

3-17

# WINDOWS AND DOORS

# 4

Perhaps more than any other products, improperly specified doors and windows make buildings inaccessible. A door may be either too wide (and thus too heavy to open) or too narrow for easy passage by people using mobility aids, luggage wheels, strollers, or carts. A vision panel in the door, so helpful in preventing accidents, may produce disabling glare for people with differences in vision. When dealing with conflicting needs, it is obvious that specialized knowledge is required to design universally. There are few simple solutions, and mistakes are easily made and expensive to correct.

## WINDOWS

## Window Types

Both the design of the window and the location of the controls can improve access for all. Casement, sliding, hopper, and awning windows with controls on the bottom are easier for adults of shorter stature, children, and people in wheelchairs to reach. Make sure latches can be operated with a closed fist and corners of sills are rounded to prevent injury. Double-hung windows can drop unex-

pectedly and are difficult for everyone to open. Their latches are often too high to be reached by adults of shorter stature, children, and people in wheelchairs. Although emergency exit is not possible through most awning windows, this design is easier to reach and open than a double-hung installation. (Fig. 4-1) An awning window can also be installed inside an existing double-hung window. Awning windows, casements, and horizontal pivot sashes are easier to clean than sliding or double-hung windows.

4-1

4-2

Many crank-type casement windows are also easier to use than sliders, although a slider with ball bearings may also be easy to operate. A longer crank or lever arm multiplies the applied force. (Fig. 4-2) Place levers so that they can be operated with the stronger hand for greater power. For those in wheelchairs, space for a side approach may necessary.

4-3

Although casement windows with levers or push rods may require more force to open, they do not require as large a range of motion as do horizontal sliders and pivoting sashes. A crank-type control can also be added to double-hung windows. (Fig. 4-3) A power window offers the easiest access, but it must have a break-out feature in case of power failure. (Fig. 4-4) The force required should be no more than 5 pounds of force (lbf), but in no case can it be more than 15 lbf. The window lock must be installed within easy reach of adults of shorter stature, children, and people in wheelchairs.

A sliding window panel or shutter on a track may be easier than a hinged panel to operate from a wheel-chair. The top panel of a double-hung shutter is often higher than 4 ft a.f.f. and not reachable by adults of shorter stature, children, and people in wheelchairs. For safety, choose windows and shutters that will not drop unintentionally or swing in the wind. Keep the sill height at or below 2 ft a.f.f. if the window could be used for an emergency egress.

People with limited circulation often need higher ambient temperatures, and children, adults of shorter stature, and people in wheelchairs are in the lower, often colder, part of a room. For these people, heat loss and solar gain are critical issues. Create an overhang to reduce solar gain in hot climates, or raise the sill height and reduce the header or window height. Double-glazed sliding

4-4

windows conserve energy but may be too heavy for many people to operate. Manually operated push-button windows are available with a vertical control to adjust the window opening.

For people who have an increased need for security, consider using bay or bow windows, which offer a more complete view of the surroundings. They also allow more light into a room. (Fig. 4-5) Glass windows can be more easily broken than plastic but do not typically provide intruder protection. Use tempered glass or Lexan in low-level windows in case of a fall. Wired glass can also be used but has a more institutional appearance and is more dangerous when cracked. Heavy-duty plastic windows with locking devices are strong and resistant to force. Locate the lock as far away from the glass or plastic as possible. Look for windows with pins or bars that insert into the frame to prevent the window from opening even if the lock is breached.

## Window Treatments

Both the type of window treatments and the location of the installation need to be considered for access by adults of shorter stature, children, and wheelchair users. Treatments mounted within the window frame block some of the light and view but free extra wall space for storage within reach. (Fig.

4-5

4-6

4-6) If drapery is stacked outside of the window frame, it consumes wall space of approximately one third of the window width.

Sheer window treatments diffuse sunlight and prevent glare. (Fig. 4-7) Direct sunlight may dazzle and cause temporary blindness. Lip reading is also difficult when the speaker is standing in front of a bright window.

4-7

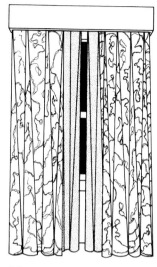

4-8

Many window treatments that insulate the space from temperature changes also block exterior noise. Consider heavy draperies with a separate liner (Fig. 4-8) or heavy roman shades that seal around the perimeter of the window. These soft surfaces also absorb the ambient noise generated within the room.

Make sure cords on roller shades and wands on blinds are long enough to be reached by children, adults of shorter stature, and people in wheelchairs. Wall-mount cords on blinds and draperies to keep them handy and within reach. Add beads to wall-mounted cords to improve grip strength. Do not mount cords over counters, especially in corners where they would be difficult to reach.

Electric drapery rod controls and wall-mounted drapery cords require less manual dexterity. Blinds and shades can also be operated electrically by switch or remote control. (Fig. 4-9) The trade-off is that electrical devices require additional maintenance.

Many people cannot respond quickly to fires. Flame-retardant fabrics are a logical choice for window treatments. Modacrylic or fire-resistant polyester fabrics drape well but cannot be laundered in hot water. Polyester has the added disadvantages of pilling, staining, and collecting static electricity. Although fiberglass is flameproof, it does not drape well and can cause skin irritations.

For people who spend some daylight hours in bed, use a reflective blackout lining to darken the room for sleeping. It reflects heat during the day and serves as a barrier to both air and moisture while protecting draperies from sun damage.

Many people cannot tolerate extremes of heat and cold. Reduce high heating and cooling costs with the right choices in window treatments. Exterior shades or awnings give the most effective protection from extremes in heat. (Fig. 4-10) Draperies, on the other hand, transfer less heat to the room than do interior blinds or shades.[1] Insulating draperies should be installed within ½ in. of the floor and ceiling or protected by a cornice for good thermal control. (Fig. 4-11) Otherwise, convention currents behind shorter draperies actually cool the space in the winter and heat it in summer. (Fig. 4-12)

4-9

4-10

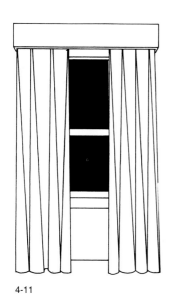

4-11

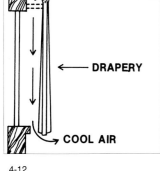

4-12

Drapery accessories can also improve energy efficiency. For example, draperies can be sealed to the wall with tacks, magnetic tape, Velcro, or moldings to reduce heat loss and gain. With fabrics that adhere to Velcro, the overlap in the center can be sealed with a Velcro strip that is hidden from view. Light-colored linings reflect solar energy and keep rooms cooler, while darker colors absorb the heat.

Insulated shades are available that seal the window for maximum control. They completely block out light and view, however, and are not appropriate for daytime light control. Solar shades allow light and view but are not as effective as shades that seal.

Specify shades that overlap the window on all sides to minimize heat and light leaks. Existing inside-mounted shades and draperies can be covered with a lambrequin, which controls light leaks and offers thermal protection.

Many people have limited time and energy, and window maintenance becomes a critical factor. Draperies require a special heading to be machine washable. A washable snap-tape system can be used so that drapery pins need not be removed and replaced. (Fig. 4-13) Vertical louvers on shutters and blinds are easy to maintain. Horizontal louvers may be dust traps and cause problems for people with allergies unless they are installed between panes of thermal glass. With fabric-filled shutters, fabric should be removable for maintenance. Fabric on padded cornices can be installed with snap tape or Velcro for easy removal and cleaning.

1. Snap Tape is sewn to the fabric, and the bottom and sides are hemmed.

2. Brackets or ceiling clips are mounted and the track is snapped into the clip.

3. Drapery panels and optional liner are snapped on the linkage.

4. Linkage pins are inserted in the carriers on the track.

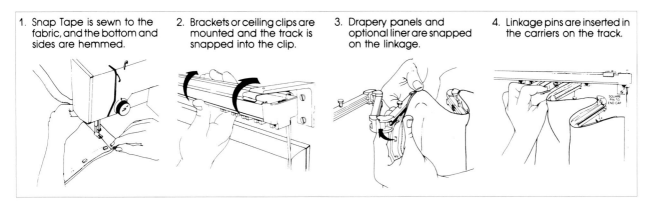

4-13

4-14

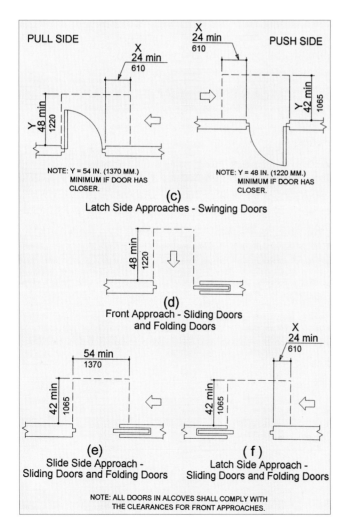

NOTE: Y = 54 IN. (1370 MM.) MINIMUM IF DOOR HAS CLOSER.

NOTE: Y = 48 IN. (1220 MM.) MINIMUM IF DOOR HAS CLOSER.

**(c)**
Latch Side Approaches - Swinging Doors

**(d)**
Front Approach - Sliding Doors and Folding Doors

**(e)**
Slide Side Approach - Sliding Doors and Folding Doors

**(f)**
Latch Side Approach - Sliding Doors and Folding Doors

NOTE: ALL DOORS IN ALCOVES SHALL COMPLY WITH THE CLEARANCES FOR FRONT APPROACHES.

4-15a

## DOORS

## Door Types

Perhaps more than any other product, improperly specified doors disable. Eliminate the vertical stop between double doors, as it is often not detected by blind people who use canes. Dutch doors are also a problem, because the top half of double-hung doors cannot be detected. Most are over 2 ft 3 in. a.f.f. and are not in compliance with the ADA. Doors that open at an angle into high traffic are hazardous for all. When the door swing cannot be changed, plan sliding interior doors to eliminate this problem. (Fig. 4-14) Pocket doors often solve space-planning problems but may not offer sound insulation to ensure privacy; some pocket door hardware is difficult to use.

To operate swinging doors, people in wheelchairs must often reach, grasp, pull, back up, turn, and go around. Maneuvering clearances are essential, and these approaches must be level and clear. (Fig. 4-15) These clearances can be

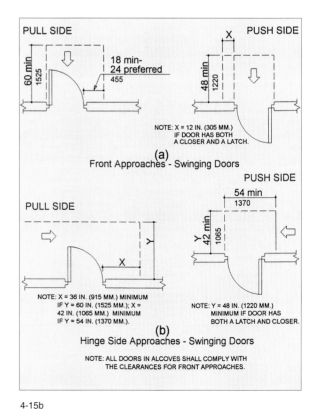

NOTE: X = 12 IN. (305 MM.) IF DOOR HAS BOTH A CLOSER AND A LATCH.

**(a)**
Front Approaches - Swinging Doors

NOTE: X = 36 IN. (915 MM.) MINIMUM IF Y = 60 IN. (1525 MM.); X = 42 IN. (1065 MM.) MINIMUM IF Y = 54 IN. (1370 MM.).

NOTE: Y = 48 IN. (1220 MM.) MINIMUM IF DOOR HAS BOTH A LATCH AND CLOSER.

**(b)**
Hinge Side Approaches - Swinging Doors

NOTE: ALL DOORS IN ALCOVES SHALL COMPLY WITH THE CLEARANCES FOR FRONT APPROACHES.

4-15b

reduced by using interior sliding doors, installing double swinging hinges, or by moving the hinges to the opposite side.

Folding doors also require less clearance, but it is easy for children and others to pinch their fingers in them. If these doors are on a track, make sure the track is recessed and is not an obstacle for entry. Accordion folding doors can also be used.

Sliding top-hung doors with bottom guides may be easier to move than those that slide on a bottom track. (Fig. 4-16) Choose nylon wheels or roller bearings with self-lubricating metal tracks.

French doors are often specified for additional clearance, but from a wheelchair or walker it is difficult to open both doors at the same time. Keep each leaf wider than 32 in. (Fig. 4-17) or replace them with folding doors or a single sliding door.

Solid-core doors require more strength to open and close than do hollow-core doors. Heavy doors should be kept to a minimum width of 3 ft to keep them easier to open. Sliding glass exterior doors can be very difficult to operate because of the width and weight of each door. Also, the accumulation of dirt in the door track can render the doors inoperable. Consider a hinged glass door as a replacement. For people who are autistic or prone to seizures and falls, use tempered glass. Glass doors should be protected from wheelchair abrasion by a bottom rail.

To measure the force necessary to open a door, attach a pressure scale, opening the door slowly and evenly. Many people cannot open exterior doors that require more than 8.5 lbf. Interior doors and all sliding doors must require less than 5 lbf to operate,[2] although this is difficult to achieve with interior fire doors. Adults of shorter stature and children are often unable to use heavy fire doors, particularly with panic hardware.

Doors that stick or drag require needless effort. The problem can often be corrected by oiling the hinges or removing the old paint on the edges of the doors. If this does not work, remove the door, plane and sand the edges, and shim the hinges or rehang the door on new hardware. Sand the sharp leading edges of doors to minimize possible injury. Specify an oil finish for easy touch-up. For people with allergies, use a water-based sealant or a hard-finish polyurethane.[3]

Doors can be selected to reduce transmitted noise and improve hearing ability within the space. Make sure all door and wall assemblies eliminate acoustical leaks. Inspect gaskets and use lam-

4-16

4-17

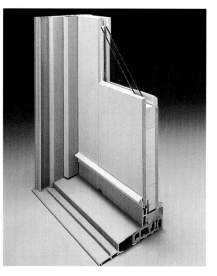

4-18

nated or double-glazed glass in doors and windows. (Fig. 4-18)

In commercial spaces, alternative doors or gates must be installed adjacent to turnstiles and revolving doors. An accessible revolving door is a more nearly universal solution. (Fig. 4-19)

For people who must spend part of the day in bed, use French or atrium patio doors in a wide width that allow the bed to be moved outdoors. (Fig. 4-20) Wider doors also allow the addition of large pieces of furniture to the room. Narrow doors may require the addition of an extra panel that can be opened when wider access is necessary.

For security purposes, the best protection is a metal door and frame. With existing sliding glass doors, add screws to the top to prevent doors from being lifted out of the frame. Wooden entry door frames (even with a dead bolt) can be forced with a well-placed kick.

## Door Hardware and Accessories

Door accessories that can assist wheelchair users include levers, door closers, thresholds, protective plates, vision panels, and hinges. Doors may be equipped with double-action hinges so they can swing both ways. Be sure the action of the door

4-19

4-20

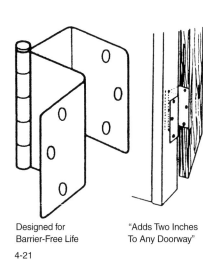

Designed for
Barrier-Free Life

"Adds Two Inches
To Any Doorway"

4-21

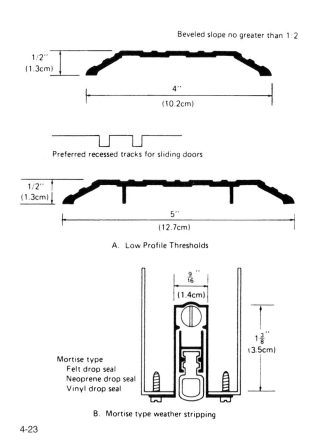

Beveled slope no greater than 1:2

1/2"
(1.3cm)

4"
(10.2cm)

Preferred recessed tracks for sliding doors

1/2"
(1.3cm)

5"
(12.7cm)

A. Low Profile Thresholds

$\frac{9}{16}$"
(1.4cm)

$1\frac{3}{8}$"
(3.5cm)

Mortise type
Felt drop seal
Neoprene drop seal
Vinyl drop seal

B. Mortise type weather stripping

4-23

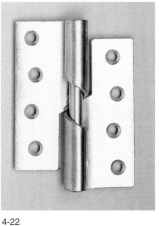

4-22

does not interfere with foot traffic, and specify a vision panel to prevent accidents.

If the door is too narrow for wheelchair or walker use, try removing the doorstop for an added amount of clearance. Offset pivot hinges increase the width of the open doorway by 2 in. (Fig. 4-21) This may be all that is required for the necessary 32 in. clear opening.[4] Whenever possible, specify a 36 in. door with 34 in. of clear space.

Rising pin-butt hinges should be specified for easy door removal in case of seizure behind a locked door. (Fig. 4-22) Residential interior locks should be easily opened with a screwdriver. This is especially important on bathroom and toilet room doors.

A rising pin-butt hinge can also be used to elevate weather stripping from floor surfaces. Negotiating

interior thresholds may be difficult for people pushing carts or using mobility aids. Thesholds are also a tripping hazard for some older users. Most interior thresholds serve no purpose and should be removed. Exterior thresholds must be no higher than ½ in. and must be beveled to a vertical slope no greater than 1:2.[5] To totally eliminate the exterior threshold on swinging doors, use movable mortise-type weather stripping, which lowers to the floor when the door is closed. (Fig. 4-23) Specify sliding glass doors that do not require thresholds. (Fig. 4-24)

4-24

4-25

On the exterior door, add a mail slot at latch height. (Fig. 4-25) Before installing the slot, make sure the post office agrees to deliver mail to the door. Attach an insulated box on the interior side of the door to catch the mail and prevent heat loss or gain. A larger insulated box could be used to keep delivered meals at the proper temperature.

On an exterior door, add a fish-eye peephole. Lower the door knocker to 3 ft 6 in. to 4 ft a.f.f. for children, adults of shorter stature, and wheelchair users.[6]

A pneumatic door closer can offer convenience for people carrying a heavy load and those using carts or mobility aids. It is also useful for people with vision differences, because a door left open at an angle into a traffic area may present an unexpected problem. A delayed-action door closer helps to keep the exterior door from blowing closed during use. (Fig. 4-26) Mount the door closer above 80 in. a.f.f. to prevent it from becoming a protruding hazard. Make sure the closer allows the door to remain open to a full 90° for 20 seconds to allow passage.[7] If it does not, substitute a lightweight spring device. Rising pin-butt hinges are not sufficiently reliable as door closers in some situations.

4-26

To close the door without a door closer, add a C-grip handle mounted on the hinge side of the door. This requires strength to use, but it does offer convenience for some. (Fig. 4-27)

The automatic door is truly universal. (Fig. 4-28) The door may be activated by a remote control, a floor mat sensor, or a photo cell. (Fig. 4-29) If mounted on the pull side of the door, the sensor or photocell must open the door before the user reaches the sweep area. This is not an issue with folding or sliding power doors. (Fig. 4-30) A wall button or switch may also be used if mounted within reach, close to the door or on the push side (but not in the frame). The button must be a minimum of ¾ in. in diameter, be flush mounted (not recessed), and require 5 lbf or less to operate. Make sure automatic doors have a break-out feature in case of power failure; force required must be no more than 15 lbf.[8]

People with balance or vision differences are often injured by swinging power doors or sliding doors with malfunctioning motion detectors. Signage with warnings and instructions should be in place. Air curtains and manually operated doors are better choices.

Texture on the door pull or lever indicates that the door leads to a dangerous area, such as a loading dock, boiler room, stage, or electrical equipment room. The texture can be made by knurling or by applying a Carborundum-epoxy-coated abrasive surface to the lever.[9] Do not use texture on the emergency exit door hardware, even if the door leads to a stairway.

Limit the height of doormats to ¼ in. and secure them to the floor with beveled metal trim or tape. Recessed carpet mats must not exceed ½ in. in pile height.[10] Rolling traffic can be immobilized

4-27

by a loose mat, the mat can be drawn up into a power wheelchair, and loose mats are also a tripping hazard. Exterior thresholds should be color contrasted; most interior thresholds should be eliminated.

To protect doors from abrasion, consider a high kickplate (16 in.) on manually operated doors. Extend the plate the full width of the door on the push side. The corners of metal plates should be filed or bent toward the door to avoid possible injury. A clear acrylic door guard scratches more easily than metal but is less institutional in appearance. A plate is preferable to projecting rails, which could catch a cart or mobility aid. With or without a kickplate, the bottom 10 in. of doors should be smooth on the push side for use with wheelchair footrests.

A metal bar or decal over a sliding glass door makes the door more visible and can prevent accidents. (For security purposes, a bar can also be used to block a sliding glass door.)

4-29

4-28

4-30

4-31

Vision panels in doors allow an adult of shorter stature, child, or person in a wheelchair to see and be seen. On an exterior door, a vision panel helps to monitor visitors. On an interior door, a vision panel or side light lets the person become oriented to ongoing activities before entering a room. (Fig. 4-31) The bottom of the panel should be mounted no higher than 3 ft 0 in. a.f.f. for use by adults of shorter stature, children, and people in wheelchairs, but it should not extend to the floor. People with vision differences can mistake panels that extend to the floor for door openings.

A glass panel above the door allows the frame to be easily adapted to the height of a taller person. The opening could also be extended to the ceiling if a ceiling track for a lift is needed.

Mount door hardware at least 34 in. a.f.f. so that it does not protrude into the arm clearance needed by people using wheelchairs. Levers (mounted at a height of 36 in.) on both interior and exterior doors are convenient for people in wheelchairs, children, adults of shorter stature, and people with strength differences.[11] They are much easier to use than doorknobs. Horizontal levers require less operating force than do vertical levers. Levers should point toward door hinges for easier access. (Fig. 4-32) They should have a slight return to keep them from catching on clothing and to prevent the hand from slipping off without trapping it. The shaft should be at least 4 in. in length

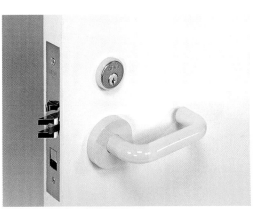

4-33

to fit the hand, and there should be no sharp edges. (Fig. 4-33)

Use extra-length doorstops to protect walls from door levers. Choose an extra-length doorstop that doubles as a hook for clothes. (Fig. 4-34) To protect walls from doorknobs, use doorstops mounted to the door hinges, or wall mount spring-loaded stops. It is easy to trip over a floor-mounted doorstop.

Paddles on doors can be specified if they can be easily maneuvered with one hand. Avoid doorknobs; never specify a knob on one side of the set and a lever on the other, because the spring of the lever is too strong for the knob. Avoid hardware requiring simultaneous two-handed operation. An example is a lock requiring the user to turn a key with one hand and pull with the other. Consider a push-button system (Fig. 4-35) or a card reader that can be used with one hand. If a dead bolt is used, specify a set that disengages

4-32

4-34

4-35

both the dead bolt and the door latch with one motion. For people who do not have the strength to operate the dead bolt, a slide bolt provides nearly the same amount of security and is easier to handle. Use a quick-release combination lock on doors to potentially dangerous areas, such as the head of a stairway or the entrance to a furnace room.

Doors without latches should have a C-grip on the pull side and a push bar on the push side. Doors with C-grips on both sides give the misleading message that both sides should be pulled. Especially avoid residential doors with knobs installed in the center of the door. These often require considerable strength to operate. They also make it difficult to determine which way the door will swing.

# FLOOR COVERING

Floor covering can make a significant contribution to the abilities of all users through prevention of slips and falls, increase in visual acuity, improvement of acoustics, and elevation of insulation value. Even wayfinding and orientation can be improved by floor covering. A variety of colors and patterns can help the individual delineate different spaces. This is especially true for people who take visual cues from lower levels, downward gazing for fear of slip and fall. Frequently a single color and type of floor covering is specified throughout an interior to add continuity to the design; this can make orientation difficult.

More effort is required to roll carts, wheelchairs, and strollers across carpeting than to roll across a hard-surfaced floor, but carpeting offers several advantages. First, it offers value as an insulator, a feature appreciated by people with limited circulation who cannot tolerate extremes of heat and cold. (It also feels warm to bare feet, which is especially appreciated by people in health care facilities.) Second, it is more comfortable for children and for people who like to spend some time out of the wheelchair on the floor. Finally, it absorbs noise, thus keeping the interior quieter. Studies show that carpeting can reduce ambient noise by up to 70 percent.[1] It also prevents generation of surface noise and reduces impact noise transmitted from level to level. Even noise from mechanical equipment can be significantly reduced by carpeting when used with floor insulation and padding. Cut pile absorbs more sound than does loop pile.[2]

Ceramic tile, wood, rubber, and vinyl floor coverings are all appropriate for rolling traffic, provided the surface is not too slick for wheelchair traction. Hard-surfaced flooring is not always the safest choice for pedestrian traffic. Vinyl and wood floors may require a nonskid polish. Surprisingly, research has revealed that hard-surfaced floors are not safer than carpet for controlling fungal or bacterial growth,[3] although it may be easier to control dust and allergens on a hard-surfaced floor.

## CARPET

### Carpet Construction

Evaluate carpets for resistance to static, flame, mildew, abrasion, fading, and permanent staining, as well as for resiliency. A resilient carpet is especially important for use with carts, strollers, and wheelchairs. (Fig. 5-1) Although nylon 6,6 is slightly less resistant to stains and fading than polypropylene (olefin) fiber, it equals or exceeds olefin in every other area, especially in resiliency, dyeing flexibility, styling versatility, appearance, and the hand or feel of the carpet.

The face weight (also called pile weight) of a carpet refers to the amount of yarn in a given area. In considering carpets of the same face weight and fiber, a lower pile and higher tuft density give the best performance. An increase in face weight increases performance to a maximum of 30 oz per sq yd in loop and 40 oz per sq yd in cut.[4] Increased

EVALUATION GUIDE: PERFORMANCE CHARACTERISTICS OF CARPET FIBERS

| Property | Nylon 6,6 | Nylon 6 | Acrylic | Olefin | Poly | Wool |
|---|---|---|---|---|---|---|
| | | | FIBER | | | |
| **HEALTH & SAFETY** | | | | | | |
| Flame Resistance | 4 | 3 | 1 | 3 | 2 | 3 |
| Static Resistance | 3 | 3 | 3 | 3 | 3 | 2 |
| Mildew Resistance | 3 | 3 | 3 | 3 | 3 | 1 |
| **WEAR LIFE** | | | | | | |
| DURABILITY | | | | | | |
| Abrasion Resistance | 4 | 4 | 2 | 3 | 2 | 2 |
| APPEARANCE RETENTION | | | | | | |
| Resiliency | 4 | 3 | 3 | 1 | 2 | 3 |
| Soil Resistance | 4 | 4 | 2 | 4 | 2 | 3 |
| Stain Resistance | 3 | 3 | 2 | 4 | 3 | 2 |
| Fade Resistance | 3 | 1 | 3 | 4 | 3 | 3 |
| MAINTENANCE | | | | | | |
| Cleanability | 4 | 4 | 2 | 4 | 2 | 3 |
| **ENVIRONMENTAL** | | | | | | |
| Dyeing Flexibility | 4 | 4 | 3 | 2 | 2 | 3 |
| Styling Versatility | 4 | 4 | 2 | 2 | 2 | 3 |

Legend = Poly = polyester, 4 = excellent, 3 = good, 2 = fair, 1 = poor

5-1

PROPERTIES AFFECTED BY THE STRUCTURE OF CARPET

| Property Affected | Tuft Density | Face Weight | Tuft Type | Face Fiber | Color | Dye Method | Texture Pattern |
|---|---|---|---|---|---|---|---|
| | Structural Components | | | | | | |
| **WEAR LIFE** | | | | | | | |
| DURABILITY | | | | | | | |
| Abrasion Res. | X | X | X | X | | | |
| APPEARANCE RETENTION | | | | | | | |
| Resilience | X | X | X | X | | | |
| Soil Hiding | | | | X | X | | X |
| Color Change | | | X | X | X | X | |
| MAINTENANCE | | | | | | | |
| Cleanability | X | | X | X | X | X | X |
| **ENVIRONMENTAL** | | | | | | | |
| Acoustics | X | X | X | | | | |
| Comfort | X | X | | | | | |
| Ambience | X | X | X | | X | | X |
| Wheeled Equip. | X | X | X | | | | |

5-2

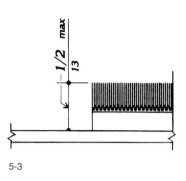

5-3

face weight also increases the sound absorption properties, but a corresponding increase in pile height can make the carpet more difficult for use by carts, wheelchairs, and strollers. (Fig. 5-2)

Carpet must not exceed ½ in. pile height in commercial spaces[5] (Fig. 5-3); ¼ in. height may be necessary for people with differences in strength. Use an uncut or tip sheer in a high-density pile for an easy traverse. (Fig. 5-4) Cut pile may pull the wheelchair, cart, or stroller in the direction of the nap.

A single-level loop pile wears best, but unless it is carefully selected, it can appear institutional. Multilevel loops and random sheer pile offer more texture, which tends to hide seams and soil. Cut pile has the shortest wear life but is the most residential in appearance. A frieze or highly twisted pile has the best appearance retention of the cut piles. A tightly twisted ply of crimped fibers in an uncut loop construction is the most resilient and retains appearance when carts, strollers, and wheelchairs are used. (Fig. 5-5)

Choose a carpet with an added biological guard to prevent bacteria growth and resulting odors. Make sure this carpet is inherently stain resistant and do not install it in areas with intense sunlight. The Centers for Disease Control (CDC) rate carpet as safe as hard-surfaced flooring in control of bacteria and fungi if maintained properly.[6] For people with dust allergies, however, hard-surfaced flooring is a better choice than carpeting, which can harbor dust and dust mites.

5-4

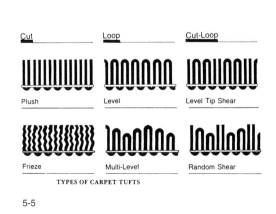

5-5

5-6

of balance. Large loops can catch on braces, canes, and walkers.

Choose synthetic primary carpet backings for areas with spills, such as bathrooms and dining rooms. Spun-bonded olefin is a good choice for the primary backing; it keeps spills on the surface of the carpet for easier cleaning while preventing rot, mildew, and shrinkage. Some people prefer carpeting in the bathroom for comfort and to cushion falls. If it is installed over a hard-surfaced floor covering using double-faced tape, the carpet can be removed easily for cleaning.

Use a woven primary and secondary back, such as stainless jute, for a stretched installation in areas where moisture is not a factor. Woven backs are an excellent choice for an installation requiring good tuft bind (with children pulling at the carpet tufts, for example). Some solid primary and secondary backs are also designed for this purpose. Woven and felted carpets provide excellent tuft bind.

A carpet with a woven secondary back can also be easily glued to a dry subfloor (without a cushion). For a softer surface, foam-rubber-backed carpets glue down well, but they are difficult to take up for replacement.

In the information age, static often interferes with data storage and transmission. It also interferes with hearing aids. Most contract carpet is inherently static free, but static-resistant carpeting must be specified in residential carpeting. Existing carpet can also be treated to prevent static.

## Carpet Installation

Do not glue down carpet over building expansion joints. As the building expands and contracts, the carpet could tear or ripple, interfering with the use of carts, strollers, and mobility aids and causing a tripping hazard. Improperly installed seams can open and trip pedestrians. Ask the installer for a plan of seam locations and make sure seams are not located in high-traffic areas. For a releasable bond, specify a carpet that incorporates its own adhesive system. These

Needle-punched polypropylene (olefin) or nylon textured flooring with vinyl backing combine the feel and appearance of carpet with the one-step cleaning of resilient flooring. (Fig. 5-6) This is especially important if incontinence is a problem. Because the carpet fibers are embedded in the backing, the result is increased tuft bind, decreased edge ravel, and moisture-proof seams. People prefer carpet because the feel of cold, hard floors may trigger the urge to toilet and reduce continence.

Olefin polypropylene can be cleaned easily, does not retain odors, and is more comfortable and safer than hard-surfaced flooring. It has a low melting point, however, and can show scorch marks from the friction generated when furniture is dragged over it too rapidly. It is less resilient than other fibers, especially when used by roller traffic.

Carpet reduces the incidence of falls and cushions any falls that do occur. The carpet should have a pile height of $\frac{1}{4}$–$\frac{1}{2}$ in., and the pile should be of a high density. A carpet surface that is too soft is easy to sink into and may cause loss systems can be rapidly installed, reducing the downtime on commercial projects.

Specifications should instruct the installer to save the scraps, which can be used to replace burns and stains. This is especially important to people with coordination differences. The installer should remove all doors before installing and ensure that the subfloor is clean and free of wax before gluing. Instruct the installer to maintain a consistent pile direction exactly parallel or perpendicular to roller traffic.

To prevent odors, seal concrete slabs with an acrylic polymer before installing carpeting. If the concrete flooring is hydrophilic, it will absorb liquids and their odors as it expands and contracts.[7] Specify a carpet with a moisture barrier. This is especially important for people with incontinence.

Area rugs and entrance mats should be permanently installed. Otherwise, the small wheels of standard wheelchairs, carts, and strollers may cause the rug to gather in front of the users. People in power wheelchairs may also be immobilized, as the rug may become tangled with the mechanism. More often, the loose corner of the area rug or mat causes a pedestrian to slip and fall, usually landing on the surrounding hard-surfaced floor. This often causes extensive injury resulting in institutionalization. Use area rugs only in low-traffic areas, and use graduated carpet strips for the installation. Never use an area rug over another carpet; the resulting surface is unstable, impossible to use with mobility aids, and a dangerous tripping hazard. Create the look of an area rug by using wall-to-wall carpeting with an inset in a contrasting color or pattern. (Fig. 5-7) Borders can be used to blend carpet colors between rooms and to serve as a guide for wayfinding, but use low contrast so that a border is not mistaken for a step. Carpeting can also be inset in tile without a change in level. (Fig. 5-8)

It is often difficult to spot a slight elevation in floor level. Single steps, thresholds, carpet strips (especially across hallways), high pile, and the edges of area rugs all present a tripping hazard, especially to people who drag their feet. Do not exceed a ¼ in.

5-7

5-8

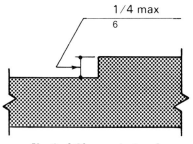

1/4 max

6

*Vertical Changes in Level*

5-9

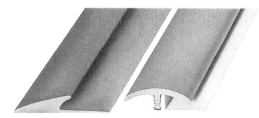

5-10

drop from one floor surface to another. (Fig. 5-9) Use a bevel if the change is between ¼ and ½ in. Use a small ramp if the change exceeds ½ in.

Avoid standard carpet strips between rooms, as they may pose a tripping hazard. Instead, sew carpets together at doorways or use graduated carpet strips. (Fig. 5-10)

## Carpet Underlayment

Padding adds comfort for children and people in wheelchairs who spend time on the floor out of the wheelchair, but it makes wheeling more difficult. If

a pad is used, specify a synthetic material with the equivalent firmness and resilience of a hair pad.

Roller traffic may cause the carpet to ripple unless latex rubber is applied to both sides of the pad. A preapplied pad adhesive system also works well. The carpet and pad are glued directly to the floor. (Fig. 5-11) The pad also reduces rippling and minimizes drag on the wheelchair if a thin, dense style is specified. Ripples in the carpet surface disable wheelchair users and trip people who walk.

For the easiest use of carts, wheelchairs, and strollers, eliminate padding in the carpet installation. Padding (and high carpet pile) may present an unstable surface for people who walk, especially when used on stairs. Padding is also responsible for many odor problems. A direct glue-down installation without a pad also prevents the rippling caused by roller traffic.

If a pad is necessary for comfort or acoustics, choose a solid synthetic style sealed to prevent absorption. Do not use a fibrous, waffle, or composite construction or a rubber pad, which can rot.

## Carpet Pattern

Visually confusing pattern and sculpture on carpeting is a problem for everyone, especially for

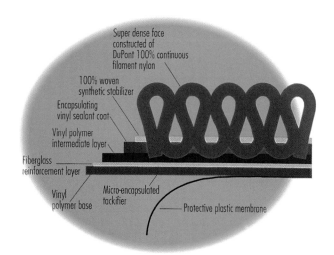

Super dense face
constructed of
DuPont 100% continuous
filament nylon

100% woven
synthetic stabilizer

Encapsulating
vinyl sealant coat

Vinyl polymer
intermediate layer

Fiberglass
reinforcement layer

Vinyl
polymer base

Micro-encapsulated
tackifier

Protective plastic membrane

5-11

5-12

people with differences in vision. Some patterns can make small objects on the surface difficult to locate. Contrast can also cause problems. Limit the contrast between carpets, as transitions and wide stripes can be perceived as a change in elevation. A carpet with high-contrast patterns may also be perceived as a variation in floor height.

Use subtle patterns in lighter colors; this increases light quantity throughout the space without increasing glare. Contrast the carpet with the wall color to highlight the edges of the room and improve spatial differentiation and wayfinding. Also choose a carpet that contrasts with the furniture to prevent collisions and falls. (Fig. 5-12)

## FLOORS

## Wood Floors

Textured wood floors in some oiled finishes offer surprisingly good traction and do not require polishing. Avoid wood floors with polyurethane finishes, which offer limited traction. They are especially difficult for people in power wheelchairs. A tongue-and-groove construction is available in

5-13

many woods and is a necessity for a stable installation on a poor subfloor. Use an oil finish on hardwood in low-traffic areas subject to scratching (e.g., under chairs); it can be touched up more easily than resin finishes. Use synthetic finishes in high-traffic areas. Acrylic-impregnated wood can be safely treated with gamma radiation to harden surfaces and prevent dents and chips. These surfaces never need waxing or protective coating and are the only wood floors that are appropriate in high-traffic areas. The acrylic saturation process also helps improve flame spread ratings and resistance to bacterial growth. The textured acrylic finishes offer better traction than polyurethane. (Fig. 5-13)

## Vinyl Floors

Solid vinyl floors with a nonskid polish are a good choice for use with carts, wheelchairs, crutches, walkers, and other mobility aids. Cushioned vinyl floors require slightly more effort to use with a wheelchair than solid vinyl surfaces. Cove vinyl to protect the kick space from wheelchair footrests. (Fig. 5-14)

Sheet flooring prevents leakage from spills and protects the subfloor better than vinyl tiles, especially if the seams are chemically or heat welded. A seamless installation is important for people with allergies, as leakage in the seams promotes bacterial growth. Monolithic high-density vinyl floor coverings are acceptable to most people with allergies if fas-

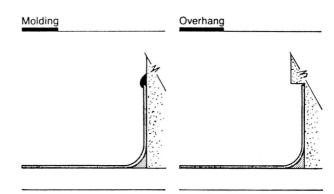

Molding        Overhang

**TERMINATION OF FLASH COVING**

5-14

## EVALUATION GUIDE: RESILIENT FLOORINGS

This table compares resilient floorings with one another. It does not compare the properties of resilient floorings with those of carpet or hard surface floorings.

| Property | TYPES OF RESILIENT FLOORINGS | | | | |
|---|---|---|---|---|---|
| | Vinyl Backed | Vinyl Solid | Vinyl Comp | Asphalt | Rubber |
| **HEALTH & SAFETY** | | | | | |
| Slip Resistance | 2* | 2* | 1* | 1* | 3* |
| **WEAR LIFE** | | | | | |
| DURABILITY | | | | | |
| Abrasion Resistance | 4 | 4 | 3 | 1 | 3 |
| APPEARANCE RETENTION | | | | | |
| Resilience | 3 | 4 | 2 | 1 | 4 |
| Static Load Resistance | 2 | 3 | 2 | 1 | 4 |
| Moisture Resistance | 4 | 4 | 3 | 2 | 4 |
| Chemical Resistance | | | | | |
|    Acids and Alkalis | 4 | 4 | 3 | 3 | 2 |
|    Oil and Grease | 4 | 4 | 3 | 1 | 2 |
| Cigarette Burn Resistance | 1 | 1 | 2 | 1 | 4 |
| MAINTENANCE | | | | | |
| Ease of Maintenance | 3 | 3 | 2 | 1 | 4 |
| **ENVIRONMENTAL** | | | | | |
| Comfort Underfoot | 2 | 4 | 2 | 1 | 4 |
| Sound Absorption | 2 | 3 | 2 | 1 | 4 |
| **INSTALLATION** | | | | | |
| Ease of Installation[†] | 3,4 | 3,4 | 4 | 2 | 3,4 |
| Flexibility | 3 | 4 | 2 | 1 | 4 |
| Cost | High | High | Medium | Low | High |

\* Varies considerably according to surface finish or polish.

[†] Tiles of any given material are easier to install than sheet goods.

Legend: 4 = excellent, 3 = very good, 2 = good, 1 = fair

5-15

tened with wood baseboards. Selection of adhesives and leveling compounds should be based on the allergy.

Floors with a large percentage of vinyl resin are the most resistant to stains.[8] Solid colors appear to be soiled more quickly than patterned floors. Soiling is also exaggerated by very light or dark colors.

Cushioned floors can be permanently dented by braces, canes, high heels, or other sharp objects, but they do reduce high-frequency noises such as footsteps. They are not durable enough to be used in high-traffic situations, however. Rubber and solid vinyl floors are the most resilient and dent resistant. (Fig. 5-15)

Self-shining synthetics eventually need touching up and should not be used in high-traffic areas. Solid vinyl floors or floors with a large proportion of vinyl resins are the best choice for abrasion resistance in such areas. Solid-colored vinyls or inlaid patterns are more resistant to abrasion than vinyl prints or rubber. Inlaid stripes are often used for wayfinding in commercial spaces. Low-voltage lighting strips can also be inserted in floor covering to aid in wayfinding.

In bathrooms or other potentially slippery areas, specify sheet vinyl impregnated with corundum chips. The seams can be chemically or heat welded to prevent leakage. This surface is easier to maintain than some other nonslip floors.

## Rubber Floors

Self-shining synthetics may be too slick for many people. Rubber and vinyl floors offer better traction with just enough shine to require only occasional maintenance with a commercial buffer.

Rubber flooring shows fewer scuff marks than solid vinyl. (Fig. 5-16) It is resistant to wear, slippage, abrasion, cigarette burns, and most oils, acids, and alkalis. Rubber surfaces are not recommended for commercial kitchens, operating rooms, or spaces subject to heavy rolling loads.[9] Patterned vinyl can be substituted, as it resists grease and oil and does not easily show scuff marks.

A rubber floor polished with a water emulsion offers better traction for users of wheelchairs, walkers, and crutches than does a smooth quarry tile. It is also a good choice for slip resistance in the bathroom. Darker colors help to hide marks left by shoes, wheelchairs, carts, and strollers, but unpatterned dark floors show dust and footprints. Dark colors also absorb light, a consideration for people with vision differences who require increased lighting.

Hard surfaces must be slip resistant or treated with a nonskid wax. Test slipping with a crutch angled at approximately 70° from the horizontal. If the floor is rated as a nonskid surface, it should have a friction coefficient no less than .6 (.8 for ramps) when wet or dry.[10] A rubber floor often exceeds this criterion and is a good selection, especially in a design with a slightly raised disk or strip. A rubber floor also lightly cushions falls. (Fig. 5-17)

5-16

5-17

## Tile Floors

Textured quarry tile, especially in small sizes with many narrow joints, is a good choice for the kitchen and offers better traction than shiny ceramic tiles. Rougher ceramic mosaic tile also provides good friction for wheeling but requires more strength to traverse than a synthetic floor without joints. Deep joints in a width greater than ¾ in. may hold the wheel of a wheelchair, cart, or stroller. The joints can also catch a crutch or walker. Protruding joints may produce a wash-boardlike effect, which can cause extreme dis-comfort, pain, or spasticity for the wheelchair user and serve as a tripping hazard to pedestrian traffic. Cobblestones and uneven surfaces resist rolling. Tile floors also increase the chance of breakage from kitchen and bathroom accidents, but tile can be a good choice for traction and durability. (Fig. 5-18)

5-18

Irregular paving and flooring materials look as if they provide good traction, but they may cause tripping, especially for users of mobility aids or prosthetic ankles. Ceramic mosaic tile can offer good traction without irregularities. Select a tile with an abrasive face, such as silicon carbide, Carborundum, or grit. (Fig. 5-19)

5-19

A slightly raised pattern also reduces slipping. Keep the joints small between the tiles to prevent tripping. (Fig. 5-20)

5-20

Use a moisture-resistant grout and vitreous tile where moisture is present and bacteria could grow. Porcelain, ceramic mosaic, and paver tiles are the most resistant to moisture.[11] Set the tile in portland cement; this is especially important in high-traffic areas and under wet conditions, where mastic is never recommended. A mixture of latex and portland cement is less permeable than other grout and should be used for shower stalls and other areas that may remain wet. The same mixture should be used in the grout. A floor grout in a darker color does not discolor as easily as lighter colors. (Fig. 5-21)

5-21

# FURNITURE

6

Manufacturers are only beginning to realize the potential of the market controlled by people who depend on universal design. These consumers are looking for products that are easily managed and that can make everyday tasks simpler and more enjoyable, not products that are complicated or bothersome to use.

## BEDS

A comfortable bed and adequate storage are basic design elements of any bedroom. Many people cannot function without a comfortable sleeping system with storage within reach. These elements are especially critical for people who spend considerable time in bed or find it difficult to sleep without pain. (Fig. 6-1)

Specify a twin-sized bed because its edges are easier to grip for turning. A shorter bed provides additional space for people who use strollers, luggage wheels, or mobility assistance devices. Many older people are comfortable with a 66 in. youth bed.

The height and stability of bedroom furniture are important considerations in universal design. If the bed is too low for transfer from a wheelchair, consider adding locking casters (Fig. 6-2) or recessing the legs in wooden blocks to raise the bed to the seat height of the wheelchair. Recess drawers under the bed for storage within reach. A fitted bedspread does not catch in the wheelchair mechanism. (Fig. 6-3)

6-1

6-2

Consider the installation of ceiling eyebolts or tracks above the bed for trapezes, frames, or lifts to aid in transfer or change of position in bed. This installation is difficult to remove, however, and requires structural support, so many people install a trapeze on the headboard even though it visually calls attention to the user.

If side rails are used on the bed, they should be removable for ease of entry and exit. Latches for the side rails should be within reach, not at the foot of the bed. They should be below mattress level to prevent injury in transfer.

Consider a hospital bed to provide a raised angle for sleeping. People who are not susceptible to pressure sores can elevate their knees to relieve lumbar pressure. Elevated beds can also be helpful to people with respiratory ailments or nausea. Some designs are more residential in appearance than others. (Fig. 6-4)

Specify footboards in a height of 34–38 in. a.f.f. to provide stability when walking around the bed (20–28 in. for children and adults of shorter stature). (Fig. 6-5) The footboard can also be used to hold the blanket or bedspread to relieve pressure on the feet. Consider nonskids to stabilize footboards and other furniture; also make sure the various pieces are of substantial weight for stability. A headboard with an upper edge approximately 10 in. above the mattress level may be used for support to rise to a standing position.

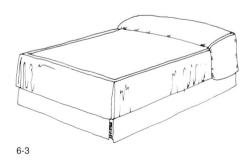

6-3

6-4

6-5

A stable headboard with vertical spindles can also be used for support when standing or transferring to a wheelchair. (Fig. 6-6) A headboard with built-in compartments or shelves can hold television controls, clocks, telephones, communication devices, bed controls, and alarm systems. Storage around the headboard can be expanded to include medical equipment such as an oxygen generator or respirator.

6-6

## MATTRESSES

A mattress should provide good heat retention, offer sufficient absorption to allow ventilation, and be flame retardant. An innerspring mattress should be firm, featuring pocket coil springs or open coil springs with little side play. Plywood under the mattress may provide good back support. The mattress cover should be changeable and washable. People with allergies often require cotton box spring covers and mattresses with cotton batting and ticking. People with limited circulation may prefer to sleep on sheepskin because the fleece serves as a soft support, conforming to the body and improving ventilation and absorption. The sheepskin should be washable.

Many water and air beds are manufactured from polyvinylchloride and other soft plastics that outgas, especially when heated. People with allergies may need to avoid these sleep systems, along with the algicides and fungicides often used with them. Although a water or air bed offers good back support and evenly distributes weight to prevent bedsores, it may be difficult to use in transferring to a wheelchair. A better choice might be another system that evenly distributes weight. Systems are also available that allow a person to lie motionless while the mattress adapts to simulate position changes.

All mattress systems should be evaluated for dressing in bed and for ease of transfer to and from a wheelchair. Specify a mattress with a firm edge at 19 in. a.f.f. to help in transferring[1] (11–17 in. for children and adults of shorter stature). When using an adjustable bed, choose a mattress that does not bunch and become lumpy at the bends.

For people who depend on the sense of touch more than vision, keep the mattress and nightstand at equal heights. Also, keep the dresser and headboard at equal heights; this way the user can slide a hand across the headboard to the dresser to locate objects.

## NIGHTSTANDS

Specify a nightstand large enough to privately store assistive devices. The top should be large enough to accommodate a telephone or call system; a gallery rail or edge around the top prevents items from being accidentally pushed to the floor. (Fig. 6-7) A console or wall-mounted countertop used as a nightstand provides clearance for wheelchair footrests, making it easier to approach the bed or answer the phone. If a drawer is used, consider specifying a lock for privacy.

Brightly colored furniture that contrasts from the background improves visual acuity. Clutter reduces visual acuity; this problem can be prevented by adequate storage.

6-7

## DRESSERS

Drawers are a good indication of quality in dressers. As a test for ease of use, grasp one corner and see if the drawer can be opened easily. Look for hardware that can be operated with a closed fist or slightly opened hand. To allow one-handed use, look for drawers narrow enough to open with one central C-grip (Fig. 6-8) Drawers under the bed may be handy for people who dress while seated or lying on the bed.

6-8

## WARDROBES

A wardrobe on wheels can be used to move clothing and shoes to a dressing area. This is particularly helpful for people who dress on the bed. Hooks and hangers in wardrobes and closets should be adjustable down to at least 4 ft a.f.f. (Fig. 6-9), although a maximum 3 ft height is optimal. The 3 ft height is also good for children and adults of shorter stature. A locking drawer in the wardrobe is a handy feature.

6-9

6-10

## BED TABLES

A cantilever table projects over the bed to keep things within reach. (Fig. 6-10) Some models attach to the headboard; others are supported by a base, which may not fit under an adjustable bed or a bed with box springs. Another choice could be a table that sits on top of the bed. Some models are adjustable for reading, writing, and working. A lazy Susan or a large bed table can improve reach. (Fig. 6-11)

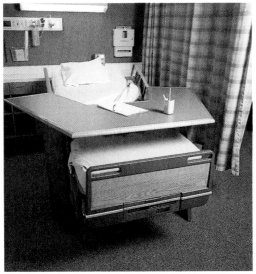

6-11

## BOOKCASES

In choosing bookcases, consider flexibility and ease of maintenance. Custom features available include carpet casters, adjustable shelves, and interior lights (a feature that improves visual acuity). (Fig. 6-12) Because laminate finishes can chip, consider using distressed finishes, which hide abrasions. Oiled wood finishes can be touched up if they have been abraded by use of strollers, luggage wheels, or mobility assistance devices. Metal trim can guard against chipping.

Look for rounded corners on case goods. The General Services Administration (GSA) Federal Supply Service requires all furniture corners and edges to be rounded to a minimum ⅛ in. Rounded corners are especially good for people with vision problems and those who bruise easily. (Fig. 6-13)

6-12

6-13

6-14

People often use bookcases for support when walking or transferring to a chair, so structural integrity is important. Cabinet quality should be tested with a full load of storage. When the cabinet is pushed to the side, it should not sway or creak as if the joints are spreading. The back of the piece should be glued, screwed, and finished, but glue smeared around a joint indicates poor craftsmanship. Interiors of cabinets, shelves, and drawers should be light colored to increase visibility. Angled storage shelves should have raised edges to prevent items from slipping.

Adjustable shelves in cabinets, bookcases, and other storage units offer maximum accessibility and flexibility as needs change. Consider a pulley system that allows shelves to be adjusted to various levels. Shallow shelves are more convenient for reach, especially from a seated position; they should be no deeper than 12 in. when placed above shoulder level. A shelf with a 12 in. depth can be further divided into two 6 in. bypassing shelves. High shelves should be of glass, wire mesh, or clear plastic so that objects can be seen from below. (Fig. 6-14) This is critical with seated use.

For seated persons, shelves should be adjustable to a reachable height, generally not exceeding 48 in. a.f.f. (36–44 in. for children and adults of shorter stature). Specify sliding or bifold cabinet doors that can swing out of the way of the people who use strollers, luggage wheels, or mobility assistance devices. Cabinets should be easy to open. Hardware should be strong, as it may be used for support.

## ROOM DIVIDERS

With proper furniture planning, large spaces need not appear institutional. Room dividers, hanging wall systems, and screens may help to temporarily divide a space and still free it for a variety of later uses. Dividers can also help to define territory or set up a transition between spaces. (Fig. 6-15) Avoid dividers with legs that extend into traffic areas. When legs are used, they should be no more than ½ in. a.f.f. and extend into the circulation area no more than 9 in.[2] Improperly designed legs can pose a tripping hazard and restrict people using carts, wheelchairs, walkers, and crutches.

6-15

## WORKSTATIONS

Workstations should allow a $5 \times 5$ ft clear floor space as a turning radius for wheelchair users. An aisle width of 5 ft should be provided on at least one side of the workstation. The underside of the work surface should be adjustable between 25 in. and 30 in. a.f.f. The depth should be at least 20 in. for leg clearance, and the work surface and cabinets (both upper and lower) should be a maximum of 25 in. deep. For a unit without a knee space, the work surface should be no deeper than 20 in. If workstations offer hanging storage for clothing, they should be adjustable between 48 in. and 66 in. a.f.f. The bottom shelf of cabinets over work surfaces should be adjustable to 44 in. a.f.f.[3] Task lighting, redundantly cued signage, sufficient contrast between surfaces, and a 15 in. a.f.f. minimum outlet height should be planned. Hardware must not require tight grasping, pinching, or twisting, or more than 5 lbf to operate.

Ventilation to control heat buildup and odor is an important feature if the room divider will be used to store a television, copier, or other appliance. For a person with allergies, the odors from the equipment may have to be vented outdoors.

To maximize strength, adjust work surfaces so that bending is not required. The height may be as low as

6-16

25 in. a.f.f. for a seated user or as high as 42 in. for a tall standing user. Heavier items like televisions can be more easily managed on swing-out shelves or turntables. Books are easier to grasp on shallow shelves, with the books protruding slightly. Deep shelves and clothing racks should roll out. (Fig. 6-16)

## WALL SYSTEMS

Wall systems with adjustable shelves, drawers, and cabinets allow storage heights to be customized to the reach of the user, which is especially important for seated persons. (Fig. 6-17) Store seldom-used objects at the extreme edges of the range of reach. (Fig. 6-18)

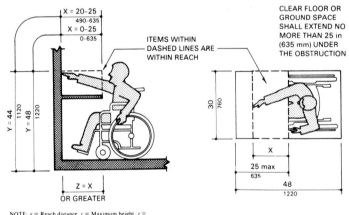

NOTE: $x$ = Reach distance, $y$ = Maximum height, $z$ = Clear knee space. $z$ is the clear space below the obstruction, which shall be at least as deep as the reach distance, $x$.

*Maximum Forward Reach over an Obstruction*

6-17

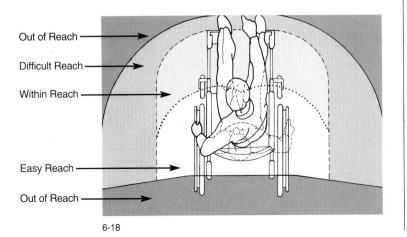

6-18

6-19

Freestanding wall systems that are accessible from both sides are more convenient than cabinets opening on one side only. Pull-out shelves and drop-lid desks are available on many wall systems, offering the option of lower work surfaces for use from a seated position. Surfaces at elbow height are useful for fine, discrete manipulations, such as writing.

For increased coordination, it may be easier to work on surfaces slightly below elbow height. For people in wheelchairs, cabinets and drawers should be raised at least 9 in. a.f.f. to allow footrest clearance. (Fig. 6-19, Fig. 6-20)

6-20

Keep drawers in wall systems at a reachable height (usually under 32 in. a.f.f.). Seated users may have trouble reaching to the back of drawers that are installed any higher.

A wall-mounted shelf for phone books is handy beneath a wall phone, which should be installed within reach. Add a clip to the shelf to secure a notepad. For planning shelf heights and depths, consider the maximum reach of a seated user. Wall-mounted shelves for parcels are helpful near a door. Install a hinged shelf on the latch side of the door slightly above the armrest of a wheelchair user. A shelf may be needed on both the inside and outside of the doorway. A standing user may prefer the shelf at elbow height, but the base must extend down to 27 in. a.f.f. or it will be a protruding hazard for blind people.

With a wall bed system, an extra bed can be added without limiting space for people who use strollers, luggage wheels, or mobility assistance devices. Some models offer a power system to raise and lower the bed. (Fig. 6-21) Be sure to specify an extendable nightstand, or cut portholes in the side of the system to allow the nightstand to be reached from bed.

## TABLES

Basic features to consider in table selection include construction, surface reflection, clearance for chair use, and height to support the task. These features are critical for people who may need to lean on the table for support, are susceptible to surface glare, or require specific heights and clearances.

A sturdy table may be necessary for support. When evaluating table construction, look for blocking in the leg joints. The joints should also be glued and screwed. Consistency of the type of wood used is a sign of quality construction.

Table and desk surfaces should reflect 30–50 percent of light that falls on them. Darker woods, including rosewood and walnut, reflect as little as 9

6-21

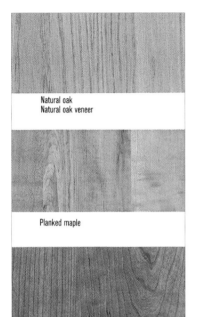

Natural oak
Natural oak veneer

Planked maple

Colonial cherry

6-22

percent. A white top reflects too much light and can tire the eyes. Shiny and glossy surfaces also produce too much glare. Select dull greens and beiges or light oak, maple, cherry, and teak for proper light reflectance.[4] (Fig. 6-22)

A round or oval top on a pedestal base allows an approach from all directions. (Fig. 6-23) Specify a stable base that will support a person who leans on the edge of the top.

Select a table with a border clearly identifying the edge. (Fig. 6-24) A slight reveal keeps spills off the floor without accumulating dirt. A raised edge makes some tasks difficult from a seated position. Specify a round table or a table without sharp corners to prevent bruising. An adjustable-height table allows a user to raise the table for detailed projects and reading.

6-23

6-24

In the dining room, a 60 in. round table can comfortably seat six, including one person in a wheelchair. (Fig. 6-25) If the diameter is increased to 66 in., seven can be seated, including one person in a wheelchair. Eight can be seated around a 72 in. table, including one person in a wheelchair. These estimates are based on dining room chairs that are 23 in. wide.

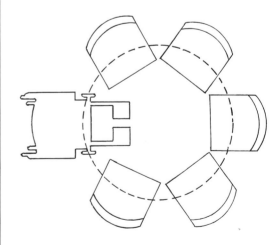

Seating, including seating for a wheelchair user, at 60" round dining table

6-25

A square table (54 × 54 in.) can seat four people in wheelchairs. For rectangular tables, allow 24 in. for each dining chair and 30 in. for each wheelchair user. (Fig. 6-26) Children's tables should be adjustable in height. (Fig. 6-27)

The size, height, shape of the top, and type of base may all limit the approach by people who use mobility assistance devices. Children and adults of shorter stature in wheelchairs typically require a knee space of 24 in. a.f.f.[5] Low crossbars between table legs may prohibit wheelchair access. Crossbars should be recessed a minimum of 19 in. from the front edge of the table. Skirt boards should be recessed a minimum of 12 in.[6] Trestle tables are often high enough to meet these requirements.

Pedestal tables allow closer access if the base does not interfere with the wheelchair footrests. Bases should be heavily weighted to prevent accidental overturning. A table with legs is more stable than a table with a pedestal base. Rubber and upholstered legs resist chair abrasion. (Fig. 6-28) A table with a minimum clearance of 27 in. a.f.f. (24 in. for children and adults of shorter stature) allows most wheelchair users to slide

6-27

under the table apron. Specify a high table (in the range of 32–34 in. a.f.f.) for a closer approach by a wheelchair user. A high table facilitates use of the shoulders and upper arms. If too high, however, it may put pressure on the back and cause eyestrain.

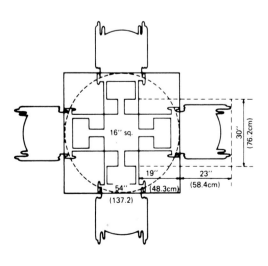

6-26

6-28

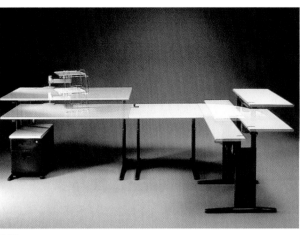

6-29

6-30

6-31

For larger projects, plan an adjustable worktable. (Fig. 6-29) For a person in a wheelchair, one large table is more accessible than a grouping of smaller tables. For smaller projects, consider an adjustable coffee table. This works well for people who choose to spend some time on the floor out of their wheelchair. High coffee tables (21–24 in. a.f.f.) do not pose a tripping hazard,[7] but low tables are easier to reach from a seated position.

Avoid table legs or supports that extend into traffic areas. Keep coffee tables lightweight or on casters if they are to be pushed out of the way by people who use carts, strollers, luggage wheels, or mobility assistance devices. (Fig. 6-30) A nest of lightweight tables can be stacked out of the way when not in use. (Fig. 6-31)

Pedestal coffee tables cannot be used for support when sitting down or rising from the sofa, and drop leaves do not support much weight. Choose a well-constructed table with straight legs for support. Specify sleigh legs to easily move the table over textured surfaces. (Fig. 6-32)

6-32

6-33

6-35

Lamp tables and side tables are often moved; they should be lightweight and mobile. For detailed work from a standing position, keep the table slightly below elbow height. Heavy manual work requires a table about 10 in. below elbow height.[8]

In planning reachability, consider the shape of the table. With a 60 × 30 in. table, only 68 percent of the surface can be easily reached.[9] A person with reduced mobility uses even less of the surface. An L- or U-shaped surface can bring all items within reach for many people (Fig. 6-33), although the corners may still be difficult.

A drop-leaf table can be closed to clear the space for access. (Fig. 6-34) To save space, use a drop-leaf table as a sofa table that can be extended for dining. (Fig. 6-35) Be sure the space between the legs is wide enough (30 in.) for a wheelchair user. Extra seating stored under a sofa table can save space for wheelchair passage. (Fig. 6-36)

Flip-top tables can be stacked against the wall to facilitate use of carts and mobility aids. (Fig. 6-37) Specify locking casters so that tables can be moved for storage. A wall-mounted table that folds flat against the wall can also help keep space clear for passage.

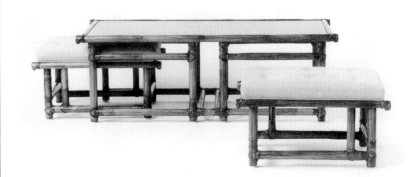

6-36

6-34

6-37

For serving food or clearing a table, specify a small cart. A toaster or microwave can also be moved on the cart from the kitchen to the dining room. (Fig. 6-38) Another handy item is a carpeted exercise table or bench at the seat height of the wheelchair to allow easy transfer. This exercise bench also works well for people who have trouble getting up from the floor after exercising. (Fig. 6-39)

6-38

6-39

# DESKS

For typing, the desk surface should be between 5½ and 7 in. above seat height. For most other tasks, the surface should be between 10 and 12 in. from seat height.[10] Desks with adjustable slanting tops can reduce fatigue and discomfort.[11] (Fig. 6-40)

Specify a desk with removable cutouts for a closer approach in a chair. Some models offer high rims to keep items from rolling off. Add a lazy Susan to improve reach. (Fig. 6-41)

Consider using a hunt table as a desk, as it offers access to a larger surface area. The surface on all sides also provides extra support for arms and shoulders.

6-40

6-41

6-42

Movable file cabinets under the desk can prevent extra trips across the room. They can also be pulled out to open the space under the desk for people who use mobility assistance devices. (Fig. 6-42) The top of a cabinet can be used as extra work space when the file is rolled out or can be opened for convenient access to both drawers at once. (Fig. 6-43). For people who need to lean on a file cabinet for stability, specify a model with locking casters.

Plan an adjustable-height workstation for computer use. (Fig. 6-44) Make sure the keyboard shelf or table can be adjusted to just barely clear the lap. Position the center of the screen slightly below eye level for maximum visual acuity and minimum neck strain. Looking up at a screen can cause neck discomfort over an extended period of time.

6-44

When specifying a reception desk in an office, keep one surface at 28–34 in. a.f.f. with clearance of 27 in. below for use by people in wheelchairs. For children and adults of shorter stature in wheelchairs, plan a height of 26–30 in. a.f.f. with clearance of 24 in. below. This provides direct visual access between the staff and visitors as well as a writing surface at a usable height. (Fig. 6-45) An accessible width of 36–42 in. should be allowed for both adults and children.[12]

6-43

6-45

## FRAME SEATING

In planning seating, consider comfort, quality of construction, and ease of maintenance. A comfortable chair should allow the user to place both feet flat on the floor. (Fig. 6-46) Most of the sitter's weight should be on the buttocks, and there should be a space between the thigh and front edge of the seat. Pressure behind the thigh over an extended period of time can aggravate circulation problems.[13]

The deeper the seat, the more slant needed on the backrest for comfort. An open space between the seat and the back is often more comfortable, as it allows extra room for the buttocks. (Fig. 6-47) The back of the chair should be adjustable from 8 to 13 in. above the seat surface. Plan chairs in a variety of sizes to accommodate both small and large visitors.

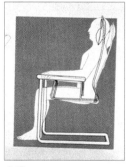

6-46

6-47

(The width of the seat should be no less than 16 in. and the depth no less than 15 in.)[14] A variety of styles can be used as visual cues to help people become oriented in large commercial spaces.

In a chair without armrests, the user is more comfortable if the back of the chair is narrower than the width of the shoulders and lower than the shoulder blades. In a chair with armrests, the user should be able to rest naturally on the arms, although lower armrests may be better with a desk or table. The armrests should be slightly below the table apron.

Armrests should seldom be higher than 8½ in. above the seat for maximum support and reduction of fatigue. Armrests alone support 12.4 percent of body weight.[15] They offer a sense of security and provide support in rising from the chair. Many people get out of a chair by first sliding forward to the edge and then pushing off. (Fig. 6-48) Make sure that the seat will not tip forward and that the arms extend slightly beyond the leading edge of the chair seat. Hard, not padded, chair arms are helpful for transferring from a wheelchair. A seat with an armrest that swivels up also facilitates transfer from a wheelchair.

Specify at least one chair in which the user can be comfortable for a long period of time. For comfort, the seat may have to be adjusted in height (between 13⅔ and 20⅔ in. a.f.f.).[16] The angle of the seat and backrest should also be adjustable.

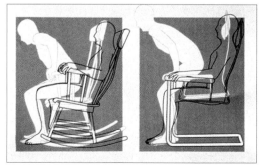

6-48

6-49

6-51

Pressure on the spine decreases as the tilt of the backrest increases. A lumbar cushion also reduces pressure and offers greater support.

An adjustable high stool may help the user maintain endurance and strength with minimal bending over a task. (Fig. 6-49) The user may also want higher dining chairs (with a seat height of 18 in. a.f.f.). The seat cushion should compress no more than 1 in.[17] A lower seat height and a sagging cushion may be hard on knees and hips when rising from the chair.

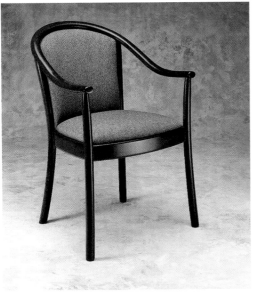

6-50

Low bracing also interferes with rising from a chair if the user's feet are tucked under the seat to push off; eliminate bracing. (Fig. 6-50) To provide extra support without bracing, specify a chair with seat stretchers. Stretchers also stabilize a chair for transfer from a wheelchair.

A seat cushion is especially helpful in the area where the spine meets the seat, and proper cushioning prevents skin ulcers. Test for proper cushioning by putting the full weight of your closed fist in the center of the seat. You should not feel a spring or supporting board. Upholstery that is too soft is not appropriate for work and can even induce sleep.[18]

Choose seating with curved edges, padded corners, and soft surfaces to prevent bruises and pressure on the backs of the knees. (Fig. 6-51) Removable cushion covers without welting, ridges, and tufts are easier to maintain. Welting at the front of the seat may hamper circulation to the legs.

EVALUATION GUIDE: PROPERTIES OF FIBERS

| Property | Wool | Nylon | Modac | Olefin | Cotton | Rayon | Acryl | Poly |
|---|---|---|---|---|---|---|---|---|
| Strength | 2 | 4 | 3 | • | 4 | • | 3 | • |
| Flexibility | 5 | 3 | 3 | 4 | 3 | 3 | 3 | 4 |
| Resiliency | 4 | 5 | 5 | 4 | 2 | 2 | 5 | 3 |
| Extensibility | 4 | 4 | 4 | • | 2 | 2 | 4 | 4 |
| Recovery | 3 | 5 | 3 | 3 | 1 | 1 | 3 | 5 |
| Elasticity | 4 | 4 | 3 | 3 | 2 | 2 | 3 | 4 |
| Absorbency | 4 | 2 | 2 | 2 | 4 | 4 | 2 | 1 |
| RESISTANCE TO: | | | | | | | | |
| Alkali | 2 | 4 | 4 | 4 | 4 | 3 | 3 | 3 |
| Acid | 3 | 2 | 4 | 4 | 2 | 3 | 3 | 4 |
| Solvents | 4 | 4 | 4 | 2 | 4 | 4 | 4 | 4 |
| Sun | 1 | 1 | 5 | 3 | 3 | 1 | 5 | 3 |
| Micro/Insects | 1 | 5 | 5 | 5 | 1 | 1 | 5 | 5 |
| REACTION TO: | | | | | | | | |
| Flame | BS | BS/M | M | B/M | BQ | BQ | BQ/M | BS/M |
| Flame Removal | SE | SE | SE | CB | CB | CB | CB | SE |

Abrasion resistance is a function of strength, flexibility, and resiliency.
Dimensional stability is a function of resiliency, extensibility, recovery, elasticity, and absorbency.

Legend: • = dependent on formulation, 5 = excellent or very high, 4 = very good or high, 3 = good or medium, 2 = fair or low, 1 = poor or very low.
Modac = modacrylic, Acryl = acrylic, Poly = polyester
B = burns, S = slowly, Q = quickly, M = melts, SE = self extinguishing, CB = continues burning

6-52

In most applications, upholstery fabrics that allow the skin to breathe and prevent slipping also make chairs more comfortable. Choose textured fabrics with corrugation for more friction. The latter can help people stay oriented by maintaining an upright sitting position.[19] However, slippery fabrics may be useful to help people slide into deep booths or automobile interiors.

Use nylon upholstery for abrasion resistance, polypropylene for stain and sun resistance (but not resistance to heat or stretching), and wool for porosity and comfort. (Fig. 6-52) Remember that vinyl and plastic coverings on chairs may become hot, slippery, and uncomfortable and should not be used on upholstery planned for long-term seating. Shiny vinyl is associated with institutional use and makes an interior appear sterile. Vinyl with a slight texture or pattern may be a better choice.

6-53

6-54

If the user is more comfortable with the hip or knee in a straight position, choose a chair with a movable thigh rest. Armrests are also available for supporting paralyzed arms.

A high-back rocker provides head support, but make sure the chair does not tip. (Fig. 6-53) Studies have shown that people with dementia benefit from access to chairs that rock or swivel.[20]

Mobile stools and chairs allow a wide range of motion in places too tight for wheelchair use. Choose a stool with adjustable seat height, seat angle, armrest, backrest, and footrest. Casters that automatically lock during entry and exit are also helpful. (Fig. 6-54) In addition, the hardware for chair adjustment should be easy to reach and operate.

People maintain eye contact and read body language more easily from swivel chairs in a group situation. (Fig. 6-55) Semicircular seating arrangements are recommended, perhaps around a table. Seating placement is critical for people who read lips.

For people who are sensitive to petrochemicals, specify hardwood or metal furniture rather than composite wood or pressboard frames. Choose pieces with mechanical fasteners instead of glue.[21]

6-55

## UPHOLSTERED SEATING

Specify couches and chairs with firm cushions; soft cushions impede transfer from a wheelchair. Down cushions, for example, are too soft. If the deck is also soft, add plywood under the cushion for support.

Bucket seats and some contour seats make it difficult to shift or change position. Rockers aid muscle tone, digestion, and circulation, but they should be lockable to aid in transferring.

To easily rearrange the room, put locking casters on all furniture. Casters also allow furniture to be pushed out of the way by people who use strollers, luggage wheels, or mobility assistance devices.

Avoid furniture that involves unusual angles of exertion to operate, like sleeper sofas and reclining rockers. To maximize strength, furniture and equipment should be selected on the basis of operation. To fold a sleeper sofa, for example, bend the knees to extend the large leg muscles to their length rather than use the weaker back muscles. Maximum effort is deployed when the greatest number of muscles are involved, when the largest muscles are used, and when muscles are resting at their length.

If the user does not have the arm strength to operate the controls of a recliner but finds the automatic legrest convenient, consider a recliner with foot controls. A recliner on casters allows the user to be pushed from one room to another on hard floors. (Fig. 6-56) For people who spend much of their time in bed but prefer to be in the living room, consider a convertible chair. (Fig. 6-57) This may be easier than rolling the bed into the living room, but the user may still need help operating the mechanism of the chair.

Make sure swivel chairs, recliners, and other movable seating have locking mechanisms. It is difficult for many people to sit and rise from a swiveling seat. Specify seats at the same height as a wheelchair seat to aid in transfer and to reduce the difference in eye level.

If a chair or couch is too low for easy transfer, raise it with blocks of wood. Recess the sofa legs into the blocks for stability. Cover the blocks with a longer skirt or add a slipcover. Make sure the base is recessed or left open for wheelchair footrests. (Fig. 6-58)

Many people lean on upholstered seating for support while standing. The legs of a sofa or chair should be at the corners of the seat. For stability, the back legs should extend outward so the feet are even with the top of the backrest. (Fig. 6-59)

6-56

6-57

6-58

6-59

For people who have trouble rising from the center cushion of a long sofa, a shorter sofa puts the user closer to an armrest for support when rising. (Fig. 6-60) Loveseats and shorter sofas also allow more flexibility in furniture arrangement.

Add a portable lift seat to an existing chair to help the user rise slowly to a 45 angle, or consider a chair with a controlled pneumatic lift. Models are available with movable seats and armrests.

A high-back chair can provide protection from drafts and a feeling of greater security, but lightweight, open chairs usually occupy less floor space and are easily moved. If the user naps in the chair, look for an adjustable head cushion. Unless the chair is very low to the floor, the user may also need a footrest. (Fig. 6-61) For people with back problems, choose a footrest that is high enough to keep the knees bent at a height slightly above the waist. When choosing a footrest, make sure it is easily removable. Low ottomans can pose a tripping hazard. Keep these well away from high-traffic areas and provide contrast from the floor.

6-60

6-61

Fire-resistant furnishings are critical for older people and others who need additional reaction time to respond to a fire. Most states require testing for flammability. California Technical Bulletin 133 requires that the product as a whole be tested, rather than its individual components. Rate of temperature increase, the amount of toxic gas produced, smoke density, and weight loss of the test sample burned may be affected by combinations of fabric, cushion, and construction. Designs with open arms and backs, for example, may be rated differently than designs with loose seat and back cushions with upholstered arms.[22] Fire rating is not often improved by applying chemical flame retardants to the fabric. This technique has not been proven effective and may even produce toxic gases when burned. The application may also change the appearance of the fabric.

# ACCESSORIES AND EQUIPMENT

7

The value of a building design may be determined by the attention that was paid to detail. Do the accessories meet the personal needs of the users? Is the telephone equipped with amplification? Does the alarm clock have large lighted numerals? Can controls be easily operated? Does the interior reflect care and concern?

## SMALL APPLIANCES

Cordless units save time and energy. They can be operated from a distance by touch control, by phone, or voice signals. Other controls for installed appliances should be set at counter level, accommodating children, people in wheelchairs, and adults of shorter stature. With smart appliances, like built-in vacuum systems, controls are eliminated. A vacuum system of this type is especially convenient because operation is easy and one-handed. Tostart, the hose is simply inserted into the inlet. Be sure to mount the inlet at a reachable height (15 in.

a.f.f.). (Fig. 7-1) A built-in vacuum system is also appropriate for people with allergies because it blows dust and other allergens out of the house.

If the cost of a built-in vacuum is not in the budget, a portable vacuum can be strapped to the back of a wheelchair for ease of use. The best offer controls located on a contoured handle, not on the machine. Specify a retractable cord and a dust bag that is easy to change. The hose should be crush resistant and long enough to reach around the wheelchair.

A cordless rechargeable vacuum cleaner saves time and effort on small cleanups. Hauling out a large vacuum and maneuvering around the cord in

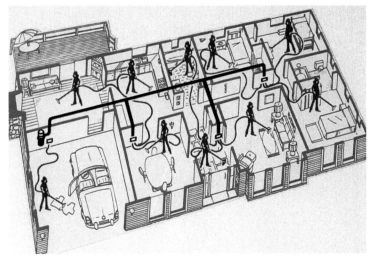

7-1

7-2

7-3

a wheelchair is much more difficult. The cordless vacuum also improves reach when a quick cleanup is in order. Consider a lightweight upright vacuum for people who may have difficulty pushing down on a handheld hose.

Select small appliances that offer such safety features as a built-in ground-fault circuit interrupter to prevent electrical shock. A handheld hair dryer, for example, can be easily dropped into the bathtub or sink, resulting in shock or fire.

Many people have a reduced reaction time to fire, and selection of an extinguisher is critical. Fire extinguishers are labeled for use with class A, B, or C fires. Class A fires are fueled by ordinary combustibles, class B by flammable liquids, and C by electrical appliances and wiring. For general use, select multipurpose A-B-C models. Choose an extinguisher that has a slight texture on the canister to improve the grip and is shaped not to roll off the lap of a seated user. Also, look for a unit that stands up on a flat bottom. Use a pedestal or mount the bottom at 27 in. a.f.f. to prevent it from becoming a protruding hazard or out of reach for seated users. It should be easily removed from the wall, and removal of the unit should automatically remove the safety catch. Use several small extinguishers rather than one large model, which is harder to handle. The diameter should be

7-4

7-5

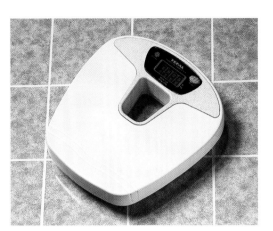

7-6

small enough to hold in one hand. Pictorial displays with sufficient contrast are preferable to written instructions.

Many small appliances and accessories originally designed for specific abilities are now being used universally. A universal alarm clock features extra-large numerals, raised indicators at each number, and audible cues. An optional bed vibrator can be added to awaken people with a wide range of hearing abilities. (Fig. 7-2) Talking calculators (Fig. 7-3) and desk clocks announce the time in a humanlike voice. (Fig. 7-4) Talking wristwatches are available with an audible or vibrating alarm, and a talking thermometer states the temperature. (Fig. 7-5) Talking scales announce current weight as well as any weight gain or loss. For convenience, look for models with toe-operated controls. (Fig. 7-6) These features help all users.

A cordless headset allows televisions to be used without increasing the ambient noise level in the room. A tape player with a cordless headset and a remote control is used by blind people in place of notes when making speeches. Tape recorders are also used by people with coordination limits to take notes.

## OFFICE EQUIPMENT

Office equipment should be specified to improve accessibility for all employees. Printers, copiers, scanners, and fax machines, for example, should be usable at 30 in. a.f.f. Touch controls should be located toward the front of the machines, and a clear

7-7A

7-7B

floor space should also be provided to access the controls, load paper, and retrieve documents.

Office equipment with wireless remote control is a convenience for all people. Most stands for slide projectors are too high for adults of shorter stature and people in wheelchairs; a height adjustment may be needed. Many projectors can easily be stored in pop-up stands for convenient access. (Fig. 7-7)

Calculators, automatic pencil sharpeners, and many other pieces of office equipment are available in designs for one-handed use, an advantage to all users. Keyboards can now be added to that list. (Fig. 7-8) In selecting a model, specify right- or left-handed use.

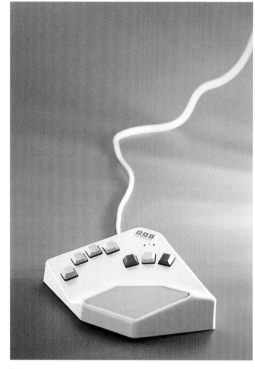

7-8

## COMPUTERS

Computers are used for a wide range of daily activities: telephoning, messaging, banking, and shopping, to name a few. Unlike telephones, computers can be used without spoken communication, a decided advantage for people with hearing or speech differences. Computers offer bulletin boards, networks, and direct communication with anyone who has a Touch-Tone phone or a text telephone (also known as TDD and TTY).[1]

A variety of accessories is available for computer use with a mouth stick or with one hand. A keyguard or wristguard stabilizes the finger, hand, or stick so that other keys are not pressed by accident. (Fig. 7-9) Software and operating systems now have built-in accessibility features that do not require users to press two keys simultaneously, as with the shift and control keys. Keyboard positions can be redefined. Other features slow down or eliminate the auto-repeat function, which may be difficult for some people to control. Voice recognition systems (which accept spoken commands) are also commonly available.[2] (Fig. 7-10) With features like these in place, a person with quadriplegia can type up to 60 words per minute.

Keyboards are available with enlarged keys for people with differences in coordination. Some have single keys for frequently used words and

7-9

7-10

phrases. For people who cannot depress keys, membrane keyboards are available. Switching systems can be operated by any movement and are used to replace keyboards. Switches are used in conjunction with scanners or with Morse code, which is faster than scanning. Scanners provide wide choices of information on a screen or separate panel. The user selects the information of interest with a switch.

People with learning differences benefit from the immediate feedback offered by computers. Learners see, hear, and feel information (on a touch screen) to reinforce the message and allow for a variety of learning styles.

A speech synthesizer offers voice output for a person who cannot use the screen or who has a speech impairment. The computerized voice lets the user hear the information printed on the screen. It provides immediate audio feedback as data are entered, so mistakes are easily identified.[3] When used with a telephone interface, a synthesizer can serve as a speakerphone, allowing two-way conversation without the use of voice. (Fig. 7-11)

Braille systems and optical readers are helpful add-ons to improve visual acuity. A Braille display reads aloud the information from the screen and also presents it in Braille. (Fig. 7-12) Printed infor-

7-11

7-12

7-13A

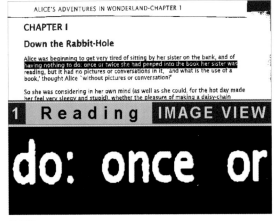

7-13B

do: once or twice
she had peeped into
the book her sister
was reading, but it
had no pictures or
conversations in it,

7-13C

mation can be scanned and displayed on a magnified screen, reprinted in Braille, or read aloud by the speech synthesizer. This is especially helpful for dated information like newspapers or correspondence that needs attention before a tape or reading service can be used.[4] Software is also available to enlarge text and images. (Fig. 7-13)

Computer peripherals are becoming more user friendly for people with varying abilities. A printer system, for example, can be operated with a mouth stick, by voice, or by hand without requiring manual dexterity. One excellent example of a user-friendly device is a disk-loading system that can be fully operated with a mouth stick.

## DRINKING FOUNTAINS AND WATER COOLERS

To minimize injuries to blind people who use canes, water coolers with floor clearances exceeding 27 in. a.f.f. must not be placed in circulation paths.[5] People in wheelchairs require a clearance of at least 27 in., so this is the exact clearance to meet the needs of both populations. Units recessed in alcoves can have higher clearances without becoming obstacles for people who sweep with a cane. A recessed fountain or cooler with a forward approach must project between 17 and 19 in. from the wall. The recess must be a minimum of 30 in. wide and a maximum of 24 in. deep. If only a side approach can be used on a fountain recessed more than 15 in., the recess must be 60 in. wide. An alternate fountain should be offered for children with a spout no higher than 30 in. a.f.f., a clear knee space of 24 in. a.f.f., and a depth of at least 14 in.[6] (Fig. 7-14)

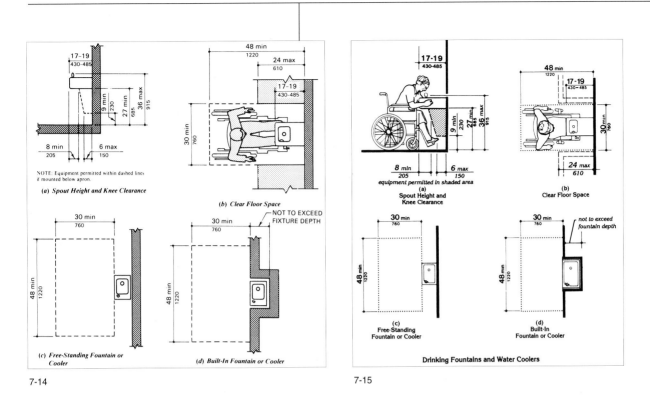

7-14

7-15

The ADA requires a combination of standard height drinking fountains and fountains lowered to the height of adults of shorter stature, some children, and wheelchair users who require a spout no higher than 36 in. a.f.f. (Fig. 7-15) The spout must be located close to the front of the unit (within 3 in., with a round or oval bowl) with water flow parallel to the front edge. The flow must be at least 4 in. high for use with a cup. A flat-bottom paper cup dispenser adjacent to the water fountain allows use by many people who can't reach the spout.

Controls must be located near the front edge of the fountain. They must be operable with one hand without tight pinching, tight grasping, or twisting of the wrist. (Fig. 7-16) An automatic sensor is most easily operated, freeing both hands to hold packages, luggage rollers, briefcases, etc.

7-16

## TELEPHONES

What was once the simple telephone is now a machine that understands specific voices, takes notes, communicates with others, and travels everywhere. When used as a component of a "smart" house, the phone can open doors, adjust heating and cooling, start the oven, and dim the lights. If water in a kettle is boiling on the stove, the level of the flame on the range can be lowered by a phone call from bed. One phone call can warm up the hot tub and start a romantic fire using a gas log in the fireplace.

7-17

In new commercial buildings, at least one forward-reach telephone is required on each floor with usable elements no higher than 4 ft a.f.f. Keep the route to accessible phones free of obstacles and make sure that the public closed-circuit phones are accessible. At least one pay phone must be accessible at each location where a pay phone is provided. Allow a 30 × 48 in. clear space in front of each for an approach in a wheelchair. (Fig. 7-17) The bottom of the public telephone and its surrounds must be no more than 27 in. a.f.f. if it is in a circulation path. (Fig. 7-18) Phones placed higher cannot be easily and consistently detected by blind people using canes. Recessed telephones offer protection for adults and children who sweep with canes as well as access for people in wheelchairs, providing the recess is a minimum of 30 in. wide and a maximum of 24 in. deep, with a clear floor space.[7]

If the existing wall phone is in an awkward location, replace it with a cordless phone. For people with reduced mobility, portable phones can prevent the race to the telephone or the frustration of a missed phone call. Choose a model with a two-way intercom for communication between the base unit and the handset. Specify a phone that searches frequencies for the clearest channel. Clarity is just as important as volume for people with reduced hearing. The phone must also switch between tone and pulse. Other features to consider are automatic redial, volume control, and a ringer that cannot be heard through the earpiece.

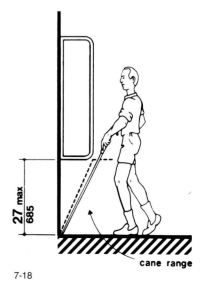

7-18

A car phone is a convenience as well as a necessary security feature for people of all abilities. Many public phones are not accessible. With a car phone, help can be reached, appointments can be confirmed, and directions can be requested, resulting in great savings of time and energy.

Touch controls on phones are easier to manipulate for people with differences in coordination. Card-dial telephones are also available. Touch controls on the headset are more convenient for use from bed. (Fig. 7-19) Make sure the cord to the handset reaches across the width of the bed and wall mount lighter-weight phones for additional stability. Specify a cord length of at least 29 in. between the handset and the base of all phones.[8] This cord length is required on accessible public phones to facilitate use with a text telephone.

Phones with large, easy-to-read push buttons are convenient for all users but essential for people with reduced vision. (Fig. 7-20) Talking caller identification devices are also available.

If touch controls are still too difficult, attach a touch plate. Pressure on any part of the plate dials an operator who in turn, places the call. Puff-and-sip dialing systems are available on some telephones; the operator is contacted by blowing into a plastic tube. (Fig. 7-21) Voice-activated dialing service is also available.[9] Some phones respond to the spoken name of the person to be called, recalling the number and dialing it.

Headsets, puff switches, lapel microphones, and pillow switches can be used by people with differences in arm motion or manual dexterity. (Fig. 7-22) An existing phone can be adapted with a telephone stand and a handset clamp. Some models have a lever-operated line interrupter that can

7-20

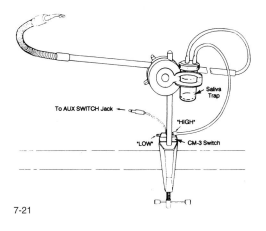

7-21

7-19

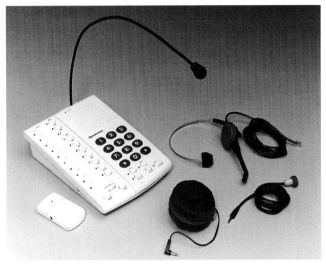

7-22

7-23

7-24

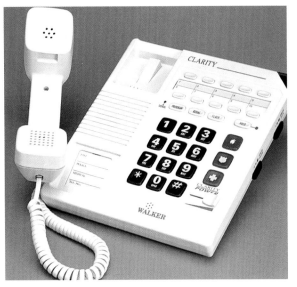

7-25

be used by pushing with the hand, elbow, or foot. With the line interrupter, the handset can be left permanently in the clamp.

Light-touch speaker phones are useful for people with varying strength and coordination who may have difficulty with a handset. (Fig. 7-23) Speakers can also be attached to existing telephones. Models are available with Touch-Tone, memory for automatic dialing, visual cuing, and an answering system.

Telephone receivers on required accessible phones must generate a magnetic field to be compatible with many hearing aids. In-line amplifiers are available and portable amplifiers can be added to an existing telephone. (Fig. 7-24) Amplified phones are also available that control background noise, volume, and clarity control, boosting high-frequency sounds. (Fig. 7-25) This feature is needed by 95 percent of people with reduced hearing.

Text telephones, tone ringers, gongs, and signals in other frequencies allow more choices in signaling an incoming call. Telephones can also be wired to room lights, flashing lights, or amplified signaling devices. (Fig. 7-26) Visual telephone signaling devices should be placed near the phone, not mounted high on a wall where they would could be mistaken for a fire alarm or obscured by smoke in the event of a fire.

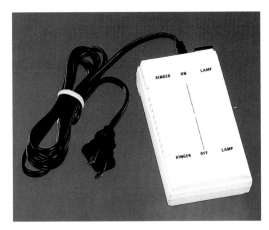

7-26

7-27

7-29

Telephones, teleprinters, and other telephonic devices are available to transmit printed messages to a teletype emphasis printer or television monitor. (Fig. 7-27) A portable text telephone with a cellular phone adapter can be used to call any location with a compatible unit or through the relay system to an incompatible unit. (Fig. 7-28) Provide a shelf for the unit with a receptacle outlet within 4 ft. (Fig. 7-29) A built-in printer provides a record of the conversation, an advantage to all users. Some phones can be easily switched from text to voice. The switch also allows users to type ahead of incoming messages.

For a person with a soft voice or with speech differences, consider a programmable speech synthesizer or a handset for speech amplification (Fig. 7-30), which plugs into any modular telephone and increases the volume of the voice by as much as 30 percent. Amplification may be critical for a person to be understood in an emergency.

7-28

7-30

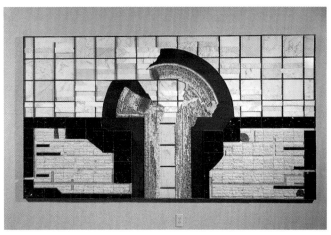

7-31A

7-31B

7-31C

## DECORATIVE ACCESSORIES

Decorative accessories may actually reduce stress when the user maintains control of the selection and chooses a "positive distraction."[10] Universal art even appeals to people who are blind. In one creative example, visitors are encouraged to touch a tile mosaic, feeling their way through a maze to the fossil "reward" at the end. (Fig. 7-31)

Art can be a source of relaxation and pleasure or a source of irritation, depending on the reaction of the individual. The choice of art can be returned to the individual in a health care setting through a mobile cabinet or art cart, which allows consumers to personalize their room with the art of their choice. A similar program can be introduced in an office setting or in any other space principally occupied by one user. (Fig. 7-32)

7-32

7-33

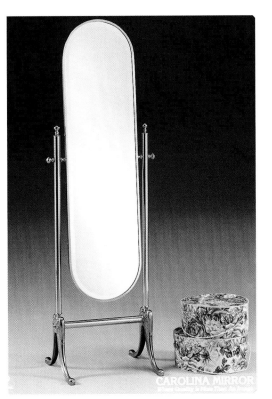

7-34

Encourage people to display wall hangings or crafts to personalize the interior. Use accessories that reflect the interests of the individual. Collections can be displayed in curio cabinets or tables. (Fig. 7-33)

Hang some artwork and other wall-mounted accessories at a lower height for children, adults of shorter stature, and people in wheelchairs. Include full-length mirrors in the bedroom and by the front door to serve all populations. Elevate glass at least 10 in. from the floor to avoid damage from wheelchair footrests. (Fig. 7-34)

Avoid tall arrangements of flowers or accessories on furniture that block a clear line of vision to interpreters or other people in the room. Tall arrangements may make it difficult to maintain eye contact and to read lips and gestures.

## SIGNS

Signs in public spaces are needed to control movement and to offer advice, information, and identification. They are important elements of both wayfinding and orientation strategies. Signs should be understandable, requiring no further clarification.[11] Simple terms like *walkway* and *general hospital,* for example, are more easily understood than *overhead link* and *medical pavilion.*[12] Signs should be consistent throughout the space, as succinct as possible, readable for all users (composed at a sixth-grade reading level), and stated in positive terms.[13]

Proportions

Display Conditions

7-35

## SUMMARY OF ADA SIGNAGE REQUIREMENTS

| ADAAG Section | Identification | Sign req'd | 4.30.2 Character Proportion | 4.30.3 Character Height | 4.30.4 Raised Braille Pictogram | 4.30.5 Finish & Contrast | 4.30.6 Location & Height | 4.30.7 Symbols of Access. (Figure #) |
|---|---|---|---|---|---|---|---|---|
| 4.1.2(7) 4.1.3(16)a | Permanent Room or Space Identification | | | | √ | √ | √ | |
| 4.1.2(7) 4.1.3(16)b | Direction or Information about functional spaces. | | √ | √ | | √ | | |
| 4.1.3(16)b | Exception: Temporary Signs (Directories, Menus) | N/A | | | | | | |
| 4.1.2(7)a 4.6.4 | Accessible Parking Spaces. "Van Accessible" below International Symbol where applicable. | Req. | | | | | | 43a/b |
| 4.1.2(7)b | Accessible Passenger Loading Zones. | Req. | | | | | | 43a/b |
| 4.1.2(7)c | Accessible Entrances where not all are accessible. | Req. | | | | | | 43a/b |
| 4.1.2(7)c 4.1.3(8)d 4.1.6(6)h | Directional Signage at inaccessible Entrance | Req. | √ | √ | | √ | | 43a/b |
| 4.1.2(7)d | Accessible Toilet where not all are accessible. | Req. | | | | | | 43a/b |
| 4.1.6(3)eiii | Directional signage to Accessible Toilets at inaccessible toilets | Req. | √ | √ | | √ | | 43a/b |
| 4.1.3(17)a | Derectional at inaccessible Telephone where accessible Telephone not visible | Req. | √ | √ | | √ | | |
| 4.1.3(17)b, 4.30.7(2) | Volume Control Telephone | Req. | | | | | | Handset w/ Waves |
| 4.1.3(19)a | Assembly: Fixed Aisle Seats w/removable armrest. | Req. | | | | | | 43a/b |
| 4.1.3(19)a | Assembly Ticket Office: Availability of accessible Seating | Req. | | | | | | 43a/b Optional |
| 4.1.3(19)b. 4.30.7(4) | Assembly: Availbility of Assistive Listening System. | Req. | | | | | | 43b |
| 4.3.11.5 | Area of Rescue Assistance identification (illuminated when exit sign illumination required.) | Req. | | | | | | 43a/b |
| 4.3.11.5 | Area of Rescue Assistance: Directional signage at inaccessible exits or as otherwise needed to indicate location of Area of Rescue Assistance. | Req. | | | | | | 43a/b Optional |
| 4.3.11.5 | Instructions on use of Area of Rescue Assistance adjoining 2-way Communication System. | Req. | | | | | | |
| 4.10.5 | Elevators: Floor designation at Hoistway | Req. | | 2″ | √ | | √ | |
| 4.10.12(2) | Elevator car: Control bottons with Braille and Raised Letters/Numerals Star @ Main Entry Floor | Req. | √ | 5/8″ Fig. 23a | √ | √ | 4.10.12(3) 4.10.12(4) | 23a |
| 4.10.14 | Elevator: Emergency Communications. | Req. | | | √ | | 4.10.14 | |
| 4.30.7.(3) | Text Telephone | Req. | | | | | | 43c |
| 4.30.7.(3) | Directional Sagnage to Text Telephone. | Req. | √ | √ | | √ | | 43c |
| 7.3.(3) | Business & Mercantile: Accessible Check-out Aisle | Req. | | | | | | 43a/b |
| 35.163(a) | Prov. info. concerning all services, activities & facilities of public entities (may be signage) | Req. | | | | | | |
| 10.4.1(2) GA4.30.1 | Signage for **Transportation Facilities**. see **Transportation Signage Form.** | Req. | √ | √ | | √ | | 43a/b Optional |

(a) Proportions: International Symbol of Accessibility

(b) Display Conditions: International Symbol of Accessibility

(c) International TDD Symbol

(d) International Symbol of Access for Hearing Loss

Volume Control [ 4.30.7(2) ]

7-36

To identify accessible facilities and parking, use the international symbol for accessibility. (Fig. 7-35) Parking signs should directly face the driver within a 60° cone of vision.[14] In addition to the international symbol of accessibility, additional signage may be required. (Fig. 7-36) For example, parking for vans requires a sign stating "van accessible," and "areas of refuge" signs are also required. Text telephones

7-37

must be marked with the international symbol for TTY, and volume control telephones and assistive listening systems must be identified by the international symbol of access for hearing loss. Inaccessible elements like entrances, exit stairways, toilet rooms, drinking fountains, and elevators must have signage offering directions to accessible features. Directional signage mounted over 80 in. a.f.f. must have 3 in. characters at a minimum.

Contrast, proportion, and redundant cuing are important signage features. Light yellow or white letters on a black background are the most readable for partially sighted users.[15] (Fig. 7-37) The ADA Accessibility Standards recommends a contrast level of 70 percent. People who are color-blind have difficulty with signs relying on contrast between red and green. People using different languages and learning skills may understand colored pictograms more easily than words.

Signs that offer tactile and audible cues as well as visual cues are important to people with differences in vision, reading, and learning abilities. Tactile signs must include letters or symbols raised a minimum of 1/32 in. and must be accompanied

7-39

with Grade 2 Braille and should be angled for ease of use.[16] (Fig. 7-38) Raised Arabic numerals and standard block uppercase letters without serif are recommended.[17] Raised characters must be ⅝–¾ in. high[18] but no higher than 2 in.[19] (Fig. 7-39)

People with reduced vision appreciate well-placed tactile signs that identify accessible routes, common use spaces (e.g., cafeterias), and public health and safety features (e.g., fire exits, toilets, and hazardous areas). In the event of an emergency, exit signs should be backed up with a middle-frequency audible signal to aid in location of an exit.[20] Tactile maps lead users from larger to smaller details about a space. The metal ball on a tactile map indicates the location of the sign. (Fig. 7-40) Required tactile signs must be mounted at a

7-38

7-40

7-41

7-42

height of 60 in. a.f.f. (48 in. for children) on the latch side of the door. (Fig. 7-41) A person must be able to approach within 3 in. of signage without encountering protruding objects or standing within the swing of a door.

Audible signs may have touch controls or, with a controlled audience, may include infrared or low-frequency radio signals. Receivers can be distributed in stadiums, auditoriums, hotels, convention centers, museums, schools, etc. The area is scanned with the receiver to pick up audible messages. Some facilities offer an interactive audiovisual tour on a handheld unit with large touch buttons and a visual printout. This unit is helpful to people with hearing, coordination, and vision differences. (Fig. 7-42)

All signs should be placed to avoid glare from windows and light sources, and glare-free materials should be selected. Proportion can also improve visibility. Letters and numbers must have a width-to-height ratio between 1:1 and 3:5. The letter $X$, for example, could be $3 \times 5$ in. The ratio of the stroke width to the height must be between 1:5 and 1:10. If each line used to make the $X$ is 1 in. wide, then the line itself could be between 5 and 10 in. in length.[21] Spacing between lines of text should be 25–30 percent of the point size.[22]

## PLANTS

Plants add a feeling of life, vitality, and growth to a space. They absorb carbon dioxide and other unwanted gases while adding oxygen to the air. Although people with mold allergies should probably avoid houseplants in moist soil, houseplants are helpful to people with other allergies. For example, ficus plants absorb formaldehyde, which outgasses from many building materials and carpeting. (Fig. 7-43) In a large planter, keep houseplants in smaller pots so that they can be easily moved. Larger potted plants can be moved if they are in a mobile plant stand.

CHEMICALS REMOVED BY HOUSEHOLD PLANTS FROM A SEALED
EXPERIMENTAL CHAMBER DURING A 24-HOUR EXPOSURE PERIOD

| | FORMALDEHYDE | | | BENZENE | | | TRICHLOROETHYLENE | | |
|---|---|---|---|---|---|---|---|---|---|
| | Initial (p/m) | Final (p/m) | Percent Removed | Initial (p/m) | Final (p/m) | Percent Removed | Initial (p/m) | Final (p/m) | Percent Removed |
| Mass Cane | 20 | 6 | 70 | 14 | 11 | 21.4 | 16 | 14 | 12.5 |
| Pot Mum | 18 | 7 | 61 | 58 | 27 | 53 | 17 | 10 | 41.2 |
| Gerbera Daisy | 16 | 8 | 50 | 65 | 21 | 67.7 | 20 | 13 | 35 |
| Warneckei | 8 | 4 | 50 | 27 | 13 | 52 | 20 | 18 | 10 |
| Ficus | 19 | 10 | 47.4 | 20 | 14 | 30 | 19 | 17 | 10.5 |
| Leak Control | 18 | 17.5 | 2.8 | 20 | 19 | 5 | 20 | 18 | 10 |

Note: Plants were maintained in a commercial-type greenhouse until ready for testing. Each test, 24-h in duration, was conducted in a sealed chamber with temperature and light intensity of 30°C +−1 and 125 footcandles +−5, respectively.

7-43

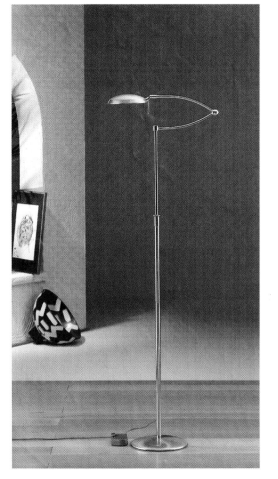

7-44

## LAMPS

Avoid installing any projecting wall lamp that can be an obstacle to people who may not see it or pick it up with a cane. Movable floor lamps are more easily detected. Lighter-weight floor lamps can be positioned from a wheelchair for task lighting, especially when they are adjustable in height. (Fig. 7-44) A touch control eliminates the switch, lighting the lamp when any metal surface is touched. Inexpensive touch converters for metal base lamps are available at many lighting stores. Squeeze switches on cords are also easily operated by many people. All lamps should have heavily weighted bases for stability.

Keep lamps at each task location, and choose designs that can be used in both the living room and bedroom for added flexibility. Use translucent shades for reading and opaque shades for accent color and ambient lighting. Plastic shades and fixtures are prone to volatile outgassing when exposed to high lamp temperatures. These gases can cause problems for people with allergies.[23]

## BEDROOM ACCESSORIES

Save energy, exertion, and time with well-organized storage. Plan a place for everything so that effort is not wasted looking for lost items. Expand reachable storage in the closet with hanging racks for shoes and sweaters. High reach for adults of shorter stature and children typically ranges from 36 in. to 44 in. a.f.f. (Fig. 7-45), while adults in wheelchairs prefer a high reach of 48 in. a.f.f. A universal solution is a pull-down closet rod. (Fig. 7-46) Keep closet shelves transparent above eye level with plastic or wire shelves. Make maxi

7-46

mum use of space at a reachable level with racks and shelves attached to the backs of doors. Add a carousel system that rotates hanging clothes. This type of system is appropriate for people in wheelchairs or anyone needing access to a tight storage space. (Fig. 7-47)

Accessories like keys, staplers, scissors, paper clips, tape, eyeglasses, pencils, and pens can be duplicated and stored in a variety of locations to save the energy required for extra trips and prolonged searches. Specify accessory holders at multiple locations. Have a pad and pencil at each telephone together with a directory.

Provide a lap stand for reading or working in bed. (Fig. 7-48) Bands on the stand hold the book firmly in place and allow the pages to be turned with one hand. Automatic page turners are also available. For ease of bed making with one hand, specify a quilt with a blanket cover that replaces the bedspread, blanket, and top sheet. With a covered comforter, the bed can be made with one easy motion, an advantage to all users. Also, a short comforter is easier to manipulate than a bedspread extending to the floor.

7-45

7-47

7-48

People who have trouble turning over in bed may require satin sheets, which are used with satin pajamas. (Fig. 7-49) People in pain can move more easily on satin sheets; some maintain that this is the only way they can sleep. Others, however, slip out of bed or have difficulty getting into bed with satin sheets and pajamas.

Many of the accessories discussed in this chapter are more adaptable than universal, but the distinction becomes less necessary with movable accessories that can be inexpensively replaced.

7-49

# KITCHENS

8-1

8-2

8-3

Flexibility is the key to successful universal kitchen design. At least one counter in the kitchen should be adjustable so that it can be occasionally changed to meet the needs of visitors and future residents. Removable cabinets also make the home easier to sell by appealing to a larger market, including people who use mobility aids and people who need to sit down to cook or wash the dishes. (Fig. 8-1) For everyday use by children or adults of shorter stature, tall adults, wheelchair users, and those with lower back pain, a variety of fixed work surface heights should be planned. (Fig. 8-2)

Work space should be planned between the sink, range, and refrigerator. Because it requires less strength to slide pans between the sink and stove, it is helpful if the sink and range are on the same level and connected by a continuous counter. Supplemental work surfaces should also be offered at a variety of heights including multiple-height tables, pull-out breadboards, islands, and pull-out carts. (Fig. 8-3)

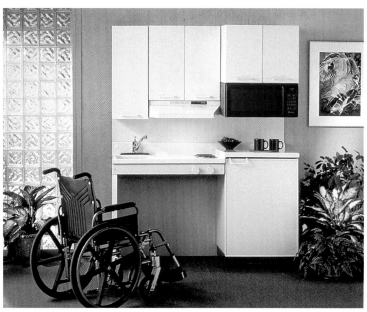

8-4

Another universal concept is the alternate kitchen plan. With this option, the existing kitchen counters remain at a height for standing users, while a second kitchen is temporarily installed for seated users as needed. A breakfast nook, dining room, utility room, or guest suite could have hot and cold water lines and a drain concealed during construction, so that the alternate kitchen can be added at a later date with minimal expense. (Fig. 8-4)

The alternate kitchen concept is also useful to anyone with a temporary injury or to a house guest in a wheelchair. If elderly parents need family assistance, for example, a temporary kitchen can be installed for use from a wheelchair with minimal expense using a portable refrigerator, a two-burner hot plate, and a small oven or microwave.

Remodeling a kitchen for wheelchair use is costly now and may be costly again in the future when the home is resold or rented to a limited market of people in wheelchairs. Rather than limiting the market, the alternate kitchen expands the market and increases the resale value of the home.

## CABINETS

When using removable cabinets under an adjustable-height counter, be sure the counter adjusts between 42 in. above the finished floor (a.f.f.) for tall users and 24 in. for children in wheelchairs. Each cabinet under this counter can be designed as a freestanding unit that is totally removable, as a unit with a removable front and base, or as a unit with a base that folds up to open the space for access by a wheelchair user. (Fig. 8-5) Adjacent cabinets should be finished on the exterior side that is exposed when another cabinet is removed. A clear kick space (8¾ in. a.f.f. × 6 in. deep)[1] should be left between the floor and all cabinets to protect them from wheelchair abrasion and to allow a closer approach. For people with sufficient mobility, drawers can be recessed into the toe space to store items that are seldom used.

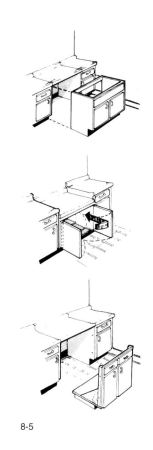

8-5

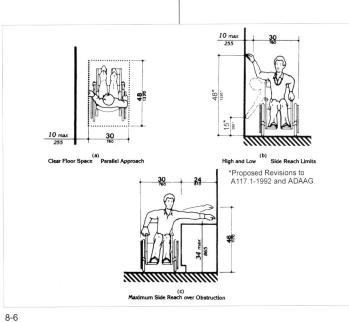

Clear Floor Space   Parallel Approach

High and Low   Side Reach Limits

*Proposed Revisions to
A117.1-1992 and ADAAG.

Maximum Side Reach over Obstruction

8-6

Install upper cabinets on heavy-duty commercial shelf brackets between the counter height and the high reach limit. (Fig. 8-6) Cabinets that lower with the push of a button are also available. (Fig. 8-7) An open shelf between a cabinet and the counter increases reachable storage space. (Fig. 8-8)

For seated use, a clear floor space of at least 30 × 48 in. must be allowed for each work area. If possible, plan slightly larger clear floor spaces (36 × 48 in.) for children in wheelchairs, who may require larger maneuvering spaces. These space allowances are also helpful for people who use other mobility aids.

One of the most convenient plans incorporating these clear floor spaces is an L-shaped kitchen with a level counter space extending between the refrigerator and the wall oven. Clear knee space should be provided under the entire counter, including the sink. The counter and sink should be adjustable (between 24 and 42 in.).

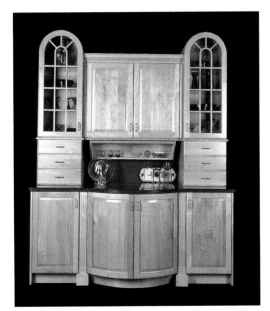

8-7

8-8

8-9

8-10

Plan a breakfast area close to the kitchen counter to shorten the distance for serving and clearing. (Fig. 8-9) Storage between kitchen and dining room should open from both sides. (Fig. 8-10) This is particularly helpful with corner cabinets, where back storage space may be out of reach from one side.

A movable cabinet under the sink can serve as a cart between the counter and the table. (Fig. 8-11) When the cabinet is moved out, the space under the counter is clear for seated users and the top of the cart can serve as extra counter space. The cabinet can also serve as a refuse container or be

8-11

8-12

used to hold other large items, like heavy roasters or small appliances that are difficult to remove from the back of the other cabinets. The cabinet should have casters and a top rail to prevent items from sliding off (Fig. 8-12) .

Prefabricated cabinets (requiring a 36 in. counter height) may be usable from a wheelchair, depending on the height of the user. It may be desirable to eliminate the 3 in. a.f.f. toe space and lower these high cabinets to the floor. This method sacrifices clearance for wheelchair footrests but saves the expense of custom work. When using this method, leave enough clearance for the doors to swing open over the kitchen floor covering.

To access the sink under existing cabinets, cut a large section out of the cabinet floor to provide a space for footrests. Remove the center stile and attach it to one of the door edges.

## Kitchen Storage Details

Plan extra storage space in the kitchen to eliminate clutter and to cut down on the number of needed shopping trips. Uncluttered space is a boon for everyone, but especially for people who wish to improve visual acuity, mobility, and concentration.

Organize items by activity; keep the coffee, coffeepot, and filters in the same area. Store baking equipment and ingredients in the same cabinet close to the oven. Keep frequently used items at

the front of cabinets and heavier items on lower shelves; eliminate items that are seldom used. Use dividers in drawers to organize utensils and kitchen gadgets. A system of this type is especially important for blind people. (Fig. 8-13)

Use high cabinets to store seasonal items and seldom-used equipment. Install clear plastic shelves or metal racks on upper cabinets to allow easy viewing. For people who are allergic to petrochemicals, use mesh shelves installed in metal or hardwood cabinets.[2] (Fig. 8-14) Existing cabinets can also be sealed to minimize offgassing of formaldehyde.

8-13

8-14

8-15

It is difficult to plan sufficient storage within the 36–48 in. a.f.f. reach of most wheelchair users, children, and adults of shorter stature. For additional storage, a built-in waste bin with automatic lid can be attached to a cabinet door. (Fig. 8-15) Wire racks can be added to cabinet or pantry doors. (Fig. 8-16) Even the space between the cabinet door and sink can be utilized. Dispensers can help bring cans and bottles within reach. Lazy Susans and slide-out rotary shelves also improve access. (Fig. 8-17) Half-circled pull-out shelves are particularly useful in corners. (Fig. 8-18) Vertical revolving shelves bring high storage within reach. (Fig. 8-19)

Shelves attached to cabinet doors also help to bring storage within reach. These shelves should have rims to keep objects from sliding off. Roll-out shelves especially need rims. (Fig. 8-20)

8-16

8-17

8-18

8-20

Removable bins offer access and flexibility on any shelf. Bins and heavy objects slide more easily on a shelf with a smooth surface. For faster access, plan shallow shelves rather than deeper kitchen cabinets. (Fig. 8-21) Reaching into deep base cabinets is difficult for most and dangerous for some. Plan a pantry in the space between studs in the wall to add shallow shelving. (Fig. 8-22)

8-19

8-21

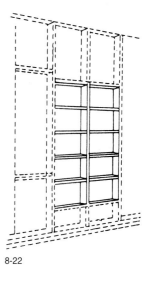

8-22

## Kitchen Drawers

A pull-out pantry can be installed in minimal cabinet space. (Fig. 8-23) A pull-out drawer for pans is also a convenience. (Fig. 8-24) Drawers should be equipped with full-extension roller-type slides, which allow access to deep storage. (Fig. 8-25) Pull-out drawers may need one lower side to allow access from a seated position. (Fig. 8-26)

8-25

8-23

8-26

8-24

## Kitchen Cabinet Doors

Most cabinets now incorporate hinges that hold the door closed but require more strength to open than touch latches. With a touch latch, the door opens with a push rather than a pull. Magnetic catches on cabinets may be difficult to open unless they are combined with touch latches. (Fig. 8-27) This system requires no pulls or knobs, which can be uncomfortable for people who may need to lean on

8-27

8-28

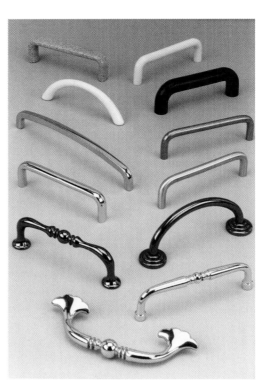

8-29

cabinets for support. (Fig. 8-28) If hardware is included, test it for strength and durability. Knobs should not protrude more than $\frac{1}{8}$ in.[3] Use a slightly textured finish on the cabinet to prevent slipping. Cabinets with handles may need extra-long C-pulls. (Fig. 8-29) Mount handles vertically on upper cabinets as close to the bottom of the doors as possible.On base cabinets, mount the pulls near the top edge of the cabinet doors. Right-angled pulls work well for a vertical or horizontal grasp. (Fig. 8-30)

Flat door handles can be marked in Braille. Spices can also be labeled in Braille and placed in alphabetical order. Mount the spice rack on the inside of a cabinet or pantry door for easy reach.

In some locations, sliding kitchen cabinet doors may be easier to operate while using a mobility aid than doors that swing out. Tambour doors do not block other storage areas when open, but they may require more force and control than standard cabinet doors. Display items can be stored in cabinets without doors, but they require extra maintenance.

Upper-cabinet doors may injure people when left open and cannot be easily detected by blind people who use canes. Install bifold, swing-up, or sliding cabinet doors to prevent injury. Self-closing hinges are also available, but they require simultaneous two-handed use; one hand must hold open the door while the other removes an item from the cabinet.

8-30

## KITCHEN COUNTERS

Three steps are often repeated in the kitchen during food preparation. First, the food is removed from the cupboard or refrigerator and sometimes washed in the sink. Next, the food is prepared or mixed. Finally, it is cooked. For this reason, the sink should be located between the stove and the refrigerator, with counter space on both sides of the sink (18 in. minimum).

Some people who are blind use counters to line up all the ingredients and utensils in logical order for the task. For this purpose, the countertop should be at least 4 ft long. People who stand with crutches or use a walker also appreciate longer clear counters to provide adequate body support. Deaf people may need extra counter space to set things down, freeing their hands for sign language.[4] Seated users may have an awkward angle for lifting objects onto counters. Unbroken counter spaces allow objects to be pulled or pushed instead, a technique also used by people with limited balance or strength.

For wheelchair users, kitchens or work areas should have a minimum clear floor space of 40 in. between opposite counters or walls if the kitchen is open on both ends.[5] It is best to plan more space between the counters and some clear floor space under the counter to permit a 5 ft diameter U-turn in a wheelchair. Three-wheelers may require a slightly larger area for a smooth turn (Fig. 8-31), and larger spaces should be planned if the kitchen is to be shared.

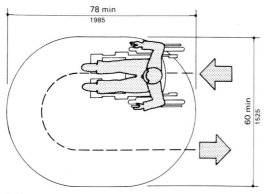

78 min
1985

60 min
1525

8-31

## Counter Heights

Counter surfaces at a variety of heights allow people of all ages, sizes, and abilities to work comfortably together. Because many people slide heavy objects on counters, the primary work surface should be continuous and adjustable in height. Adjustable surfaces offer flexibility to provide just the right position to improve strength and coordination. Counters can be mounted on recessed heavy-duty shelf standards screwed into studs or solid blocking.[6] Specify a finish on adjacent counter ends and cabinets, as these are exposed when the counter is lowered.

Adjustable counters can be lowered for use by children and future residents. Taller people may prefer counters up to 42 in. a.f.f. for some tasks. The minimum knee clearance required for adult wheelchair users is 27 in. a.f.f. (with 24 in. required for children). An adjustable counter no more than 2 in. thick allows a cook in a wheelchair to work comfortably. (Fig. 8-32) If the counter has a skirtboard, recess it a minimum of 12 in. from the front edge, but design the counter to support front-edge loads.[7]

If only one adjustable-height counter is installed, place it next to the latch side of the refrigerator. The resulting clear floor space next to the refrigerator improves reach for people using wheelchairs or scooters. A counter lowered for seated users may be at a supportive height for a standing person to knead dough or perform other heavy manual work. The ideal height for this work is calculated to be about 10 in. below elbow height (from a standing

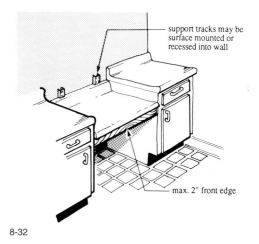

support tracks may be surface mounted or recessed into wall

max. 2" front edge

8-32

### CONVENIENT HEIGHTS OF WORK SURFACES FOR SEATED PEOPLE*

| Conditions of Use | SHORT WOMEN | | TALL MEN | |
|---|---|---|---|---|
| | in | mm | in | mm |
| Seated in a wheelchair: | | | | |
| Manual work: | | | | |
| Desk or removable armrests | 26 | 660 | 30 | 760 |
| Fixed, full-size armrests† | 32‡ | 815 | 32‡ | 815 |
| Light, detailed work | | | | |
| Desk or removable armrests | 29 | 735 | 34 | 865 |
| Fixed, full-size armrests† | 32‡ | 815 | 34 | 865 |
| Seated in a 16-in. (405 mm) high chair: | | | | |
| Manual work | 26 | 660 | 27 | 685 |
| Light, detailed work | 28 | 710 | 31 | 785 |

*All dimensions are based on a work surface thickness of 1-1/2 in. (38 mm) and a clearance of 1-1/2 in. (38 mm) between legs and the underside of a work surface.

†This type of wheelchair arm does not interfere with the positioning of a wheelchair under a work surface.

‡This dimension is limited by the height of the armrests: a lower height would be preferable. Some people in this group prefer lower work surfaces, which require positioning the whheelchair back from the edge of the counter.

8-33

position).[8] Writing and light work can best be done on a work surface 1–3 in. below elbow height when standing. When seated, surfaces for light work should be slightly higher than surfaces for heavy manual work. (Fig. 8-33) With limited counter space, consider a motor-driven countertop that can be changed in height for a variety of tasks and abilities. (Fig. 8-34)

## Counter Finishes

Specify a heat-resistant counter next to the cooktop to prevent surface burns. Ceramic tile is a good choice, but it is more difficult to slide pans over tile joints than over a smooth surface. Many people cannot lift heavy pans and need to slide them between the range and the sink. Smooth, heat-resistant solid-surface counters are available for this purpose.

Surface burns, scratches, and cuts can be removed from some solid-surface counters with a light sanding. Matching sinks can be fabricated with angled sides and in custom depths to improve access. Solid-surface counters are also needed by people who are allergic to laminate tops adhered to chemically offensive substrates. (Fig. 8-35)

High-maintenance products waste valuable time and energy. A slight texture or pattern on the counter conceals water spots and scratches, but too much texture (like deep leather grains) hold dirt. Remember that very light or very dark colors show smudge and grease marks. Use a slight pattern to conceal marks, with a medium light color to increase ambient light levels, and be sure to specify a low-glare finish.

8-35

8-34

## Details

Corners are often difficult to reach, especially for those using mobility assistance devices. An L-shaped counter design has only one corner, but a person who uses the counter for support may have trouble leaning into it. Add a straightedge to the corner of the counter for better support and more reachable work space, even from a wheelchair. (Fig. 8-36)

Because a person in a wheelchair must rest his or her arms on the edge of the counter while working, bevel or round the edge for comfort. (Fig. 8-37) This also protects those who may fall against the counter or use it for support. Elevated rolled edges prevent spills but make it difficult to work directly on the counter from a wheelchair. Rolling out a pie crust, for example, is almost impossible on an elevated edge. Add a bevel instead or slope the counter slightly to drain toward the sink. This slope also helps people slide heavy pots from the work area to the sink.[9]

8-36

8-37

Add a rail to the edge of the counter as a safety feature, as many falls occur in the kitchen. The rail also protects the counter from chipping and can be used to hold towels or to pull up to the counter in a wheelchair. (Fig. 8-38)

8-38

## Alternatives to Counters

A fold-down work surface can be added to increase counter space within reach without taking up floor space needed by people who use mobility aids. (Fig. 8-39) Additional fold-down or removable shelves can be located under the counter to increase storage without creating a problem for seated users. A sliding shelf over the counter can greatly increase work space.

8-39

8-40

Extra counter space can also be created by replacing a drawer with a pull-out work surface. If a lower counter height is required for stirring, cut a hole in the surface to hold the mixing bowl. Line the hole with a rubber strip to keep the bowl from slipping. (Fig. 8-40)

A movable chopping board over the sink can also increase usable counter space. Choose one with a vegetable basket on the side for drainage. Acrylic boards can be cleaned more easily and completely than wood, but wood boards can be customized for one-handed use. Nails can be driven into the wood to impale vegetables so they can be peeled with one hand, or a potato peeler can be clamped on. A raised edge can be added to one corner to help hold bread in place when cutting. (Fig. 8-41)

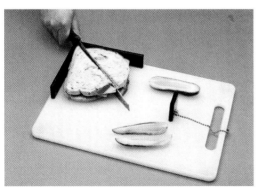

8-41

## FIXTURES AND APPLIANCES

To save time and energy, choose labor-saving devices like self-cleaning ovens, frost-free refrigerators, and microwave ovens. The microwave should be free of leakage that can interfere with hearing aid operation. Specify a model with visual, tactile, and audible controls. To improve reach, place it on a pull-out shelf. Avoid low-contrast displays. Light-emitting diodes (LEDs) with amber letters are easier to read than liquid crystal displays (LCDs). Look for a display with a letter height of at least $\frac{5}{16}$ in.[10]

People who are blind also appreciate the safety of a microwave, as no flames are involved. Non-metallic cooking containers and utensils do not get as hot in a microwave as in a standard oven, a safety feature that is especially important for people with reduced sensation. Take care to avoid steam burns when opening a container from the microwave. The door release mechanism should protrude far enough so that it is easy to depress with a fist, arm, or hand. The most difficult controls are squeeze triggers and pull handles with no opening in the handle.

Ice dispensers are easier for most people to use than ice trays. Door-mounted models bring ice and cold water within reach and are helpful for people who have the strength and coordination to use them. Before purchasing, make sure that these features can be plumbed into a nearby water supply and test the operation of controls with a closed fist.

## Controls

Switches should be cued with warning lights to show that appliances are on. Redundant cuing like this makes controls more noticeable by all people. It may be helpful to include automatic turn-off switches on appliances. Controls should also be large, easy to read, and well located. (Fig. 8-42) Choose appliances with controls and accessories on the side or front, not in the back, where users would have to reach over a hot element. Built-in

8-42

appliances should have controls at counter level, not on the fascia, which can be too easily reached by children.

Some appliances may need to be used with an electrical outlet under the counter. For use from a seated position, mount an electric can opener on the inside of a lower-cabinet door. Store a mixer on a pop-up shelf under the counter. Consider installing a motor base on the countertop for stable operation of many attachments. A food processor,

for example, can be operated with one hand from a permanently installed motor base. (Fig. 8-43) Locate the motor between the cooktop and the sink, where most food preparation takes place.

Specify push bars rather than pull-out buttons, touch controls with raised tactile surfaces (Fig. 8-44) rather than dials, and controls that can be operated with the palms up, not down. Test a control to see if it can be operated with a fist using light pressure. Where greatest accuracy is required, hand and arm motion should be used rather than foot and leg movements. The hand should be held close to the body at approximately elbow level to maximize accuracy.

Avoid controls that can be activated accidentally. Although touch controls are the easiest to use, they are also easier to turn on by accident. Remember that touch controls can also be easily used by children.

Specify controls that do not require sustained effort. Some push-type faucets, for example, require sustained holding to operate. Also, keep in mind that it is easier to operate controls in front of the body rather than at the side and easier at the waist than overhead.

8-43

8-44

# Faucets

A faucet with a single lever can be easily operated with one hand. Paddles, blades, or push-type mechanisms are also easier to use than knobs and are good choices for people who may be confused by single-lever controls. Many faucet controls can be mounted on the front apron of the counter for easier access by a seated user.

To eliminate controls, consider a faucet that incorporates an infrared sensor to initiate water flow. A faucet with a spring-loaded push knob or push rod can be operated with the palm of one hand. The rod attaches to the faucet and is operated by pressure from a cup or glass. A gooseneck faucet can be used to fill a pan on the counter, which is easier than lifting the pan into the sink and out again. (Fig. 8-45)

One innovative faucet design combines a gooseneck style with a pull-out spray on a retractable hose. Both the faucet and the spray can be installed in an existing sink with a single hole, and the unit is designed around the natural motion of the hand and wrist (Fig. 8-46)

8-47

Faucet controls should be located uniformly on all sinks throughout the home to prevent accidental scalding. Hot-water taps are normally on the left, cold on the right. Green, red, and blue color coding can be used to differentiate filtered, hot, and cold taps respectively. (Fig. 8-47)

# Sinks

Access to a sink can be improved by the placement of the drain control, the depth of the sink, and the location of the installation. The drain control may be located on the countertop to improve reach. (Fig. 8-48) The sink must be no deeper than 6½ in.[11] (5½ in. for children). If an existing sink is

8-45

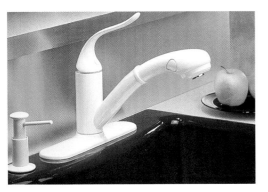

8-46

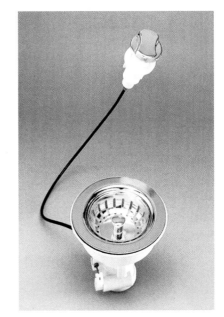

8-48

8-49

8-51

8-50

Specify a sink with the drain to the back and to one side so that connecting pipes are either to the left or right, not in the center, allowing a closer approach in a wheelchair. (Fig. 8-51) With a double sink, only one side needs to be accessible to seated users.

It is easier to move pots and pans out of a sink with angled sides. A stainless sink is thinner and allows more knee clearance than a porcelain sink. (Fig. 8-52) Also, it does not chip, an advantage for people prone to dropping things.

deeper, recess the front of the countertop for a closer approach. From a wheelchair, the user should be able to place one hand flat on the bottom of the sink. A removable rack can also be used to improve reach. (Fig. 8-49)

Consider installing two sinks in the kitchen, one at the correct height for the cook, the other for the rest of the family. If the cook is standing with arms relaxed, the bottom of a shallow sink should be 2 in. higher than wrist height.[12] If the main sink is not accessible, add a bar sink on a lowered counter. (Fig. 8-50)This bar sink is also accessible to children if the controls are within a 14 in. reach from the front of the counter.

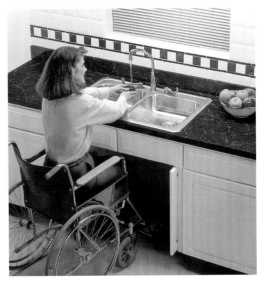

8-52

8-53

Adjustable-height sinks are available in prefabricated models with manual or automatic controls. (Fig. 8-53) When customizing an installation, simply change the tailpiece to alter the height. To do so, a flexible supply line must be in place and the trap must be low enough to receive the tailpiece at the lowest position of the sink. (Fig. 8-54) Insulate metal sinks and exposed pipes to prevent burns, or add a nonmetallic panel that can be removed for maintenance. The cover also keeps the pipes out of sight. (Fig. 8-55)

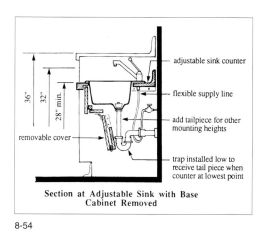

adjustable sink counter

flexible supply line

add tailpiece for other mounting heights

removable cover

trap installed low to receive tail piece when counter at lowest point

36"
32"
28" min.

**Section at Adjustable Sink with Base Cabinet Removed**

8-54

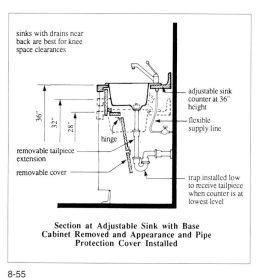

sinks with drains near back are best for knee space clearances

adjustable sink counter at 36" height

flexible supply line

removable tailpiece extension

hinge

removable cover

trap installed low to receive tailpiece when counter is at lowest level

36"
32"
28"

**Section at Adjustable Sink with Base Cabinet Removed and Appearance and Pipe Protection Cover Installed**

8-55

8-56

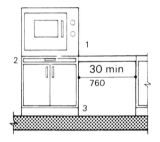

*(a) Side-Hinged Door*

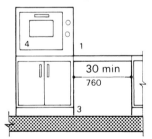

*(b) Bottom-Hinged Door*

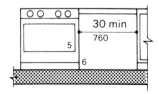

*(c) Range Oven*

SYMBOL KEY
1. Countertop or wall-mounted oven
2. Pull-out board preferred with side-opening door
3. Clear open space
4. Bottom-hinged door
5. Range oven
6. Preferred clear open space

8-57

## Ovens

Specify wall-mounted ovens instead of floor models. Wall ovens are easier for all people but are critical for wheelchair users. The hot oven door of a conventional oven is a dangerous barrier to access. Ovens mounted above shoulder level are often unusable from a wheelchair or scooter, as it is difficult to lower heavy pots and pans with arms extended above shoulder height. For increased lifting ability, the arms should be bent at a right angle, not extended above the shoulder. Mount the oven door just above lap height and insulate both sides of the oven to prevent burns. Install one rack at counter height for easy transfer of food. Install drawers under the oven for convenient storage. Above the oven, add a cabinet with vertical dividers for baking pans, broilers, trays, and lids.

It is easier to reach into the back of an oven with a side-hinged door. (Fig. 8-56) Plan the door latch and lever controls on the side next to the open counter. Install a pull-out shelf under the side-hinged door to hold a heavy pan after it is removed from the oven. The shelf should pull out to a minimum of 10 in.[13]

Next to the oven, plan a counter with knee space. This space can be used to reach fully into the oven, which is necessary for maintenance. (Fig. 8-57) To improve visual acuity, install wall ovens with controls at eye level.

## Ranges

Cooking is easier from a wheelchair with a clear floor space below a cooktop, but the danger of accidental burns caused by spills increases. Raised heating elements should be avoided; it is easier to tip a pan off an elevated surface. Smooth glass surfaces work well, and the newer models heat quickly and offer redundant cuing. (Fig. 8-58) One unit can be secured against accidental operation by children or by adults with dementia.

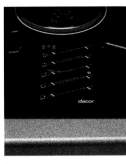

8-58

Clear floor space can be allowed under the range by planning an open knee space or by specifying a range that pulls out. With this type of unit, storage is not sacrificed to knee space. Make sure that a clear floor space of at least 30 × 48 in. is maintained when the range is open.

It may not be necessary to provide clearance under the cooktop for seated users if cooking elements and controls are in line along the front of the counter. Spills and burns often occur when reaching for controls at the back of the range. Controls should be highly contrasted and redundantly cued with tactile markings on the on-off position.

As an alternative, to prevent burns, stagger back elements so that they are accessible without reaching over a front element. (Fig. 8-59). Do not plan storage in a cabinet over the cooktop.

Magnetic induction cooktops are more expensive and require special cookware, but they greatly reduce the danger of burns and fire. They eliminate hot elements, an obvious boon to the blind person, a child or a person with dementia. They

also offer more stability for pots and pans than raised elements. (Fig. 8-60) Install magnetic induction cooktops level with counters. To prevent burns, electrical shocks, and abrasions, insulate surfaces under and on both sides of the range.

A small wall-mounted mirror can be used to monitor pots on back burners. The mirror eliminates the need for adults of shorter stature and wheelchair users to reach over a hot element to check the food. Make sure the mirror is removable for easy cleaning.

Mount the exhaust fan on the counter with controls within reach. (Fig. 8-61) A higher fan mounted close to the ear is often too noisy for people with reduced hearing. Vent the fan outdoors for more efficient control of smoke and odors.

For people who depend on the sense of touch, install guardrails around gas burners and electric elements. Gas offers auditory and olfactory cues as well as visible flames. A person who is unable to smell gas or is hypersensitive to gas odors needs an electric range. People with dementia or mental retardation may need a fire suppression system or a system that cuts off power to the range if smoke is detected.

8-60

8-61

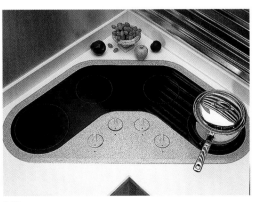

8-59

## Refrigerators

A side-by-side refrigerator allows greater access to the freezer from a wheelchair or scooter, but it is more difficult to wheel around two swinging doors. This refrigerator is often wider than a conventional model and may take up too much space. If space if limited, use a refrigerator with the freezer below even though it may be difficult for tall users. (Fig. 8-62) Install the handle side toward the sink.

8-62

8-63

Plan a clear floor space under the counter next to the refrigerator. Make sure the refrigerator door can swing back 180° to allow maximum access, which is especially important for cleaning and defrosting. A shallow horizontal refrigerator with a top door can be mounted on a countertop with clear floor space below, or a refrigerator drawer can bring food within reach. A number of these smaller units can be distributed around the kitchen and throughout the house where needed. (Fig. 8-63)

Small details on a refrigerator can make a big difference, especially for wheelchair users. Make sure the controls are toward the front of the unit. Look for stops on shelves; swing-out adjustable shelves are an option. Permanent shelves should not be deeper than 13 in. If the shelves are too deep, add lazy Susans as needed.

Refrigerators with magnetic door catches require less strength to open than those with latches, but sometimes even the magnetic seal is too difficult. As a temporary measure, a portion of the seal can be blocked with tape or a plastic clip. Also try a looped strap over the handle for people with reduced strength.

8-64

Extra shelves, especially in the freezer section, make it easier to reach more items without moving others. Adjustable door shelves can hold gallon-size containers and larger bottles, putting these heavy items in the most accessible location. (Fig. 8-64) Two small crispers in the refrigerator are easier to handle than one large unit. Specify crispers on roller guides.

For adults of shorter stature, children, very tall people, and those using mobility aids, it is often difficult to reach the bottom of a chest freezer. Specify an upright model and use lazy Susans for items in the back.

## Dishwashers

Specify a dishwasher with a recessed motor so that the toe space can be elevated to clear wheelchair footrests. Front-loading dishwashers with side-hinged doors allow a closer approach when using a mobility aid. If space is available, provide access on both sides of a standard front-loading dishwasher and elevate the unit at least 6 in. (Fig. 8-65) All of the rack space should be accessible from the front of the machine. The silverware basket should be equipped with a handle.

Portable top-loading dishwashers and their sink attachments are difficult for many people to use. Specify front-loading dishwashers with porcelain or plastic interiors (Fig. 8-66); stainless steel interiors may become too hot.

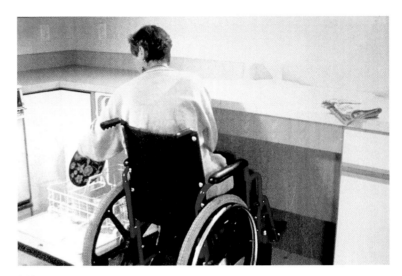

8-66

Redundant cuing should be specified on the dishwasher. A visual off-on indicator is an advantage to people with a wide range of hearing abilities. Quiet dishwashers are also available to reduce the ambient noise in the kitchen.

## Garbage Disposals

Garbage disposals save frequent trips to empty the garbage outdoors. A disposal can be installed on the deep side of a double sink (Fig. 8-67), leaving knee space below the other side for seated users. A continuous-feed model with a separate switch is easier to control than a batch-feed model with the switch in the drain. Keep the switch within easy reach. The unit should be installed with the drain to the back and to one side for use from a seated position.

8-65

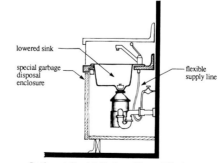

Section at Special Garbage Disposal Enclosure

8-67

## Trash Compactors

Although trash compactors also save trips to empty the garbage, the compacted bag may be too heavy to handle. For wheelchair users, the compactor takes up valuable space under the counter.

## Hot-Water Dispensers

Hot-water dispensers eliminate the need to heat, carry, and pour boiling water. Specify a model equipped with a lever. (Fig. 8-68)

8-68

8-69

## Small Appliances

Select small appliances on the basis of weight, balance, and control. Specify rechargeable models to avoid the limits of a cord. A cordless electric carving knife is usually easier to use than a regular knife. A cordless scrubber is helpful for people who have trouble exerting enough pressure to clean pots and pans. A mixer can be too heavy for many people to lift; look for a lightweight model. The mixer should have good balance, an upright rest, and controls that can be operated with one hand, an advantage for all users.

Recess small-appliance cabinets in the splash at counter level for extra work space. The appliances can then be moved out on the counter without lifting. To save counter space, a microwave oven, toaster, coffeemaker, or other appliance can be suspended from the cabinet above (Fig. 8-69) or used from a pull-out cart. The cart can also be moved to the dining area, allowing use of appliances at the table.

Toaster ovens become dangerously hot, while a manual toaster requires coordination and dexterity. An automatic toaster may be the best answer for most.

Some small kitchen appliances offer user-friendly controls; the C-grips and paddle controls on many food processors are good examples. Also appropriate are electric frying pans, available with Braille dials and large baffled controls. (Fig. 8-70) Such pans are designed for stability and are available with two handles to improve strength and grip.

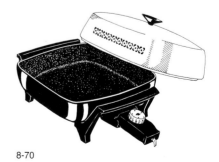

8-70

An electric can opener that requires sustained squeezing for operation can be too difficult for many people; choose a model that locks in the on position and can be used with just one hand. (Fig. 8-71) Beaters are also available for use with one hand. (Fig. 8-72)

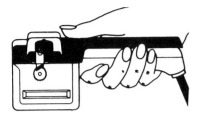

8-71

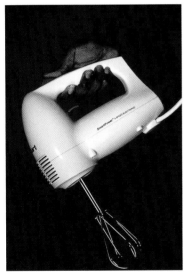

8-72

8-73

Many items are designed for one-handed use, helping all users. A breadboard and knife set is available to help in slicing. A rotary recipe file, for example, can be mounted on the inside of a cabinet door to keep recipes reachable, yet off the counter. Another example of a one-handed utensil is a pizza cutter (Fig. 8-74), which can also be used to cut meat, bread, and vegetables.

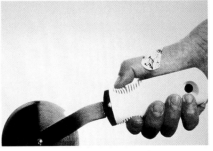

8-74

## KITCHEN ACCESSORIES

## Utensils

To keep utensils within the reach of adults of shorter stature, children, and wheelchair users, consider installing pegs or wall-mounted racks between the counters and cabinets. (Fig. 8-73) Slanted pegs are easier to use than hooks, which can catch on pan handles. Utensils can also be stored in hanging baskets.

## Cookware

Glass pots and pans, because they are see-through, allow adults of shorter stature and wheelchair users to monitor cooking food. Glass cookware can be used to cook, store, and serve food, reducing the number of cooking items needed. Choose lightweight cookware for people with reduced strength and heavier sets for people with tremors. Pans with double handles are easier to lift.

## Dining Accessories

For increased grip strength, choose smaller drinking glasses. Use larger glasses for people who have trouble tilting their heads; two-handled cups may be easier to hold. For increased coordination, select cups with large handles and dinner plates with deep sides to help in scooping the food onto the spoon. (Fig. 8-75) Although heavier dishes, like stoneware, retain heat better, they are usually more difficult to lift. For people with coordination difficulties, sectioned plates make eating easier. (Fig. 8-76)

Silverware with pistol grips or handles that conform to the hand improve grip strength. To improve

8-77

strength in slicing, consider a knife that operates with a rocking motion instead of a slicing motion. (Fig. 8-77)

To improve visual acuity, be sure dishes contrast with tablecloths. Specify plates with borders so that the edges of plates can be easily seen.

## Kitchen Maintenance Accessories

Everyday products can be used to enhance a variety of abilities. To save energy, trays can be used to clear tables so dishes do not have to be carried separately. To clean up spills, pails of water can be moved more easily on caster frames. A sponge mop with a wringer mechanism requires less strength and coordination than a cloth mop. A dustpan with a long handle requires less bending, and a feather duster with a telescoping handle increases reach. A wastebasket with a nonslip foot control can be opened without the use of hands.

## Accessories for Kitchen Safety

Every kitchen should be equipped with a fire extinguisher. Specify a multipurpose A-B-C model to combat electrical and grease fires as well as ordinary combustibles. Because people with reduced sensation cannot easily feel burns, select cookware with handles that do not become hot. Ovenproof mittens are easier to use than potholders. Insulated rubber gloves can improve grip strength on dishes while protecting hands from hot, irritating dishwater.

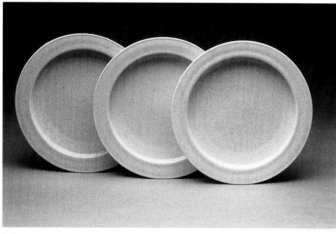

8-75

8-76

# BATHROOMS, TOILET ROOMS, AND UTILITY SPACES

In public rest rooms, space for people in wheelchairs offers convenience for many users. These larger stalls offer travelers enough room to roll in luggage or strollers and parents enough space to help children. People using crutches, canes, walkers, and guide dogs have more room to maneuver. (Fig. 9-1) With so many people benefiting from these stalls, consider installing more than the minimum number. A universal stall is a minimum size of 5 × 5 ft and includes a recessed lavatory in the stall. It may also include an emergency call button connected to the 911 operator.

In every residence at least one of the bathrooms should be adaptable to a variety of abilities. Plan removable cabinets, adjustable counters, an accessible shower, and reinforced sidewalls. Bathroom walls should be reinforced floor to ceiling with ¾ in. plywood or with wood blocking installed between the studs. This inexpensive reinforcement, if properly placed, allows for future installation of grab bars, lavatory, towel bars, and shower seat.

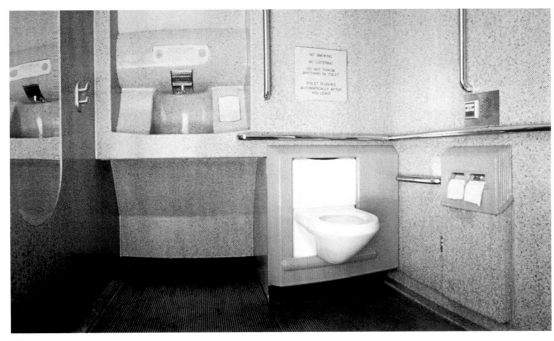

9-1

# SHOWERS

## Shower Enclosures

A shower is quicker, easier, and safer to use than a bathtub. After one transfer to a shower wheelchair, the user can roll into the shower, under the lavatory, or over a toilet without additional transfer. A wheel-in shower can be installed in the enclosure space of a bathtub (30 × 60 in.). This elongated shower design provides more maneuvering space than a standard square shower. (Fig. 9-2) It should be equipped with a handheld shower system and with temperature and surge controls to provide a safe flow of water.

This enclosure can also be planned in a square or round design. (Fig. 9-3) A corner shower open on two sides allows access from more than one direc-

9-4

tion. (Fig. 9-4) The wheel-in shower floor must be sloped rather than curbed, as a curb may block wheels or become a tripping hazard. A flexible curb offers one solution (Fig. 9-5). Another uses a 2 percent slope on the entire bathroom floor draining into the shower. A steeper slope makes it too difficult to maneuver a shower wheelchair or gurney. Be sure to specify nonslip flooring.

Water can also be contained by recessing the floor of a wheel-in shower. Use a grating to raise the floor height back to that of the bathroom. (Fig. 9-6)

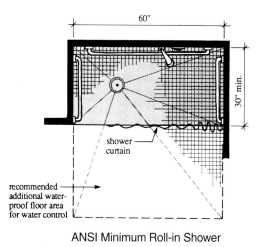

ANSI Minimum Roll-in Shower

9-2

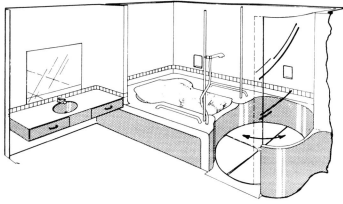

9-3

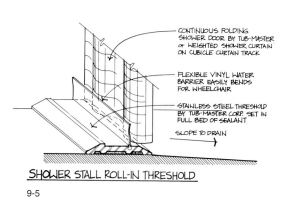

CONTINUOUS FOLDING SHOWER DOOR BY TUB-MASTER or WEIGHTED SHOWER CURTAIN ON CUBICLE CURTAIN TRACK

FLEXIBLE VINYL WATER BARRIER EASILY BENDS FOR WHEELCHAIR

STAINLESS STEEL THRESHOLD BY TUB-MASTER CORP. SET IN FULL BED OF SEALANT

SLOPE TO DRAIN

SHOWER STALL ROLL-IN THRESHOLD

9-5

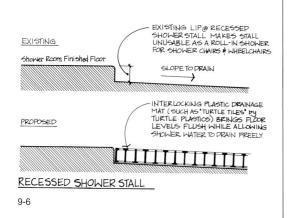

RECESSED SHOWER STALL

9-6

9-8

If a recessed floor is not practical, plan a slight ramp up to a grating placed on the finished floor. A grating and ramp can also be used to access an existing shower with a lip. In addition, a grating can be used to level the trench in a gang shower without restricting drainage.

Plan showers with curtains, not doors. (Fig. 9-7) Curtains on showers without curbs may be longer than floor length to prevent water from escaping. (Fig. 9-8) Ceiling-mounted shower curtains have a clean appearance, especially when they curve around two sides of the shower. Shower curtains can also be mounted on a swinging rod, which can be used to protect the attendant. (Fig. 9-9)

A shower that requires neither curtains nor doors is easily accessible and is helpful for people with allergies. Shower frames and curtains may retain moisture and encourage mold growth depending on the climate; furthermore, plastic shower curtains may release irritants when heated.

A transfer-in shower takes up less space than a wheel-in shower or a bathtub (as little as $3 \times 3$ ft), but it requires a shower seat for transfer from a wheelchair. The dimensions of this shower are critical for some people to reach grab bars, shower controls, and accessories while leaning into the corner.[1] (Fig. 9-10) Others can manage a longer reach to the grab bars for a transfer from a wheelchair, and a more open universal design becomes possible. (Fig. 9-11)

9-7

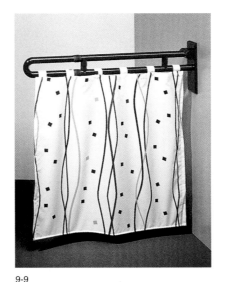

9-9

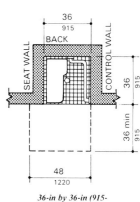

*36-in by 36-in (915-mm by 915-mm) Stall*

**Shower Sizes and Clearances**

9-10

9-11

9-12

9-14

The transfer-in shower may have up to a ½ in. high curb to contain water.[2] During transfer, the front wheels of the wheelchair are placed over the curb to prevent the chair from sliding backward. Shower controls must be mounted on the wall opposite the seat.

The shower must be slip resistant (Fig. 9-12) and equipped with a fold-up shower seat to clear the space for standing users. (Fig. 9-13) The shower seat should also be slip resistant, with small openings for good drainage. (Fig. 9-14) Make sure the edges and corners are rounded.

## Shower Fixtures and Controls

New construction should include an additional connection for the future installation of a handheld system. Such a fixture is ideal for seated use and can also be clipped to a bracket for use as a conventional shower. (Fig. 9-15) A valve should be selected that does not catch the shower hose, and it must require only one hand to regulate water flow and set the desired temperature. (Fig. 9-16) Install controls within 18 in. of the entrance to a 36 in. square shower to allow users to adjust the water prior to transferring.

Select a lever control that prevents high temperatures if the control is bumped by accident. This feature is also helpful to children just learning to use the controls. Another option is an integral thermometer, which allows the temperature to be preset. Both systems should include a pressure-balancing feature that prevents surges of hot and cold water. (Fig. 9-17)

Wall mount a handheld unit to allow adjustable height. The flexible hose must be at least 5 ft long,[3] but some users may require a hose as long as 7 ft. Choose a model with a water-volume control in the shower head. For people who do not require a handheld system, specify a multidirectional shower head that rotates 360°. (Fig. 9-18)

9-15

9-16

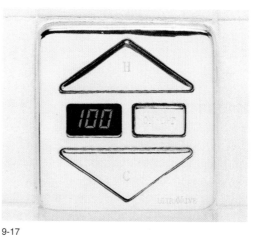

9-17

9-18

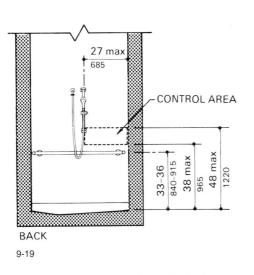

27 max
685

CONTROL AREA

33–36
840–915

38 max
965

48 max
1220

BACK

9-19

Specify a shower head bar for vertical adjustment that does not obstruct the grab bars. Controls must be carefully placed. (Fig. 9-19) For children, a second set of controls should be installed at a height no greater than 3 ft a.f.f. As an alternative for children, a sensor could be used to automatically start the shower upon entering. The temperature can be preset to prevent burns.

## Shower Accessories

A shower shelf or caddy can prevent soap, shampoos, and accessories from slipping out of reach. Choose one in solid brass, solid surface material, or stainless steel to prevent corrosion and rust, and make sure that it drains easily. (Fig. 9-20)

9-20

9-21

Recess a soap holder so that it does not interfere with wheelchair use and transfer, and plan multi-level soap dispensers. A liquid soap dispenser may require less coordination. (Fig. 9-21) A self-draining storage space for hair care products is also helpful.

## BATHTUBS

A soak in the bathtub relieves pain for many people, but standard bathtub design can make it difficult to get in and out. It can be especially difficult to transfer from a wheelchair into a poorly sized tub or a tub with a track. For a combination of a tub and shower, specify a trackless installation. (Fig. 9-22) For seated users, the height of the tub should match the height of the chair seat. The most nearly universal height is 17 in. a.f.f., but needs may vary from 11 in. for children to 19 in. for an adult.[4]

9-22

## Bathtub Seats

A seat installed on the end of bathtub is most help-ful when transferring from a mobility assistance device. (Fig. 9-23) A platform on the approachable end of the tub allows the user to enter the tub. The extra length of the tub and seat may extend the space in the bathroom to allow a 5 ft turnaround space for wheelchair users.

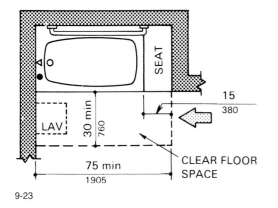

9-23

Bevel the edge of the seat so that it can be used as a headrest, and slant the end of the tub to make it easy to slide slowly into the tub from the seat, using the adjacent grab bars. For additional comfort, the slant may be contoured for extra back support. A fold-down utility tray is another conve-nience.

Install a handheld shower to use from the seat. This is useful to people who do not have the strength to lower themselves into the tub. It also helps others with washing and rinsing in the bath-tub. The controls should be lowered and installed on the long wall of the tub.

If a platform cannot be added to the end of the tub, consider a movable seat that fits over the tub. The seat is used with a handheld shower, not for trans-fer into the tub. The shower curtain should have a slit to fit over the seat. Seats are available without backs if this support is not necessary. If a back is needed, make sure it is textured. Some seats have adjustable legs with nonskid rubber tips; others can be fastened to the edge of the tub.

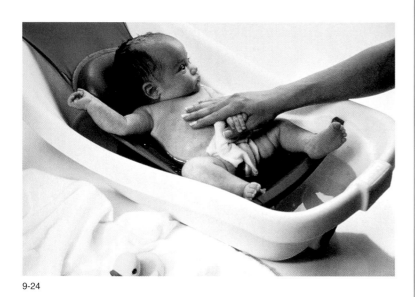

9-24

Children can be bathed in a child seat or on a bathing table that fits in the tub. (Fig. 9-24) One innovative bathtub design incorporates a stationary tray and a rotating tub to ease entry and exit.

## Types of Bathtubs

Generally, a bathtub should have a flat (not round) bottom for stability. The floor of the tub must be slip resistant. (Fig. 9-25) If it is not, add a nonslip bath mat that runs the full length of the tub. Look for

9-26

tubs with narrow rims or handles that can be grasped when getting in and out. (Fig. 9-26) Soft tubs provide a nonslip surface that may prevent falls and certainly cushion the blow if a fall does occur. (Fig. 9-27)

Use a contrasting stripe to identify the bathtub rim and base perimeter. Vertical stripes in the tub help to identify the amount of water through refraction or bending of the stripes at the level of the water.

9-25

9-27

9-28

Some doors on tubs swing up or open out for easy access. (Fig. 9-28) These doors are tightly sealed and can be used with a whirlpool bath. Make sure that drain controls are within reach and that it drains rapidly. A tub with a swing-up door can be ordered for a left or right approach, allowing full use by a person with hemiplegia. The strong side of the body can be used while transferring and accessing tub controls. A high-volume drain allows the tub to be quickly emptied before the bather exits.

9-29

A spa can be made accessible to many people through the addition of a lift (Fig. 9-29) or a series of steps, the highest of which should be at the height of a wheelchair seat (17–19 in. a.f.f.).[5] The user can slide from one step to the next, employing natural buoyancy to help with transfer.

## Bathtub Controls

Choose a lever-type faucet and drain control for easy operation. Controls must be installed toward the approach side. (Fig. 9-30) To eliminate controls, specify an automatic fill system, which can be used to preset the water temperature and level. This is especially helpful if sensitivity to temperature is a factor. (Fig. 9-31)

9-30

9-31

## TOILETS AND BIDETS

### Public Toilets

UFAS and the ADA covering public toilet installation require a turning space in each toilet room but not each stall. The National Building Code of Canada, however, requires a stall nearly 5 × 5 ft,[6] and Florida requires a minimum space of 5 ft 8 in. × 5 ft 8 in. with a lavatory,[7] the most nearly universal solution. Provide at least 42 in. of adjacent clear floor space on the approach side of the water closet for people with wheelchairs, walkers, or assistants. Some people are stronger on one side than the other, so the approach should be alternated throughout the

building. Stalls of minimum size must have toe clearance of 9 in. a.f.f. (12 in. for children). In larger stalls, a partition to the floor can provide a positive stop for a person using a mobility aid.

Doors should swing out of the stall. Stalls must also be equipped with gravity-closing hinges and hardware that is usable without tight grasping, pinching, or twisting. (Fig. 9-32)

A lavatory in the toilet space allows for additional privacy to clean up. (Fig. 9-33) Consider installing a unisex or family toilet room, which allows a spouse or aide to accompany a child or a person who needs assistance. (Fig. 9-34) To save space, recess the lavatory in the clear space required next to the toilet. (Fig. 9-35)

9-32

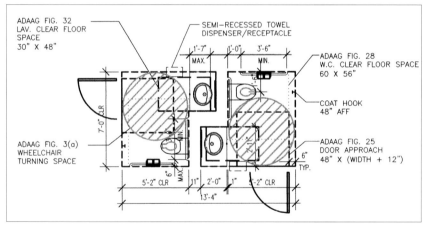

9-33A

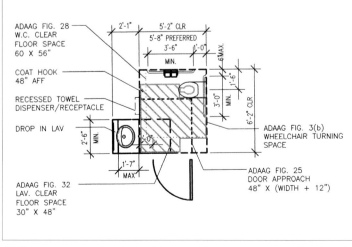

9-33B

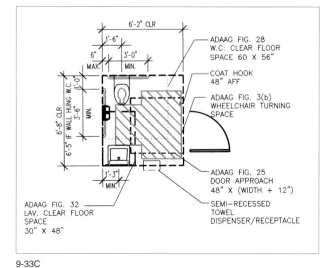

9-33C

9-34

Urinals must be specified with a maximum rim height of 17 in. a.f.f., but a floor-mounted urinal is more accessible to small boys and others who need a lower rim. A clear floor space of 30 × 48 in. must be provided in front of each urinal. Children in wheelchairs require a rim height of 14 in. a.f.f., with flush controls no higher than 32 in.[8] and a clear floor space of 36 × 48 in.

A urinal in a stall is preferable for privacy in empty-ing a leg bag. In public urinals, the privacy shields must not extend past the front edge of the urinal into the clear floor space. The urinals should be wall-mounted a minimum of 14 in. from the wall.[9] (Fig. 9-36)

9-35

9-36

## Toilets

The design of the toilet, the height of the installation, and the approach must all be considered for use with mobility aids. The toilet can be approached in several ways. In a residence or health-care facility, the user may first transfer into a shower wheelchair, which can roll over the toilet. Alternately, the individual may choose to transfer directly from the wheelchair to the front or side of the toilet. (Fig. 9-37)

Elongated toilets are easier to use when transferring or aligning with the shower wheelchair. (Fig. 9-38) Choose a toilet seat adjustable to wheelchair height for adults and children (11–19 in. a.f.f.). The lower height range may also be necessary to allow clearance when using a shower wheelchair. An existing toilet seat can always be replaced by an elevated seat if necessary.

For bowel and bladder care, specify a lower toilet with a higher seat, leaving a gap between the two. It may be necessary to reach into this gap for digital manipulation or to empty a leg bag. Specify a seat with an opening in the front. (Fig. 9-39) The seat must be firmly attached for stability when transferring. The seat must not be sprung to return

to a lifted position, but it should remain up independently when raised. Men with hemiplegia or one hand do not have a free hand to hold up the toilet seat while using the toilet. A flat or padded lid is more comfortable to lean against than one that is crowned or dished.

Most toilets are too high for easy emptying of a leg bag. The lip of the toilet needs to be below the level of the drainage tube and the leg may have to be elevated to this level to empty the bag. Wall-mounted toilets can be installed at the proper height and are easier to clean because they have no base. The clearance below also provides extra floor space for wheelchair footrests. (Fig. 9-40)

For ease of maintenance, the toilet can be installed in the shower and used as a shower seat in some installations. The toilet seat must be padded or nonslip, and a bench-type seat eases transfer. A toilet in the shower also simplifies cleanup after a bowel and bladder program. (Fig. 9-41) Plan the lavatory and mirror outside this area to keep the mirror from fogging.

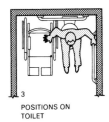

42
1065

18
455

1
TAKES TRANSFER
POSITION,
REMOVES
ARMREST, SETS
BRAKES

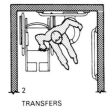

2
TRANSFERS

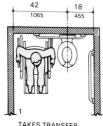

3
POSITIONS ON
TOILET

9-37

9-38

9-39

One toilet model uses warm water for washing and warm air for drying rather than toilet tissue. (Fig. 9-42) This type is especially helpful for people who find it difficult to manipulate tissue. A portable bidet is also available.

A wall-mounted toilet can be installed as high as necessary for people who have trouble sitting andrising. With a high toilet, a low stool may be required for the bowel program, elevating the feet to facilitate elimination.

Make sure the stop valve (or cutoff valve) on the toilet is easy to use and within reach. The flushing lever must also be on the approach side.[10] A flush valve in the center of the tank is harder to reach but more neutrally handed. Flush valves in back of the toilet can be uncomfortable for people who lean back for balance unless a toilet seat lid is provided. All controls must require less than 5 lbf for operation; a toilet flush lever extension may be needed. A universal design is a sensor for automatic flushing.

For a quieter water flow, specify pipes with as large a cross section as possible, and install low-pressure cisterns instead of high-pressure heads.

9-41

Quieter toilet rooms serve people with a wide range of hearing abilities. People with speech differences who need to be clearly heard and people with reduced vision who depend more on their sense of hearing also appreciate lower ambient noise levels.

9-40

9-42

## Toilet Accessories

A transfer board may help in sliding from a wheelchair onto a toilet. Select a toilet seat with a wide bench that is easier to grasp when transferring.

If a seat with arms is needed for support, make sure the arms are adjustable to the most comfortable height. Arms that extend to the floor are more stable than arms that rest on the toilet bowl.

A tissue dispenser must be at least 19 in. a.f.f. and yet low enough so that grab bars do not interfere with its use. It must be installed 7–9 in. in front of the toilet. The toilet tissue holder must permit continuous paper flow and be usable with one hand. Dispensers must be avoided that might require users to reach into a hole to initiate paper flow, and no dispenser should have a sharp or serrated edge. The dispenser should be recessed, if possible, to avoid injury when using a mobility aid. (Fig. 9-43) Consider two tissue dispensers for a constant supply, with one at a lower height for children (2–6 in. above the toilet seat).

## LAVATORIES

The type of lavatory, the location, and the accessories are all important factors in access. Lavatories with pedestals to the floor can be used, in some cases, with wheelchair footrests spread apart, but clearance for wheelchair footrests is required by most standards to extend the full depth of the lavatory.

Lavatories with legs limit access. Wall-mounted lavatories are easy to wheel under if properly installed. (Fig. 9-44) In the past, accessible lavatories were cantilevered up to a depth of 27 in. without additional bracing. If the lavatory was ever needed for support or if an electric hospital bed caught under the edge, the cantilever could break loose. A better solution is a countertop installation with a slight cantilever. (Fig. 9-45)

9-43

9-44

9-45

Water supply- and drainpipes can be plumbed in a horizontally offset position to free knee space. Sharp or abrasive surfaces below the lavatory may injure a seated user. Insulate pipes under approachable lavatories or add a removable cover to prevent burns. Plastic pipe may not require insulation if the maximum hot water temperature does not exceed 120°F,[11] but people with circulation limits can be burned by metal pipes at this temperature. Because of reduced blood flow, the heat cannot be carried away from the skin as rapidly; thus these people are burned at lower temperatures. The burn also takes a longer time to heal because of the limited blood supply. Thermostatic controls limit maximum temperature and prevent sudden changes.

The height of the lavatory is critical in accommodating the needs of people with varying ranges of motion. To be used from a standing position, the top of the lavatory should be from 30 to 42 in. a.f.f., depending on user height. Adults in wheelchairs need a lavatory no higher than 34 in. a.f.f., with knee clearance of 29 in. at the front edge.[12] (Fig. 9-46) Children in wheelchairs require a lavatory that is no higher than 30 in., with a knee space of at least 24 in.[13] To meet all of these needs, one option is to specify an adjustable-height lavatory. (Fig. 9-47) A clear floor space of at least 30 × 48 in. must be provided, extending under the lavatory a maximum of 19 in. For children in wheelchairs, the clear floor space should be at least 36 × 48 in. extending under the lavatory a maximum of 14 in. Mount controls within 14 in. of the front of the lavatory. Clear floor space for adults or children must never be obstructed by the door swing; however, the required turning space may overlap both the clear floor space and the door swing in most states.[14]

To improve visual acuity, identify the edge of the lavatory area by contrasting with a color. (Fig. 9-48) Color-coded hot and cold water controls are also helpful. Avoid glass lavatories, which may be visually confusing.

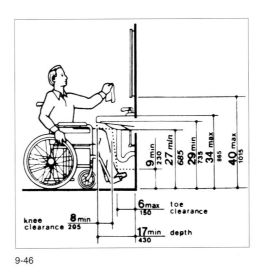

9-46

9-47

9-48

9-49

## FAUCETS AND CONTROLS

A single-lever faucet can be easily controlled with one hand (Fig. 9-49); spring-loaded faucets often take too much strength to operate. To improve reach, mount faucets and controls on the front apron of the counter or to the side of the lavatory. If the lavatory is used to wash hair, use a gooseneck design, which is easier to control than a handheld spray. (Fig. 9-50) The most nearly uni-

versal faucet controls are operated without use of the hands. These controls sense any object underneath and set flow at a safe, preset temperature. (Fig. 9-51) These valves can also be set to open and close the flow at preset intervals without the use of external controls. If a self-closing valve is used, the faucet must remain open for at least 10 seconds.[15] A temperature control prevents burns. Set the mix valve at a temperature of 115°F to start, and do not exceed 120°F.[16]

The noise created by water flow should be minimized to serve people with a wide range of hearing abilities. Specify quiet ball cocks designed to give a smooth flow and aerating nozzles on taps. Also, reduce the water pressure to further quiet the flow.

## VANITIES

A wall-mounted vanity with a knee space is useful for people in wheelchairs as well as for others who may need to sit while using the lavatory. (Fig. 9-52) To meet the needs of a wide range of users (includ-

9-50

9-51

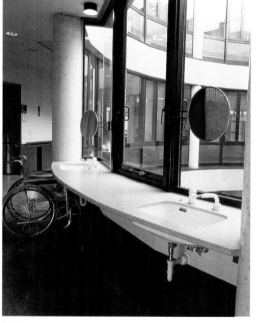

9-52

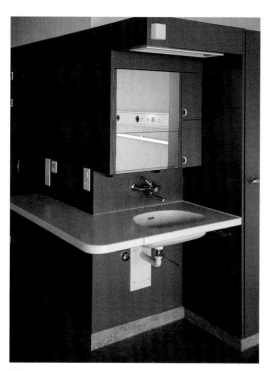

9-53

ing children), the height should be adjustable from 26 to 34 in. a.f.f. The corners of the vanity should be rounded if they extend into the room. (Fig. 9-53) It is easy to bump into a corner when approaching the toilet or bending over while dressing.

For people with allergies or chemical sensitivities, solid-surface vanity tops are preferable to laminates adhered to pressboard or particleboard, as both may offgas formaldehyde.

## BATHROOM STORAGE

Storage areas in the bathroom are often insufficient and require creative planning. With higher cabinets, interior shelves should be of tempered glass or clear plastic to make the contents more visible from a seated position. Keep medications in a medicine cabinet, not on the lavatory. Medications can serve as a constant reminder of illness and also may pose a danger to children. People with reduced manual dexterity should store medication in plastic vials rather than breakable glass bottles.

A medicine cabinet mounted to the side of the lavatory is more convenient for adults of shorter stature, wheelchair users, and children. If space is at a premium, mount the medicine cabinet over the lavatory, with the bottom shelf no more than 44 in. a.f.f. (34 in. for children). The cabinet should have sliding panels suspended on nylon rollers or a door with spring-loaded hinges.

Drawers beside the lavatory area, perhaps in a cabinet on wheels, can fill most remaining bathroom storage needs. Extra drawers can be mounted in the kick space that is elevated for wheelchair footrest clearance. These drawers may be difficult to reach, especially from a wheelchair, but they can provide needed space for seldom-used items. On all drawers, C-grip handles should be horizontal and centered, and cabinets should have slide-out shelves or bins. (Fig. 9-54)

It may be more convenient to store towels in a cabinet close to the shower (and close to the washer and dryer, if these are located in the bathroom). A roll of paper towels in the bathroom is helpful for a fast cleanup.

9-54

## GRAB BARS

Grab bars, lavatories, and towel bars must withstand at least 250 lbf including bending, shear, and tensile forces.[17] To help meet this standard, install grab bars with wood screws into studs, blocking, or plywood reinforcement. (Fig. 9-55) Molly bolts, nails, or screws into gypsum board are not adequate. With prefabricated showers, the blocking or plywood should contact the plastic over the entire reinforced area.[18]

Grab bars should not chip, and they may not have sharp or abrasive edges. They must not rotate within their fittings, and an oval design requires less strength to grasp than a circular bar. (Fig. 9-56) A flatter shape on top is easier for those who push up with their forearm. Textured finishes are available for a sure grip.

In public spaces, the color of the grab bars should contrast with the wall to ensure quick and accurate eye-hand coordination in an emergency. (Fig. 9-57) Chrome and metallic bars may produce reflected glare or blend in with the wall.

A grab bar is often used by bracing the forearm between the bar and the wall for support. Install the grab bar exactly 1½ in. from the wall or the entire arm could slip through the opening.[19]

Many standards require one horizontal grab bar at the foot of the tub when a tub seat is used at the head. Two horizontal grab bars must be placed on the long wall. (Fig. 9-58) The height of the grab bars varies according to the size and ability of the user. Diagonal grab bars may also be necessary but must not be used to replace those required by the standards. (Fig. 9-59) Grab bars may have to be as low as 18 in. a.f.f. for use by children depending on age.

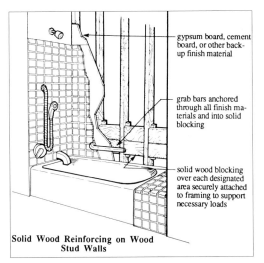

gypsum board, cement board, or other back-up finish material

grab bars anchored through all finish materials and into solid blocking

solid wood blocking over each designated area securely attached to framing to support necessary loads

**Solid Wood Reinforcing on Wood Stud Walls**

9-55

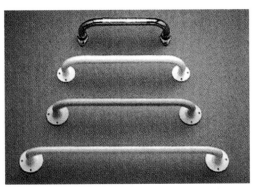

9-56

9-57

9-58

A transfer bar may be helpful over the bathtub; it should be installed on a ceiling trolley track or a ceiling eye-bolt above the tub (with a minimum capacity of at least 300 lbf). The ceiling may need to be reinforced to install this bolt or track and its strength checked periodically to verify that it has not been compromised by rust or wood rot.

Grab bars may also be necessary for transferring to a shower wheelchair. If the doorway to the bathroom cannot be widened for wheelchair users, the individual may have the strength to transfer to the shower wheelchair through the doorway with grab bars installed on both sides.

Use a textured finish on shower grab bars. In most showers, grab bars must be installed at a height of 33–36 in. a.f.f. on all sides, with 18 in. of clear space above the grab bar. (Fig. 9-60) Only shower controls and fittings can protrude into this space. When a shower seat is wall mounted, no grab bar should be placed along that wall, as users typically

balance themselves by leaning against that wall. Grab bars for children should be mounted 18–27 in. a.f.f. depending on age.[20] For standing users, grab bars should be installed just below elbow height.[21] A vertical grab bar at the entrance may be desirable

9-59

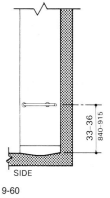

33–36
840–915

SIDE

9-60

9-61

9-62

for a standing user if placed to meet individual needs. Vertical grab bars must not conflict with the required horizontal grab bars. (Fig. 9-61)

For the easiest approach to the toilet, grab bars must usually be located behind the toilet and on one side. (Fig. 9-62) Install them at a height of 33–36 in. a.f.f. depending on the user (18–27 in. for children). The bars must be long enough to allow an unobstructed movement and 18 in. of clear space must be provided above the grab bar.

People with reduced strength often prefer grab bars on both sides of the toilet, but people with wheelchairs, walkers, or assistants need one side clear for the approach. A swing-up assistance bar can meet these varied needs. (Fig. 9-63)

## BATHROOM AND TOILET ROOM ACCESSORIES

In public spaces, installed waste receptacles and recessed towel dispensers must not project into the clear space required at fixtures unless they are mounted above 34 in. a.f.f. Then they must project no more than 4 in. or they present a protruding hazard for blind people. (Fig. 9-64) Coin slots and

9-63

9-64

9-65

controls should be no higher than 42 in. a.f.f. and must be no higher than 4 ft (3 ft for children).[22] Install soap and towel dispensers within reach of the lavatories, perhaps on the same wall or on the surface of the counter.

A vanity stool can be used with lavatories designed for wheelchair users. A lightweight stool on legs with glides is more stable than a stool on casters. Add a $2 \times 4$ ft bench in the bathroom to help in transfer and dressing. Hooks and shelves are also helpful and should be located between 40 and 48 in. a.f.f. (Fig. 9-65)

The toilet room mirror should be low enough to be used by a child, a seated user, or an adult of shorter stature. In most cases, it should be installed to the top of the splash. The bottom of a permanently installed mirror over an accessible sink must be no higher than 40 in. a.f.f.[23] (34 in. for children[24]). If the mirror cannot be placed at this height, it should be tilted with a wedge-shaped shim. A tilted mirror distorts the image of the user but offers a fuller view than a high, flat mirror. A full-length mirror is a convenience for everyone. It should be installed no lower than 10 in. a.f.f. (12 in. for children) to prevent damage from wheelchair footrests.

## UTILITY SPACES

If ambient noise is not a problem, save needless trips to the hamper by placing the washer and dryer in the bathroom. The bathroom lavatory can be used for touch-ups and the counter for clothes sorting. Install an ironing board that swivels out from under the counter, drops down from the wall, or pulls out of a drawer. (Fig. 9-66) Portable ironing boards are awkward for most people to set up, and they are bulky to store.

9-66

Most children, wheelchair users, and adults of shorter stature cannot reach the bottom of a top-loading washer. The most nearly universal solution is one front-loading machine that serves as both the washer and the dryer. Front-loading machines improve reach and also make it easier to lift wet and heavy clothes. (Fig. 9-67) Side-hinged doors allow a closer approach for a seated user than do bottom-hinged doors. Choose appliances with doors mounted 15–34 in. a.f.f.

9-67

An existing top-loading washer can be recessed in the floor to improve reach. Be sure to install a drain in the recessed area, because an overflow can harm the motor. A stacking washer and dryer maybe especially helpful for users who have difficulty bending.

If small items are still out of reach, wash them in a zippered mesh bag that can be lifted out of the washer or dryer with tongs. A retractable clothesline or wall-mounted hanger over the bathtub is also helpful in handling clothes, as is a pull-out basket under a counter, to be used as a hamper.

Specify a dryer with the lint filter on the side or front, not in back. Look for models with the controls on the front as well. Touch controls are easier to use but may be too accessible to children. Raised labels can be used on controls marking the start of each cycle. Some manufacturers have control covers in Braille or large lettering. Most washers and dryers are also equipped with bells or buzzers that redundantly cue the completion of the cycle.

# CASE STUDIES

10

In addition to the universal design criteria already mentioned, a number of special occupancies have supplemental needs. In the design of airports, courthouses, and correctional facilities; for example there is constant tension between security and accessibility requirements. In historic properties, the tension is between the need to preserve and the need to change for access. Hospitality design must balance commercial and residential universal design needs.

In other occupancies, conveniences become requirements. A covered entrance must be installed in health-care facilities, while an assistive listening system is mandated in most assembly areas. Line of sight is required for seated customers in stadiums, and a bench must be added to each stadium dressing room. Counters must be planned at heights accessible by tall, average, and short users as well as by people in wheelchairs and children. (Fig. 10-1) These details often make the difference between empowerment and disability by design.

## HEALTH-CARE FACILITIES

Health-care facilities are held to a higher standard of universal design. From the required passenger loading zone with a covered entry to a lowered clothes rod in the patient room, universal design empowers. Specific design details like

10-1

these improve patient outcomes by returning authority to the patient. Universal design can reduce liability by leaving responsibility with the patient. Finally, it can reduce costs as patients take responsibility for their health while reliance on staff decreases.

Universal design saves needless questioning of staff for directions. It addresses orientation and wayfinding with landmarks, signage, redundant cuing, and spatial differentiation. The latter is defined by changes in lighting, color, sound, and spatial volume.

Universal design acknowledges that health-care spaces should feed the body as well as the soul. Restaurants and kiosks should be close to all treatment areas, and a chapel or meditation space should be planned. Accessible art should be planned in waiting areas. Patients should also have the opportunity to experience nature while waiting.

People in health-care facilities wait. They wait for providers, for family members, and for test results. They try to find a place to rest on lengthy pathways. There never seems to be enough seating in health-care facilities. Universal design accommodates this need, increasing the quantity as well as the quality of seating. It offers firm, well-dispersed seating for people of all sizes as well as space for people seated in wheelchairs.

Finishes are planned to protect walls from a wide range of footrest elevations, from 9 in. to 18 in. a.f.f. Most standards require patient rooms to provide a turning space and a 36 in. access aisle on each side of the bed. But how does one move a patient on a gurney with a 7 ft turning radius? How does one evacuate a sleeping patient in an emergency? Do the patients really need to hear "code blue"? Are alarms acknowledged or ignored? Can signals be heard and seen in the environment? Universal design addresses these questions.

Acoustics and lighting are overlooked in most accessibility standards. Amplified telephones may be offered, but ambient noise levels are not controlled. Lighting levels are generally too low, especially for older users. Waiting areas seldom provide task lighting or reading materials in large print.

Patients also require access to text telephones and assistive listening devices. In long-term care, visual door knock alerting devices may be needed, together with smoke detectors with a visual cue. At a minimum, a closed-caption television decoder should be available and all controls, including the remote, must be operable with limited fine motor skills. Many people prefer a long wand to a drapery cord and a touch control to a lamp stem. Eventually, a voice command option will control HVAC, door locks, television, beds, and call switches as well.

## INDEPENDENCE SQUARE
by Guynes Design, Inc., Phoenix, Arizona

**CASE STUDY**

Patricia Moore is a renowned gerontologist and universal designer, and is president of Guynes Design. Patricia and David Guynes, the chief executive officer, have developed and designed more than a hundred healthcare facilities with an emphasis on geriatric, industrial, and pediatric rehabilitation.

Appearing as small towns and homes within the hospital, Independence Square® (Fig. 10-2) does not accommodate disability—rather, it enhances ability. Clinicians, families, and patients relearn the necessary skills for independent living in safe and friendly settings. These environments assist individuals to actually regain competencies lost to illness or injury by exposing them to a variety of environmental challenges. An obstacle course is offered with dirt, sand, grass, gravel, cracked concrete, grates, curb cuts, slopes, and steps. (Fig. 10-3) In addition, users climb aboard a bus, load groceries in a truck, and transfer to a car from a wheelchair. All of this practice takes place in the hospital, developing confidence in new abilities before discharge.

10-2

A life-size game board called Rehab 1,2,3® includes Mr. Pipes® (Fig. 10-4), one of the pediatric rehabilitation components designed to engage children while offering rehabilitation. The elements of the system pop up from the floor. Rehab 1,2,3® may also include stepping-stones, logs, cubes, ramps, and toadstools used in upper body exercise, fine motor skills development, coordination, and cognitive training.

10-3

10-4

# TRANSPORTATION FACILITIES

Rail stations, airports, and bus terminals place a priority on accessible parking, an accessible route throughout the facilities, usable seating, and redundant communication systems.

Plan accessible loading zones with security bollards separating pedestrian and auto traffic. This type of curbless installation is a much better solution for people using wheelchairs and scooters as well as for the many travelers using luggage carts and strollers. Curbs require curb cuts, which can be blocked by parked cars.

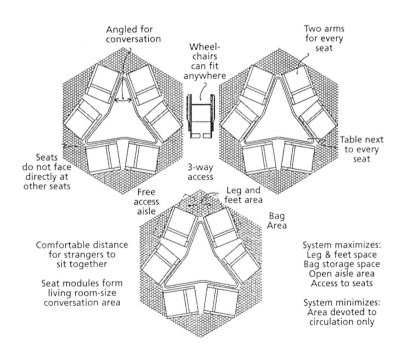

10-5

The accessible route continues through the entrance to ticketing, baggage handling, and departure gates. Vending and ticketing machines must be accessible, and if the ticketing gate must be pushed open by a person using a mobility aid, its surface must be smooth and continuous between 2 and 27 in. a.f.f. to prevent injury. Escalator treads should be marked with a stripe of contrasting color, and platform edges bordering drop-offs must have detectable warnings if they are not protected by platform screens or guard rails. The platform height must nearly align with the floor height of the transit vehicle, and the horizontal gap between the two must be minimal.

When jetways are not available at airports, lifts must be provided to the planes. Baggage check-in tables and baggage claim carousels should be designed in a low profile without a lip. Clustered seating should be conveniently located near baggage claim, check-in, and all accessible telephone locations. Universal seating provides space for wheelchairs as well as luggage (Fig. 10-5) in a configuration designed for relaxed conversation. Rest areas with universal seating should be planned on longer routes.

For wayfinding, make available carry-along information and tactile maps rather than requiring individuals with vision loss to rely on one central tactile map within a facility. Audible paging should be supplemented with visual paging. Visual alarms are essential to alert people with differing levels of hearing. Televisions should be equipped with visual captioning for the benefit of all. Open captioning in noisy concourses and bars enables all passengers to receive information when they cannot hear the audible page above the ambient noise level.

## PORTLAND INTERNATIONAL AIRPORT ACCESSIBILITY
by Pamela Pflueger & Associates, Phoenix, Arizona

CASE STUDY

10-6

10-7

Pamela Pflueger and Associates served as the project management firm for accessibility for the 400,000 sq ft expansion of this airport. The communication systems are the real highlights of the project, but the airport also includes areas of rescue assistance, accessible ticket counters, and an accessible gate adjacent to the security checkpoint. Wheelchair users are not forced to use the concourse exit as an entry, which is a violation of security provisions as well as inconvenient and potentially embarrassing.

A unique visual paging system (Fig. 10-6) is displayed on accessible information kiosks strategically placed throughout the airport. The system offers the ability to read printed messages that are usually only announced over the public address system. Readable messages include personal pages, flight changes, general information, and emergency announcements. To pick up a page, a passenger calls the paging office from a volume-controlled paging telephone or a TTY. The paging telephones are hearing-aid compatible and lowered for adults of shorter stature, children, and people in wheelchairs.

Each elevator is equipped with a distinctive emergency two-way communication system. (Fig. 10-7) This visual system supplements the phone, enabling a person with hearing differences to send and receive programmed messages. Free-form messages can also be received from the operator in the communications center. Additional communication equipment includes an audiotape to orient passengers to airport destinations. This information is also available in Braille and large print. Text telephones are located in the accessible telephone booths. Each booth is equipped with a flip-down seat, enabling a person to use the text telephone at the same height required by adults of shorter stature, children, and wheelchair users. (Fig. 10-8) This truly universal design also accommodates the needs of tired travelers and people of all ages who prefer to phone from a seated position.

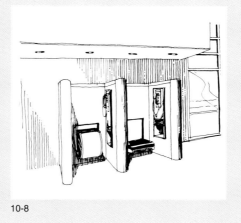

10-8

## RECREATIONAL FACILITIES

An element of fun and mystery must be balanced against the functional requirements of recreational facilities. Heavy vegetation may surround a bumpy path that is barely accessible, but to a child in a wheelchair, the trip becomes a fun ride through the jungle. Running or wheeling through a fountain can be an adventure or an unwelcome surprise to a blind person when there is no tactile warning. (Fig. 10-9) Play areas may allow children of all abilities to develop their skills or prevent them from participating. Designers must tread the fine line between creating exciting challenges and creating barriers.

Accessible fun often involves a degree of challenge, but the risk must be based on anthropometric data and existing safety standards. When there is a conflict between safety and accessibility, err on the side of safety. Accessible routes must be stable, firm, and slip resistant, with surfaces like decomposed granite, asphalt, wooden boardwalk, resilient mats, and concrete. The route may end in a fishing platform, for example, but risk must be minimized with edge protection and railings lowered in some areas for casting.

Higher platforms can be used by children in wheelchairs to safely transfer to play structures. Swings can provide safe body support and sand play areas can be offered in a variety of heights for play on the ground or in a wheelchair. Boulders or posts can provide back support in the play area. Accessible benches in a variety of heights should offer back support as well.

Supportive signage and audible cues for orientation provide perceptible information about recreation facilities. A wind chime offers a sense of direction to all users, not just to people with low vision or reduced cognitive skills. A tactile map reinforces the high-contrast lettering on the visual displays, and talking signs explain the expansive choices that universal design offers all users.

10-9

## IBACH PARK
by Moore Iacofano Goltsman (MIG), Berkeley, California (main offices)

MIG designs community facilities for play and recreation. Known for their universal design approach, MIG keeps people of all abilities participating in the same activities at the same time. At Ibach Park, consumers were involved at the very beginning of the project with a series of community meetings. These meetings defined the basis of the design concept: the archaeological context of the site.

In recognition of the universal attraction of water, a river runs through the entire play area, offering equal access to children with and without disabilities. By pressing on a bollard, children cause the water to flow at ground level on one side (for wading) and at a raised height on the other side (for access by children in wheelchairs). (Fig. 10-10) A mastodon ribcage provides a climbing structure; a missing rib creates access for children who use wheelchairs and walkers. The archeological dig offers a fossil discovery, a stimulating tactile experience for sighted and unsighted children. (Fig. 10-11) Native Indian drums provide auditory stimulation and are

10-11

installed at a variety of heights for standing and seated users. The swing area offers accessible surfacing and a bucket swing for younger children or those with balance limitations. The park integrates all children, improving their physical, social, and intellectual abilities. (Fig. 10-12)

10-10

10-12

## LIBRARIES

Sadly, library books are seldom required to be within reach of children, wheelchair users, and adults of shorter stature. However, the required 3 ft wide access aisles, lowered check-out counters, and accessible fixed seating, tables, and study carrels all contribute to the universal access of libraries. Card catalogs must be installed between 48 in. and 18 in. a.f.f., but, most importantly, libraries must provide access to computers, software, scanners, and copiers used by the patrons. In this information age, universal design of libraries is increasingly found in electronic access.

## CASE STUDIES

### LIBRARIES
by Shepley Bullfinch Richardson and Abbott (SBRA), Boston

Some firms go beyond the minimum requirements. The architects of SBRA offer unique universal design solutions for libraries. As part of their general design philosophy, SBRA creates original universal furnishings and millwork for their projects. The tabletop lamps at the Sterling Memorial Library at Yale offer universally accessible integral power and data access. (Fig. 10-13) Because they are user controlled, the task lighting levels can be increased to improve visual acuity. At the Shelby County Public Library in Memphis, Tennessee, doors to the rest rooms were eliminated by the addition of privacy screening. (Fig. 10-14) The Public Library of Cincinnati features a covered passenger loading zone without curbs or ramps (Fig. 10-15).

SBRA has also designed a tilted-up bottom shelf for easier reading of the book titles. This feature benefits all, but it is essential for people on crutches, those who use wheelchairs and walkers, and older visitors who have trouble bending.

10-13

10-14

10-15

## HOSPITALITY

Many leaders in the lodging industry believe the key to success in the twenty-first century will be their ability to attract international tourism. The ADA redefined the United States as the most accessible travel destination in a world of aging baby boomers. The universal design of guest rooms not only follows the law but makes good business sense.

Universal design begins with a warm reception for guests of all heights and abilities. (Fig. 10-16) Bathrooms should functionally and visually integrate universal design requirements such as knee clearance, lowered mirrors, and turning space. (Fig. 10-17) Restaurants must offer accessible seating and lowered service counters. Tray slides at 34 in. a.f.f. are helpful to people using wheelchairs, adults of shorter stature, and some children. Tray slides are also helpful to anyone who cannot hold a tray while moving down a cafeteria line, including those using luggage wheels, strollers, crutches, or walkers. A cart on wheels is an alternate solution. Tableware, condiment areas, self-service shelves, and dispensing devices must be approachable and within reach of children, wheelchair users, and adults of shorter stature.

An accessible hotel provides at least 32 in. of clearance at all doorways throughout the facility, not just in the accessible rooms. With these wider doors, people in wheelchairs can enter an otherwise nonaccessible room to visit a friend, and some can even use these rooms when fully accessible rooms are not available.

Hotel guest rooms challenge designers to develop solutions that support a variety of abilities while appealing to the taste and lifestyles of general users. Because the use is personal rather than public, an additional layer of complexity must be considered. Guest rooms are a home away from home, space where one dresses, sleeps, bathes, and even dines. Every design detail presents an opportunity to make the lodging experience a pleasure or a disappointment.

For security purposes, install door levers in a vertical position and make certain levers rotate away from the frame. A lowered peephole is appropriately named when one considers the view from a wheelchair. A door scope offers a wider field of view. (Fig. 10-18) People of all heights can see outside the door from up to seven feet inside the room.

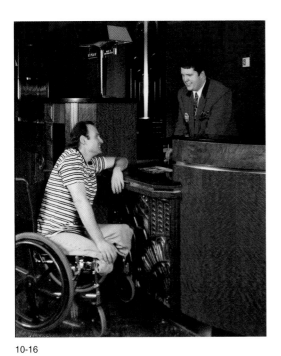

10-16

10-17

10-18

Clear floor space must be planned for access to the convenience bar, kitchen area, and all other amenities. All controls must be accessible, including those for the television, radio, HVAC, draperies, and alarm. For guests with differing levels of hearing, a variety of warning and communication equipment is available. A flashing light alerts a guest that someone is at the door or that the phone is ringing. A strobe light reinforces the smoke alarm, and a pillow or bed shaker replaces an alarm clock. A decoder for closed-captioned television and a text telephone may also be required. An electrical outlet must be provided within 4 ft of the telephone connection to accommodate the text telephone. All electrical and communication outlets for occupant use must be within reach, not under furniture.

## CASE STUDIES

### LODGING GUEST ROOM
Designed by Universal Designers and Consultants, Inc. (UD&C), Takoma Park Maryland

John Salmen of UD&C designs guest rooms that are detailed to meet a wide range of user needs. Most firms manage to meet the basic requirements: an accessible path of travel and sufficient maneuvering clearances. UD&C supplements the basics with technologies that redefine user control. An intriguing safe incorporates the same type of keypad normally found on a telephone. (Fig. 10-19) It provides tactile, visual, and auditory feedback as the numbers are punched in, yet its use is simple and intuitive for nearly everyone. It eliminates the need for keys and cards and the accompanying concern that they will be lost or duplicated. Other universal detailing includes drapery wands that extend to within 36 in. of the floor, D-pulls on drawers, several choices in lowered clothes rods, and reachable storage ideas.

UD&C offers a unique toilet room configuration that serves a wide range of users. (Fig. 10-20) In this plan, the back wall of the toilet is moved forward toward the front edge of the lavatory. This provides clearance for a side transfer from a wheelchair, an approach for a walker, and space for an assistant. The grab bar behind the toilet can be also used for support by a person standing at the lavatory. A hinged grab bar can be added to the rear wall for the user who needs support on both sides of the toilet. The plan also offers shelf space for personal toiletries.

10-19

10-20

## RESIDENTIAL

### RESIDENCE
by Anmahian Winton Associates, Boston

10-21

10-22

10-23

10-24

What happens when the sky's the limit on a universal design project? In the case of this Cambridge, Massachusetts, residence, the answer is innovation. How about a hydraulic ramp that serves both the basement (Fig. 10-21) and the foyer? (Fig. 10-22) Try a bathtub with a subsurface ledge to replace grab bars. The client is a wheelchair user who does not want visible grab bars in his house. He prefers to use the ledge to push himself up to the tub seat. (Fig. 10-23) From here, he can turn on his waterfall, which offers a 68 gallon per minute massage to soothe those sore upper body muscles. Then he slides across the recessed door track (Fig. 10-24) to exit the tub. To make dressing easier, why not elevate the bifold doors to clear the wheelchair footrests? (Fig. 10-25) Because the counters

10-25

10-26

10-27

in the kitchen are lower anyway, let's round the edge so that friends can perch on them. Then we'll add a pass-through to the garage (Fig. 10-26) to prevent all those trips with groceries on the lap. As a final indulgence, why not build two electric garage doors, one for cars and the other for a wheelchair or racing tricycle? (Fig. 10-27) No more need to wheel around cars on the way out of the garage.

## RESIDENTIAL SPACE PLAN (FIG. 10-28)

1.  Install a bathroom window to the side of the lavatory to allow children, people of shorter stature, and wheelchair users to reach window controls and to see out the window. Remember, however, the window takes up wall space that could otherwise be used for low storage within reach.
2.  Leave clear floor space around windows to allow operation of window hardware.
3.  Windows and strong lights should not be in the direct line of sight when entering the front door. This can dazzle a person whose lenses do not adjust rapidly.
4.  Stacking closets can be used as an elevator space if the need for such arises at a later date.
5.  To save effort, limit the number of doorways or plan to leave doorways open. Replace some doors with curtains where sound control is not a problem.
6.  Doors to confined spaces (e.g., bathrooms and wheel-in closets) should swing out. In-swinging doors are more difficult to close behind wheelchairs and walkers. An in-swinging door could also be blocked by a person who has taken a fall, delaying help.
7.  Remember that a doorway width of 3 ft allows extra elbow room when using a wheelchair.
8.  In the entry, plan a 5 × 5 ft turning space. If the entry has two hinged doors in a series, make sure there is clearance of at least 4 ft between the open doors.
9.  Each room should include a turning space. It can extend under the bathroom lavatory or kitchen counter without compromising function because wheelchair footrests require more turning space than armrests.
10. Accessible routes should be considered between rooms in the house and between the entryway and the garage.

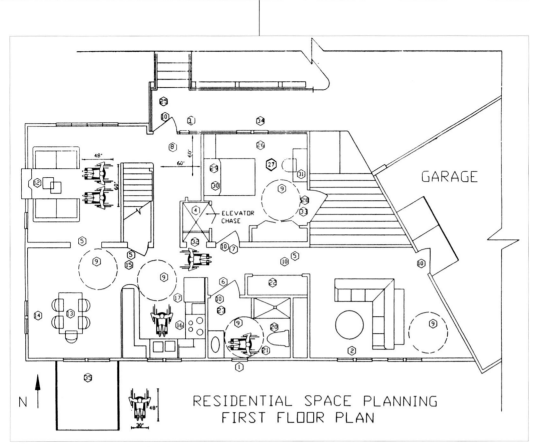

10-28a

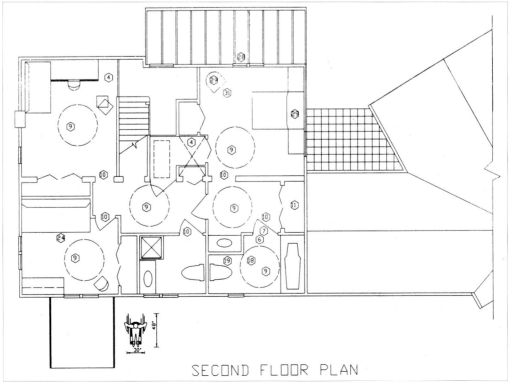

10-28b

11. A closet between the bedroom and bathroom is a nice convenience.

12. If planning a fireplace, use tempered glass doors to prevent damage from the use of mobility aids. A deep hearth (9 in.) with rounded corners serves the same purpose. Allow a 4 × 5 ft clear floor space in the furniture floor plan to accommodate two people using wheelchairs or walkers.

13. Plan the breakfast area close to the kitchen counter to shorten the distance for serving and clearing.

14. If possible, plan a window with a view in the dining room. This is particularly appreciated by a person who dines alone.

15. Plan a minimum width of 42 in. for the traffic lane from the kitchen to the dining table to allow space for use of a serving cart with a wheelchair, stroller, or walker. If there is no table in the kitchen, keep the dining room table close to the kitchen so that it can be used for food preparation.

16. Plan a U-shaped kitchen with open counter space next to the refrigerator and the oven and under the sink. Counters should be adjustable (between 26 and 42 in. a.f.f.) or offered at a variety of heights.

17. Allow a clear floor space of 2 ft 6 in. × 4 ft to approach all installed appliances.

18. Where possible, the bathroom should connect to the bedroom to allow privacy while dressing. Many people dress on the bed after using the bathroom.

19. Consider the preferred transfer technique in planning the bathroom. Space can be arranged to allow either a left-handed or right-handed approach for a person who uses a mobility aid or assistant.

20. The shower may need to be placed close to the toilet for cleanup after changing a leg bag or other aspects of a bowel program.

21. Allow clear space for a forward approach to the lavatory.

22. Consider installing the washer and dryer between the bathroom and bedroom. This design is convenient and saves time and effort. To prevent transmitted noise, insulate the closet and wall between the bedroom and the hall.

23. Isolate or soundproof noisy rooms. Locate a utility room or workshop away from such areas as the living room, bedroom, and den. Position the bathroom to achieve olfactory and acoustic isolation.

24. Privacy can be improved by planning children's bedrooms away from the master bedroom.

25. Make sure the entryway is designed to provide visual privacy to the rest of the house when the front door is open.

26. Include guest facilities if possible and attendant care facilities if necessary.

27. There should be clearance of 3 ft at the foot and at least one side of the bed for use of mobility assistance devices.

28. Plan an accessible emergency exit from the bedroom.

29. Because glare can be distracting, the bedroom should be planned so that the bed does not face a window. Reading chairs should be placed so that light comes over the shoulder, not on the face, of the person seated.

30. To prevent exposure to drafts, never place the head of a bed against or under a window. Make sure walls are well insulated if the bed is to be placed against an outside wall. For people who spend more time in the bedroom than in other living spaces, enlarge the bedroom and include extra storage to prevent needless trips.

31. Provide a comfortable seat near the bed for visitors. Consider an arrangement that allows work to be done in the bedroom.

32. Provide a centrally located closet for storing maintenance equipment. A clear floor space (2 ft 6 in. × 4 ft) should be provided in front of all storage areas.

33. Specify a wide door (at least 39 in.) to accommodate large pieces of furniture. People who spend daytime in bed may wish to move the bed outdoors for a change of pace. This doorway can also be an emergency exit.

34. Plan windows as part of escape routes. The sill width, window position, frame design, and outside landing should all be considered. For children, people in wheelchairs,

and adults of shorter stature, the view may be limited from windows higher than 3 ft a.f.f. A shallow exterior windowsill allows an even clearer view.

35. A person with limited circulation may prefer warmer rooms. Choose a house plan with southern exposures in the areas where the occupant spends the most time.

## COURTHOUSES, ASSEMBLY AREAS, AND STADIUMS

The supplemental universal design requirements for courthouses, assembly areas, and stadiums include assistive listening systems, seating to accommodate a variety of abilities, and a balance between access and security. Each courthouse, for example, must provide at least one accessible holding cell. Correctional facilities must provide at least one accessible cell of each type and security level. Each type of visiting area must be accessible as well.

In the courthouse, access can be easily and invisibly provided to the witness stand, judge's bench, and jury box through the use of an invisible lift™ (Fig. 10-29). It offers flexibility to meet access needs while concealing the entire lift mechanism. An adjustable-height lectern should also be planned for attorneys in wheelchairs and those of short stature.

A permanently installed assistive listening system (ALS) must be in half of each type of courtroom, hearing room, jury deliberation room, and jury orientation room. Portable systems may be available in the other half. The three most common types of ALS are infrared, magnetic induction loop, and radio transmission. A universal receiver can be used with all three types. (Fig. 10-30) ALS additionally requires signage that notifies users of the availability of receivers.

10-29

10-30

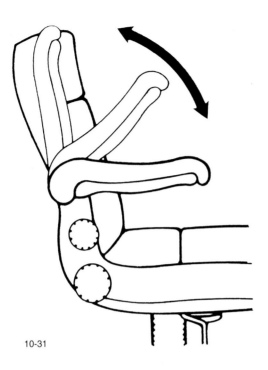

10-31

The logical transmission choice for a courtroom is the infrared ALS, which is the only system appropriate for confidential transmission.[1] However, infrared light is found in both natural and artificial

lighting sources, sometimes resulting in interference. Because the infrared receiver must be in line of sight from the transmitter, FM radio systems are the logical choice for large assembly areas and stadiums. FM produces an excellent sound quality and is available with multiple channels to broadcast alternate languages. It is not subject to electrical interference and is highly portable. AM radio and loop systems have relatively poor sound quality.

In addition to the ALS requirements, assembly areas and stadiums must also offer an accessible route to arena floors, dressing rooms, locker rooms, stages, and other spaces used by performers. Seating options and spaces for people in wheelchairs must also be provided. A companion fixed seat must be in place next to each accessible space. Some fixed seats must be available without armrests on the aisle side. Folding or removable armrests on the aisle side can also be used to ease entry by older people as well as transfer from a wheelchair. (Fig. 10-31)

A single-access space may be as small as 36 by 48 in., but each of these spaces can be reduced to a 33 in. width when paired. In larger auditoriums and stadiums the spaces must be dispersed, and each space must adjoin an accessible route or another accessible space. Readily removable seats may be placed in accessible spaces when the spaces are not being used by people in wheelchairs. (Fig. 10-32) Line-of-sight issues are particularly difficult for wheelchair users when others stand (Fig. 10-33); these are addressed in the following case study.

10-32

New Agreed Upon Dimensions
Line of Sight

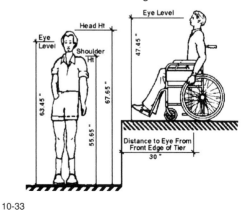

10-33

### ORIOLE PARK AT CAMDEN YARDS
by Hellmuth, Obata + Kassabaum (HOK) Sports Facilities Group, Kansas City, Missouri

## CASE STUDY

Since 1994, HOK Sports Facilities Group has designed venues to provide wheelchair users full line of sight in certain locations over standing spectators. (Fig. 10-34) A complex relationship exists between dispersement of spaces and the line-of-sight issues for people in wheelchairs. The eye height of a viewer in a wheelchair averages 43 to 51 in. To see over a standing spectator, the wheelchair user must be raised at least the difference between their eye height and a standing spectator's eye height. In addition, the horizontal viewing angle in a stadium or arena is considerably larger than that of a theater, for example. It is more easily blocked by the elevated spaces for wheelchair users, so an aisle is typically planned between these spaces and the ambulatory spectators to widen the viewing angle. Seating behind these access spaces must be placed to allow an accessible route to the space and a line of sight over the wheelchair user. The issue becomes even more complex as the line of sight changes in the higher seating bowls.

10-34

## RETAIL AND BUSINESS

Some of the most interesting universal design ideas are emerging from this sector. Braille and raised lettering are being sandblasted into glass signage (Fig. 10-35), while handrails can offer Braille directions as well as physical support. (Fig. 10-36) In addition, the handrail can be used to activate audio messages using photosensors. Displays are lowered for access by adults of shorter stature, children, and wheelchair users (Fig. 10-37). Elevated displays now incorporate lifts (Fig. 10-38). With a lift, all users can climb aboard an airplane, for example, and watch the rudder, ailerons, and elevator move as they manipulate the controls.

10-35

10-36

10-37

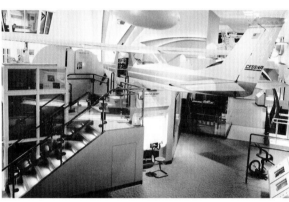

10-38

10-39

Many businesses are surpassing the minimum requirements by keeping all merchandise below 48 in. a.f.f. Thirty-six-inch clear width must be provided in aisles. Back-to-back checkout stations with shared customer aisles offer accessibility while reducing the space requirements. Checkout and reception counters are offered at a variety of heights (Fig. 10-39) and dressing rooms are planned without doors or tight spaces. This per-

10-40

mits two or three people in wheelchairs to use lockers in close proximity. (Fig. 10-40) Unisex dressing rooms allow a spouse or aide to accompany a child or a person who needs assistance.

Curtains are easier to use than doors. When a door is used, it must swing out of the dressing room and a turning space must be provided inside the room. Benches should be offered at a variety of seat heights ranging from 17 in. to 19 in. a.f.f. for adults and 11 in. to 19 in. for children. A full-length mirror should also be provided. It should be installed no lower than 10 in. a.f.f. (to protect it from wheelchair footrests) and should be viewable from the bench. Grab bars adjacent to the bench are helpful for wheelchair users and for those who have difficulty bending and stooping.

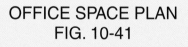

## OFFICE SPACE PLAN
## FIG. 10-41

1. For people who have trouble adjusting from light to dark areas, allow natural light into entrance areas through windows and glass doors. People with differing levels of hearing need as much natural light as possible to read lips and to see facial expressions and body movements. At least one window wall per room is recommended if the glare is controlled.

2. Consider U-shaped, V-shaped, or circular seating arrangements with swivel chairs to allow clear vision.

3. Without blocking transfers, keep the lavatory as close as possible to the toilet for easy cleanup after a bowel and bladder program.

4. Closets with a full front opening are more accessible than closets with walls returning to the doors on either side. Heavy or bulky objects should be stored below shoulder height and above hip height. Shoes are most easily reached on shelves 9 in. above the floor. In a clothes closet, place another shelf directly above the clothes rod, and be sure the rod is at a reachable height. An adjustable rod may be helpful.

5. Provide an accessible closet that is large enough to store a collapsible wheelchair, and then allow sufficient space around the door (5 × 5 ft) to place two wheelchairs side by side for transfer.

6. A sideways approach to storage areas usually allows maximum accessibility. A clear floor space should be provided in front of all storage areas.

7. Remember that a doorway width of 3 ft is necessary for wheelchair passage. This allows the required 2 ft 8 in. of clearance together with a little extra room for elbows and fingers.

8. It is difficult to provide sufficient storage space reachable by children, wheelchair users, and adults of shorter stature. Install doors 1 ft away from room corners and hinge them on the corner side of the room. This allows additional storage space behind doors.

9. Seating should not be planned facing windows, as glare can be distracting. Reading chairs should be placed so that light comes over the shoulder, not on the face of the person seated.

10. Plan seating positions that allow conveniently close conversations (seating no farther apart than 5 ft 6 in.). For people with differing visual abilities, even closer seating may be necessary. Avoid arrangements that face such distractions as outside doors or glaring windows.

11. Provide a clear turning radius of 60 in. for wheelchair use.

12. Allow sufficient clear floor space for a wheelchair or walker in alcoves on the perimeter of the room.

13. Plan sufficient space to open drawers. This may require a wider hallway to allow clearance past an open drawer.

14. Plan family bathrooms (unisex) and a lavatory in the toilet stall. Always allow clear floor space for a forward approach to the lavatory.

15. A minimum hallway width of 4 ft is required to allow passage of a wheelchair user and ambulatory person. This wider width is also appropriate for those who use other mobility aids.

16. Collisions often occur at hallway intersections. If these areas cannot be eliminated from the design, be sure corners are beveled, rounded, or transparent.

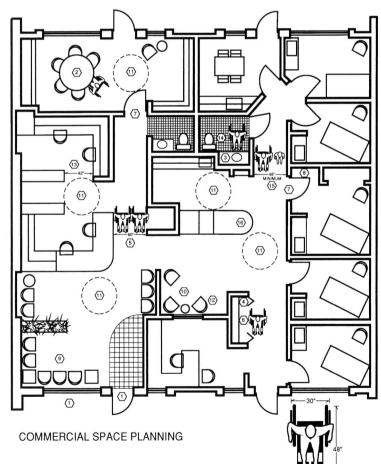

COMMERCIAL SPACE PLANNING

10-41

# CASE STUDIES

## BANK ACCESSIBILITY
by Evan Terry Associates (ETA), Birmingham, Alabama

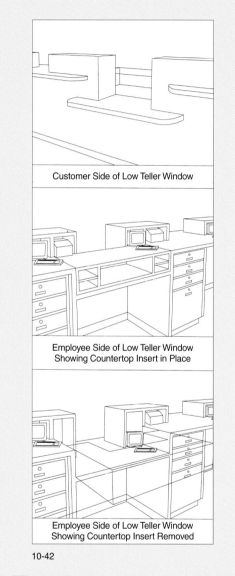

Customer Side of Low Teller Window

Employee Side of Low Teller Window
Showing Countertop Insert in Place

Employee Side of Low Teller Window
Showing Countertop Insert Removed

10-42

ETA specializes in innovative universal de-sign solutions. A variety of heights is offered at service and checkout counters of banks, and the lighting illuminates all counter surfaces as well as the faces of the tellers. A person with a differing level of hearing must often see the face of a speaker to read lips and facial expressions. A unique teller window can be easily converted to a variety of heights. (Fig. 10-42) It can be elevated to prevent back strain for tall standing users and lowered for a seated customer, child, or adult of shorter stature. The check-writing areas also offer surfaces at a variety of heights (Fig. 10-43), and accessible safe deposit booths are planned in an area outside of the vault when the vault is not accessible. Each such viewing area includes a 5 ft turning radius and an accessible counter.

Other innovations in bank design include Citibank's automatic teller machine (ATM), which is equally accessible to wheelchair users and standing customers. It is lowered by touch control for use by people in wheelchairs and adults of shorter stature. (Fig. 10-44) Braille keys are now standard on ATMs. Standard transaction codes allow users to key in instructions without reading the screens. For example, each time the user wishes to withdraw $100, the number 11110000 might be keyed in after the user's personal access code. For people with vision impairments, some machines offer choices in letter sizes and screen background. Keyboard echoing

10-43

repeats each customer selection, and voice guidance systems and tactile keypads will soon offer additional cues. Voice recognition software provides security while leaving both of the user's hands free. The software also assists people who have difficulty grasping cards.

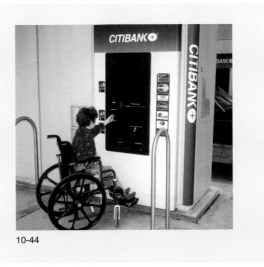

10-44

## HISTORIC PRESERVATION

Perhaps the most difficult challenge to the universal design philosophy is the integration of historic properties. The process starts with a thorough review of the defining elements of historic significance. Less important features should also be identified, defining the parameters of alteration. The success of the project often turns on the issue of establishing priorities. Features of lower historic significance may include later additions, previously altered spaces, service areas, and secondary pathways. It may be permissible to modify these elements for access.

An accessibility survey should be completed, and the design program must then attempt to accommodate both access and preservation. The most difficult problems arise in making infrastructure improvements. Level changes, including placement of ramps, lifts, and elevators, are frequently the most challenging issues. Elevators are expensive and lifts have limited capacity. They frequently require maintenance and often cannot be operated independently. Ramps and lifts segregate users to a "separate-but-equal" path. The best solution may be exterior regrading to a slope of less than 5 percent, eliminating the need for ramps and allowing all visitors to approach in the same way. Even this may be problematic, depending on the site and the historic significance of the landscape.

If at all possible, access to the historic property should be offered by the front door. Sometimes offset pivot hinges can be used to widen the doorway, and friction hinges can be retrofitted with ball-bearing inserts to reduce door pressure. Door closers can also be rethreaded for this purpose.[2] Frequently, power-assisted door openers must be installed and thresholds replaced. If the threshold is of historic significance, a bevel can be added to each side to reduce the effective height.

Unisex or family toilet rooms are permitted to preserve historic significance, and they are growing in popularity. An accessible family toilet room can frequently be installed in existing space, and the design allows a spouse or aide to accompany a child or a person who needs assistance. Such rooms offer private access to a lavatory, a help when changing a baby or maintaining a leg bag. Signs should clearly mark the route to accessible rest rooms as well as to other accessibility features not on the main routes.

When additions are required to achieve access, the priority should be to preserve the historic structure by minimizing the connection points between the addition and the existing building. Although accessibility modifications should be in scale and visually compatible, they should also be clearly differentiated from the historic structure. There should be no question about the progression of the building over time, and the modifications should be reversible if better solutions are found.

## CASE STUDY

### COOPER-HEWITT NATIONAL DESIGN MUSEUM, SMITHSONIAN INSTITUTION
by Polshek & Partners, New York

10-45

10-47

The Cooper-Hewitt is hailed as a model for providing accessibility in landmark buildings. Tim Hartung, a partner with Polshek & Partners, New York, recently designed a renovation of the museum that respects the historic fabric of the building while ensuring its accessibility. A ramp to the museum's main entrance is discreetly placed in a planting area. (Fig. 10-45) Three years were spent by various design firms looking at solutions just to provide access through the front door. According to Mr. Hartung, "The solution seemed so easy after it is discovered, but believe me, it was hard to find! There was never a formula to follow."

The ramp leads to a real treasure: the original 650-pound bronze doors. A new mechanical assistance system had to be designed to offer access. (Fig. 10-46) The architect notes, "To make the entrance accessible, we had to request a variance to allow the two sets of double doors to open at once, which compromises energy conservation. It's always a balancing act. In this example, accessibility and historic preservation were a higher priority."

Other accessibility features include areas of rescue assistance and a new accessible connection between two parts of the museum, the mansion and the adjacent townhouses. The connector offers access to the collection resource center and the garden while creating a new service approach. (Fig. 10-47) To access all areas, an elevator variance was also needed. The elevator now has three doors and makes eleven stops to access six floors. In the opinion of Mr. Hartung, "Lineal thinking seldom works in historic preservation. We have to be holistic at every level, thinking of all the needs at once and pushing the envelope with each decision. Each accessibility feature affects all of the other building requirements, not just the access requirements. A project master plan is critical when taking the holistic view, finding the ideal solutions, and reducing the number of compromises that must be made."

According to Dianne H. Pilgrim, museum director, "Every human-made object is designed, and the built or designed environment affects our lives every second of every day. The designs from the past can be not only be inspirational, but can possibly lead us to new and better solutions today . . . solutions that take into consideration function, aesthetics, social and moral values, as well as adaptable and universal concerns for the planet."

10-46

## PREFACE

1. Elizabeth Church, (comments delivered at the Universal Design Education Planning Conference, Boston, November 1994).
2. Polly Welch, ed., *Strategies for Teaching Universal Design* (Berkeley, CA: MIG Communications, 1995).
3. Ibid., 2.
4. T.J.M. Van der Voordt, "Accessibility by Means of Ramps," *Proceedings of the Built Environment and the Handicapped: Toward a Normal Life for the Disabled and Elderly* (Gotheberg, Sweden: Swedish Council for Building Research, 1981), 38–40.
5. Lou Harris and Associates. *ICD Survey of Disabled Americans, 1986* (New York: International Center for the Disabled.)
6. Kim Beasley, "Design Lines: The Cost of Accessibility," *Paraplegia News* (June 1990): 42.
7. Internal Revenue Service, Department of the Treasury, *Medical and Dental Expenses Publication #502* (Washington, D.C.: Government Printing Office, 1990), 1.
8. RIA Group, *1999 Federal Tax Handbook* (New York: RIA Group), 401 paragraph 2330.
9. U.S. House of Representatives, Select Committee on Aging, *America's Elderly at Risk* (Washington, D.C.: Government Printing Office, 1985), 20.
10. *AARP: A Profile of Older Americans, 1997* (Washington, D.C.: American Association of Retired Persons, 1997), 5.
11. Life Care Centers, *Our Commitment to Serving the Elderly* (Cleveland, Tenn.: Author, 1988), 4.
12. Gerry M. O'Connor, "Design: Remodeling for the Handicapped and Elderly," *Remodeling Contractor* (November 1986): 48.
13. Walter B. Kleeman, *The Challenge of Interior Design* (Boston: CBI Publishing, 1981), 149.
14. *AARP: Profile of Older Americans,* 12.
15. J. Neil Russell et al., "Trends and Differential Use of Assistive Technology Devices: United States, 1994," *Advance Data* 292: 1–10.
16. Gail Sheehy, *Mapping Your Life Across Time* (New York: Random House, 1995).
17. Hiroko Machida, "Why Housing Coordinator(s) for the Elderly" (paper delivered at Internation Conference of Living Environment, Health and Well Being for the Elderly Izu, Japan, March 1997).
18. Satoshi Kose, "Aging in Place: From Barrier-Free to Universal Design Dwellings" (paper delivered at the International Longevity Center Conference, "Living Environment, Health, and Well-Being for the Elderly: Cross National Perspective," Izu, Japan, 10 March 1997).
19 Markle Foundation, *Pioneers on the Frontier of Life: Aging in America* (New York: Markle Foundation, 1988), 1.
20. Meredith Minkler, "Gold in Gray: Reflections on Business' Discovery of the Elderly Market," *The Gerontologist* 29(1): 17–23.
21. U.S. Bureau of the Census, *Statistical Abstract of the United States: 1997* (Washington, DC: U.S. Government Printing Office, 1997, V. 117): 143.
22. Ibid.
23. Ibid.
24. U.S. Office of the Federal Register, "Americans with Disabilities Act Accessibility Standards," *Federal Register,* July 1, 1994: 467–618.
25. Jain Malkin, *Hospital Interior Architecture* (New York: VNR, 1992), 289.
26. Roger S. Ulrich, "Effects of Interior Design on Wellness: Theory and Recent Scientific Research" (paper delivered at the Third Symposium of Healthcare Interior Design, San Francisco, 15–18 November 1990), 13.
27. O'Connor, "Design," 47.

## CHAPTER 1

1. Uniform Federal Accessibility Standards, *24 CFR subtitle A 4-1-90* (Washington, D.C.: Government Printing Office, 1990).
2. ADA, 1994.
3. UFAS, *24 CFR,* 1990.
4. Department of Justice, "ADAAG for Buildings and Facilities; Children's Facilities; Proposed Rules," *Federal Register* (22 July 1996).
5. Denise Hofstedt, ed., "Accessible Trails: Consistency Still a Question," *Universal Design Newsletter* 2, no. 6 (April 1996): 8.
6. ADA, 1994.
7. T.J.M. Van der Voordt, "Accessibility by Means of Ramps," *Proceedings of the Built Environment and the Handicapped: Toward a Normal Life for the Disabled and Elderly* (Gotheberg, Sweden: Swedish Council for Building Research, 1981), 38–40.
8. Ibid.
9. Robert Sorensen, *Design for Accessibility* (New York: McGraw-Hill, 1979), 158.
10. ADA, 1994.
11. National Center for Accessibility, *Swimming Pool Accessibility Project* (Martinsville, Indiana: National Center for Accessibility, 1997).
12. American National Standards Institute, *American National Standard for Buildings and Facilities Providing Accessibility and Usability for Physically Handicapped People, ANSI A117.1-1986* (New York: American National Standards Institute, 1986).
13. ADA, 1994.
14. ADA, 1994.
15. Theo J.M. Van der Voordt et al., *Checklist for Adaptable Renovation* (Delft, Netherlands: Technical University of Delft, Dept. of Architecture, 1996).

16. ADA, 1994.
17. North Carolina State Building Code Council, *North Carolina State Building Code,* vol. 1-C (Raleigh, 1989).
18. Ibid.
19. Ibid.
20. Ibid.
21. ADA, 1994.
22. Ibid.
23. Ibid.
24. NCSBCC, 1989.
25. ADA, 1994.
26. Ibid.
27. Ibid.

## CHAPTER 2

1. Evan Terry Associates, *ADA Facilities Compliance Notebook Supplement* (New York: Wiley, 1995).
2. ADA, 1994.
3. Janet Reizenstein Carpman, Myron A. Grant, and Deborah A. Simmons, *Design That Cares* (Chicago: American Hospital Publishing, 1986), 228.
4. Lorraine G. Hiatt, "Long-Term-Care Facilities," *Journal of Health Care Interior Design* 2 (1990): 200.
5. Robert J. Kobet, "Allergies in Architecture" (paper delivered at the regional conference of the American Association of Otolaryngologic Allergists, San Antonio, Tex., 18 May 1987).
6. Hiatt, "Long-Term-Care," 199.
7. Walter B. Kleeman, *The Challenge of Interior Design* (Boston: CBI Publishing, 1981), 79.
8. Hiatt, "Long-Term-Care," 200.
9. Carpman, Grant, and Simmons, *Design That Cares,* 228.
10. Kleeman, *Challenge,* 76.
11. Robert J. Kobet, "The Tight House Syndrome: Causes and Cures" (paper delivered at the American Society of Interior Designers National Conference, Washington, D.C., August 1988).
12. Kobet, "Allergies."
13. ADA, 1994.
14. Kobet, "Allergies."
15. Carol Venolia, "Healing Environments," *Journal of Health Care Interior Design* 2 (1990): 133.
16. Hiatt, "Long-Term-Care," 201.
17. Kobet, "Tight House Syndrome."
18. Robert Marshall, "Carpet as an Acoustical Material," *Canadian Interiors* 1 (1970): 36–39.
19. G. W. Evans and S. Cohen, "Environmental Stress," in *Handbook of Environmental Psychology,* ed. D. Stokols and I. Altman (New York: Wiley, 1987), 571–610.
20. Carpman, Grant, and Simmons, *Design That Cares,* 228.
21. ADA, 1994.

22. U.S. Architectural Transportation Barriers Compliance Board, *Bulletin #2: Visual Alarms.* (Washington, D.C.: Government Printing Office, 1994).
23. ADA, 1994.

## CHAPTER 3

1. Beth Frankowski Jones, "Lighting and the Elderly," *Interior Sources* (September 1996): 98–100.
2. Walter B. Kleeman, *The Challenge of Interior Design* (Boston: CBI Publishing, 1981), 61.
3. Leon A. Pastalan, *Aging and Human Visual Function* (New York: Alan R. Liss, 1982), 324.
4. Lorraine G. Hiatt, "The Color and Use of Color in Environments for Older People," *Nursing Homes* 30, no. 3 (1981): 18–22.
5. Pastalan, *Aging,* 325.
6. Lorraine G. Hiatt, "Long-Term-Care Facilities," *Journal of Health Care Interior Design* 2 (1990): 200.
7. JoAnn L. Shroyer and J. Thomas Hutton, "Alzheimer's Disease: Strategies for Designing Interiors," *American Society of Interior Designers Report* 15, no. 2 (1989): 10–11.
8. Mayen Spivack, *Institutional Settings* (New York: Human Sciences Press, 1984).
9. Judith K. Mousseau, "Design Specialty: A Case for Color," *American Society of Interior Designers Report* 13, no. 2 (1987): 16.
10. Kleeman, *Challenge,* 152.
11. Shroyer and Hutton, "Alzheimer's Disease," 12.
12. Sara Marberry and Laurie Zagon, *The Power of Color* (New York: Wiley, 1995), 12.
13. Susan Gilbert, "Harnessing the Power of Light," *New York Times Magazine,* 26 April 1992.
14. Gary Coates and Susanne Siepl-Coates, "Vidarkliniken," *The Healthcare Forum Journal* (September/October 1992): 27–29.
15. Hiatt, "The Color and Use of Color," 21.
16. Pastalan, *Aging,* 324.
17. Robert J. Kobet, "The Tight House Syndrome: Causes and Cures" (paper delivered at the American Society of Interior Designers National Conference, Washington, D.C., August 1988).
18. Coates and Siepl-Coates, "Vidarkliniken."
19. Margaret Milner, *Breaking Through the Deafness Barrier: Environmental Accommodations for Hearing Impaired People* (Washington, D.C.: Physical Plant Department, Gallaudet College, 1979), 9.
20. Robert Sorensen, *Design for Accessibility* (New York: McGraw-Hill, 1979), 214.
21. Janet Reizenstein Carpman, Myron A. Grant, and Deborah A. Simmons, *Design That Cares* (Chicago: American Hospital Publishing, 1986), 223.
22. Virginia Beamer Weinhold, *Interior Finish Materials for Health Care Facilities* (Springfield, Ill.: Charles C. Thomas, 1988), 125.

23. Weinhold, *Interior Finish Materials,* 127.
24. Weinhold, *Interior Finish Materials,* 135.

## CHAPTER 4

1. Walter B. Kleeman, *The Challenge of Interior Design* (Boston: CBI Publishing, 1981), 192.
2. ADA, 1994.
3. Robert J. Kobet, "The Tight House Syndrome: Causes and Cures" (paper delivered at the American Society of Interior Designers National Conference, Washington, D.C., August 1988).
4. ADA, 1994.
5. Ibid.
6. North Carolina State Building Code Council, *North Carolina State Building Code* vol. 1-C (Raleigh, 1989).
7. ADA, 1994.
8. Ibid.
9. NCSBCC, *Building Code.*
10. ADA, 1994.
11. Evan Terry Associates, *ADA Facilities Compliance Notebook Supplement* (New York: Wiley, 1995).

## CHAPTER 5

1. Walter B. Kleeman, *The Challenge of Interior Design* (Boston: CBI Publishing, 1981), 243.
2. Virginia Beamer Weinhold, *Interior Finish Materials for Health Care Facilities* (Springfield, Ill.: Charles C. Thomas, 1988), 25.
3. Julia S. Garner and Martin S. Favero, "CDC Guidelines for Handwashing and Hospital Environmental Control, 1986," *Infection Control* 7, no. 4: 231–243.
4. Weinhold, *Interior Finish Materials,* 24.
5. ADA, 1994.
6. Garner and Favero, "CDC Guidelines," 233.
7. Lorraine G. Hiatt, "Long-Term-Care Facilities," *Journal of Health Care Interior Design* 2 (1990): 203.
8. Robert J. Kobet, "The Tight House Syndrome: Causes and Cures" (paper delivered at the American Society of Interior Designers National Conference, Washington, D.C., August 1988).
9. Roger Yee, "Almost Indestructible Floors with Goose Bumps," *Contract Design* (February 1991): 66.
10. ADA, 1994.
11. Weinhold, *Interior Finish Materials,* 85.

## CHAPTER 6

1. Lorraine G. Hiatt, "Long-Term-Care Facilities," *Journal of Health Care Interior Design* 2 (1990): 199.
2. Vivian P. Woofter, "HEW Seeks Optimal Furnishings for Handicapped Workers," *Contract Magazine* (June 1978).

3. Ibid.
4. Walter B. Kleeman, *The Challenge of Interior Design* (Boston: CBI Publishing, 1981), 118.
5. North Carolina State Building Code Council, *North Carolina State Building Code,* vol. 1-C (Raleigh, 1989).
6. Ibid., 7.2(d).
7. Bettyann Boetticher Raschko, *Housing Interiors for the Disabled and Elderly* (New York: Van Nostrand Reinhold, 1982), 105.
8. ADA, 1994.
9. Kleeman, *Challenge,* 121.
10. Ibid., 99.
11. M. C. Eastman and E. Kamon, "Posture and Subjective Evaluation at Flat and Slanted Desks," *Human Factors,* 18, no. 1 (1976): 15–26.
12. NCSBCC, 1989.
13. Kleeman, *Challenge,* 94.
14. Ibid., 109.
15. Ibid., 101.
16. Ibid., 103.
17. Ibid., 265.
18. Ibid., 106.
19. Ibid., 265.
20. Hiatt, "Long-Term-Care," 205.
21. Robert J. Kobet, "Allergies in Architecture" (paper delivered at the regional conference of the American Association of Otolaryngologic Allergists, San Antonio, Tex., 18 May 1987).
22. California Department of Consumer Affairs, *Flammability Test Procedure for Seating Furniture for Use in Public Occupancies: Tech. bulletin no. 133* (North Highlands, 1988).

## CHAPTER 7

1. IBM National Support Center for Persons with Disabilities, *Technology for Persons with Disabilities: An Introduction* (Atlanta: IBM, 1991), 1–8.
2. Ibid.
3. Ibid.
4. Ibid.
5. ADA, 1994.
6. North Carolina State Building Code Council, *North Carolina State Building Code,* vol. 1-C (Raleigh, 1989).
7. ADA, 1994.
8. Ibid.
9. For additional information, call the Voice Dialing Product Manager at Bell Atlantic at (212) 395-8534.
10. Roger S. Ulrich, "Effects of Interior Design on Wellness: Theory and Recent Scientific Research" (paper delivered at the Third Symposium of Healthcare Interior Design, San Francisco, 15–18 November 1990).
11. Janet Reizenstein Carpman, Myron A. Grant, and Deborah A. Simmons, *Design That Cares* (Chicago: American Hospital Publishing, 1986), 26.

12. Ibid., 27.
13. Ibid., 28.
14. Ibid.
15. John Salmen, ed. "Low Vision Print Legibility," *Universal Design Newsletter* (January 1994): 8.
16. ADA, 1994.
17. NCSBCC, 1989.
18. ADA, 1994.
19. Ibid.
20. Carpman, *Design That Cares,* p. 52.
21. ADA, 1994.
22. Salmen, John. Ed. "Low Vision Print Legibility," 8.
23. Robert J. Kobet, "The Tight House Syndrome: Causes and Cures" (paper delivered at the American Society of Interior Designers National Conference, Washington, D.C., August 1988).

## CHAPTER 8

1. North Carolina State Building Code Council, *North Carolina State Building Code,* vol. 1-C (Raleigh, 1989).
2. Robert J. Kobet, "The Tight House Syndrome: Causes and Cures" (paper delivered at the American Society of Interior Designers National Conference, Washington, D.C., August 1988).
3. Walter B. Kleeman, *The Challenge of Interior Design* (Boston: CBI Publishing, 1981), 42.
4. Kenneth R. Tremblay, "Housing and Design Considerations for the Deaf," *Dimensions* (Fall/Winter 1989): 7.
5. American National Standards Institute, *American National Standard for Buildings and Facilities Providing Accessibility and Usability for Physically Handicapped People, ANSI A117.1-1986* (New York: American National Standards Institute, 1986).
6. HUD, *Barrier Free Environments, Adaptable Housing: The Technical Manual for Implementing Adaptable Housing Unit Specifications, 023-000-00760-6* (Washington, D.C.: Government Printing Office, 1989), fig. 22.
7. NCSBCC, *Building Code.*
8. ADA, 1994.
9. Anne Patterson, ed., "Beautiful Designs for the Handicapped," *Kitchen and Bath Concepts* (January 1987): 36.
10. Molly Follette Story, *Microwave Ovens* (Raleigh, N.C.: The Center for Universal Design, North Carolina State University, 1995), 5.
11. ADA, 1994.
12. Health and Welfare, Canada, *Plumbing Fixtures, H74-18/11-1985E* (Ottawa: Ministry of Supply and Services, Canada, 1985).
13. ANSI, 4.32.5.7.

## CHAPTER 9

1. ADA, 1994.
2. Ibid.
3. Ibid.
4. Ibid.
5. Ibid.
6. Associate Committee on the National Building Code, National Research Council of Canada, *National Building Code of Canada 1990* (Ottawa: Ministry of Supply and Services, Canada, 1990).
7. Department of Community Affairs, Florida Board of Building Codes and Standards, *Accessibility Requirements Manual* (Tallahassee, 1990).
8. North Carolina State Building Code Council, *North Carolina State Building Code,* vol. 1-C (Raleigh, 1989).
9. Ibid.
10. ADA, 1994.
11. NCSBCC, 1989.
12. ADA, 1994.
13. NCSBCC, 1989.
14. ADA, 1994.
15. Ibid.
16. NCSBCC, 1989.
17. ADA, 1994.
18. *Barrier Free Environments, Adaptable Housing: The Technical Manual for Implementing Adaptable Housing Unit Specifications, 023-000-00760-6* (Washington, D.C.: Government Printing Office, 1989), 46.
19. ADA, 1994.
20. NCSBCC, 1989.
21. Health and Welfare, Canada, *Showers H74-18/7-1985E* (Ottawa: Ministry of Supply and Services, Canada, 1985).
22. NCSBCC, 1989.
23. ADA, 1994.
24. NCSBCC, 1989.

## CHAPTER 10

1. Architectural and Transportation Barriers Compliance Board, *Assistive Listening Systems* (Washington, D.C.: Government Printing Office, 1991), 4.
2. Thomas C. Jester and Sharon C. Park, "Making Historic Properties Accessible," *Preservation Briefs* 32 (September 1993).

| Figure No. | Illustration Credit |
|---|---|
| 1-1 | Courtesy of Evan Terry Associates, P.C.; Photography: Gary Knight & Associates, Inc. |
| 1-2 | Reprinted by permission from the Veterans Administration, VA pamphlet 26-13, April 1978. |
| 1-3 | Americans with Disabilities Act Standards for Accessible Design (ADAAG) |
| 1-4 | Reproduced with permission from American National Standards for Buildings and Facilities Providing Accessibility and Usability for Physically Handicapped People A117.1-1986, copyright 1986 by the American National Standards Institute. |
| 1-5 | Reproduced by permission from the 1984 Uniform Federal Accessibility Standards by the Publications Division, U.S. General Services Administration. |
| 1-6 | Courtesy of Heather Cram—Hilderman Thomas Frank Cram |
| 1-7 | Courtesy of Talking Signs, Inc. |
| 1-8 | Photo courtesy of Pella/Rolscreen Company. |
| 1-9 | © 1998 Chicago Botanic Garden. Courtesy of Carolyn Latteier. |
| 1-10 | Courtesy of Carolyn Latteier |
| 1-11 | Courtesy of Dana K. Stockwell, U.S. Army Corps of Engineers, John H. Kerr Reservoir |
| 1-12 | Courtesy of Industrial Fabrics Association. |
| 1-13 | Reproduced by permission from the 1984 Uniform Federal Accessibility Standards by the Publications Division, U.S. General Services Administration. |
| 1-14 | Courtesy of Mat Factory, Inc. |
| 1-15 | Courtesy of Evan Terry Associates, P.C. |
| 1-16 | Reproduced with permission from American National Standards for Buildings and Facilities Providing Accessibility and Usability for Physically Handicapped People A117.1-1986, copyright 1986 by the American National Standards Institute. |
| 1-17 | Courtesy of Evan Terry Associates, P.C. |
| 1-18 | Courtesy of Nichols Design Associates, Inc. |
| 1-19 | Reproduced by permission from the 1984 Uniform Federal Accessibility Standards by the Publications Division, U.S. General Services Administration. |
| 1-20 | Reproduced with permission from American National Standards for Buildings and Facilities Providing Accessibility and Usability for Physically Handicapped People A117.1-1986, copyright 1986 by the American National Standards Institute. |
| 1-21 | Courtesy of Nichols Design Associates, Inc. |
| 1-22 | Courtesy of Nichols Design Associates, Inc. |
| 1-23 | Courtesy of Evan Terry Associates, P.C. |
| 1-24 | Reproduced with permission from American National Standards for Buildings and Facilities Providing Accessibility and Usability for Physically Handicapped People A117.1-1986, copyright 1986 by the American National Standards Institute. |
| 1-25 | Courtesy of Smith Carter Architects and Engineers; Photography: Gerry Kopelow/WPG |
| 1-26 | Courtesy of Loren Greenhill; Photography: Sally Reynolds |
| 1-27 | Courtesy of Frank J. Colgan |
| 1-28 | Courtesy of American Stair-Glide Corp. |
| 1-29 | Courtesy of Access Industries |
| 1-30 | Reproduced with permission from American National Standards for Buildings and Facilities Providing Accessibility and Usability for Physically Handicapped People A117.1-1986, copyright 1986 by the American National Standards Institute. |
| 1-31 | Reproduced by permission from the 1984 Uniform Federal Accessibility Standards by the Publications Division, U.S. General Services Administration. |
| 1-32 | Reproduced by permission from the 1984 Uniform Federal Accessibility Standards by the Publications Division, U.S. General Services Administration. |
| 1-33 | Reproduced by permission from the 1984 Uniform Federal Accessibility Standards by the Publications Division, U.S. General Services Administration. |
| 1-34 | Courtesy of EVAC+CHAIR Corp. |
| 1-35 | Courtesy of Jack Bowersox, AIA. |
| 1-36 | Courtesy of Coco Raynes Associates, Inc., Boston, MA; Photography: Bill Miles, Boston, MA |
| 1-37 | Reproduced with permission from American National Standards for Buildings and Facilities Providing Accessibility and Usability for Physically Handicapped People A117.1-1986, copyright 1986 by the American National Standards Institute. |
| 1-38 | Courtesy of Richard Gibbs, N.B.T. Wiz |
| 1-39 | Americans with Disabilities Act Standards for Accessible Design (ADAAG) |
| 1-40 | Americans with Disabilities Act Standards for Accessible Design (ADAAG) |
| 1-41 | Courtesy of Johnsonite |
| 1-42 | Courtesy of HEWI, Inc. |
| 2-1 | Courtesy of Leviton Manufacturing Co. |
| 2-2 | Courtesy of Honeywell |

| | | | |
|---|---|---|---|
| 2-3 | Photo courtesy of Jenn-Air | 3-5 | Courtesy of Genon Wallcoverings |
| 2-4 | Courtesy of Lutron Electronics Co., Inc. | 3-6 | Courtesy of Eurotex |
| 2-5 | Courtesy of The Ironmonger, Inc. | 3-7 | Courtesy of C/S Group |
| 2-6 | Courtesy of Tempo Industries, Inc. | 3-8 | Courtesy of Barbara Matthes |
| 2-7 | Courtesy of Lutron Electronics Co., Inc. | 3-9 | Courtesy of C/S Group |
| 2-8 | Courtesy of Cynthia Leibrock, MA, ASID, Easy Access, Fort Collins, CO; Illustration: Susan Behar, ASID, Universal Design | 3-10 | Courtesy of Eurotex |
| 2-9 | Courtesy of Leviton Manufacturing Co. | 3-11 | Courtesy of Cynthia Leibrock, MA, ASID, Easy Access, Fort Collins, CO; Illustration: Susan Behar, ASID, Universal Design |
| 2-10 | Reprinted by permission from Bettyann Boetticher Raschko, Housing Interiors for the Disabled and Elderly. New York: Van Nostrand Reinhold, copyright, 1982. | 3-12 | Courtesy of Bannerscapes |
| | | 3-13 | Courtesy of Bannerscapes |
| | | 3-14 | Courtesy of Architect: Schamu, Machowski, Doo & Associates; Photographer: Frik Kvalsvik; Millwork: Walker/Welsh Associates Inc |
| 2-11 | Courtesy of The Hon Co. | | |
| 2-12 | Courtesy of Holtkötter International, Inc. | | |
| 2-13 | Courtesy of Nutone Inc. | 3-15 | Courtesy of C. Harris, Dictionary of Architecture and Construction, copyright 1975, McGraw-Hill. Reproduced with permission of McGraw-Hill, Inc. |
| 2-14 | Courtesy of HEWI, Inc. | | |
| 2-15 | Courtesy of Smith Carter Architects and Engineers; Photography: Gerry Kopelow/WPG | | |
| | | 3-16 | Courtesy of Winona Mfg. Inc. |
| 2-16 | Reprinted by permission from Van Nostrand Reinhold, The Challenge of Interior Design. Boston: CBI Publishing Company, Inc., 1981. | 3-17 | From Interior Finish Materials for Health Care Facilities, 1988. Courtesy of Charles C. Thomas, Publisher, Springfield, Illinois. |
| | | 4-1 | Courtesy of Andersen Windows, Inc. |
| 2-17 | Courtesy of Halo Lighting | 4-2 | Courtesy of Truth Hardware |
| 2-18 | Courtesy of Lightworks | 4-3 | Courtesy of A-Solution |
| 2-19 | Courtesy of Tempo Ind., Inc. | 4-4 | Courtesy of Truth Hardware |
| 2-20 | Americans with Disabilities Act Standards for Accessible Design (ADAAG) | 4-5 | Courtesy of Anderson Window Corp. |
| | | 4-6 | Courtesy of Joanna Western Mills |
| 2-21 | Courtesy of Research Products Corp. | 4-7 | Courtesy of Wonderfully Made |
| 2-22 | Courtesy of Honeywell | 4-8 | Reprinted by permission from Leona K. Hawks, Housing and Home Equipment Specialist, Utah State University |
| 2-23 | Courtesy of Jean Roy | | |
| 2-24 | Courtesy of C. Harris, Dictionary of Architecture and Construction, copyright 1975, McGraw-Hill. Reproduced with permission of McGraw-Hill, Inc. | | |
| | | 4-9 | Courtesy of Hunter Douglas Window Fashions |
| | | 4-10 | Courtesy of Industrial Fabrics Industries |
| 2-25 | Courtesy of AVSI | 4-11 | Reprinted by permission from Leona K. Hawks, Housing and Home Equipment Specialist, Utah State University |
| 2-26 | Courtesy of Aiphone Corporation | | |
| 2-27 | Courtesy of Cynthia Leibrock, MA, ASID, Easy Access, Fort Collins, CO; Illustration: Susan Behar, ASID, Universal Design | 4-12 | Reprinted by permission from Leona K. Hawks, Housing and Home Equipment Specialist, Utah State University |
| | | | |
| 2-28 | Courtesy of Nutone Inc. | 4-13 | Courtesy of Baker Drapery Corp. |
| 2-29 | Courtesy of Senior Technologies | 4-14 | Courtesy of The Maiman Company |
| 2-30 | Courtesy of The Chamberlain Group, Inc. | 4-15 | Americans with Disabilities Act Standards for Accessible Design (ADAAG) |
| 2-31 | Courtesy of Lutron Electronics Co., Inc. | | |
| 2-32 | Courtesy of Unity Systems, Inc. | 4-16 | Courtesy of Susan Behar, ASID Universal Design |
| 2-33 | Reprinted by permission from Bettyann Boetticher Raschko, Housing Interiors for the Disabled and Elderly. New York: Van Nostrand Reinhold, copyright 1982. | | |
| | | 4-17 | Courtesy of Andersen Windows, Inc. |
| | | 4-18 | Courtesy of Andersen Windows, Inc. |
| | | 4-19 | Courtesy of Horton Automatics |
| 2-34 | Courtesy of Fyrnetics Inc. | 4-20 | Courtesy of Brown Jordan |
| 3-1 | Courtesy of Space Planning and Interior Design, Jain Malkin Inc.; Photography: John Christian | 4-21 | Courtesy of Duro-Med Industries Inc. |
| | | 4-22 | Courtesy of Albert Constantine and Son, Inc. |
| | | 4-23 | Reprinted by permission from Bettyann Boetticher Raschko, Housing Interiors for the Disabled and Elderly. New York: Van Nostrand Reinhold, copyright 1982. |
| 3-2 | Photo courtesy of Andersen Windows, Inc. | | |
| 3-3 | Courtesy of Gail Finkel, M. Arch.; Photography: Gerry Kopelow/WPG | | |
| 3-4 | Courtesy of York Wallcoverings, Inc. | 4-24 | Courtesy of Sekisui House, Ltd. |

| | | | | |
|---|---|---|---|---|
| 4-25 | Courtesy of Pinecrest | | | Image Studios |
| 4-26 | Courtesy of The DORMA Group | | 5-18 | Photo courtesy of Kohler Co. |
| 4-27 | Courtesy of Barrier Free Environments; Photography: Ron Mace | | 5-19 | Courtesy of American Olean Tile Company. Project: Pennsylvania West Chapter ASID. Interior design: Nancy Hoff Barsotti, ASID. |
| 4-28 | Courtesy of The DORMA Group | | 5-20 | Architecture: Brown Gimber Rodriquez Park; Interior Design: Jain Malkin Inc.; Photography: Sandra Williams |
| 4-29 | Courtesy of Horton Automatics | | | |
| 4-30 | Courtesy of Dor-O-Matic | | | |
| 4-31 | Photo courtesy of The Lighthouse Inc., New York, NY; Photography: ©Jeff Goldberg/Esto | | 5-21 | Courtesy of Summitville Tiles, Inc. |
| | | | 6-1 | Courtesy of Ligne Roset USA; Designer: Peter Maly, 1983 |
| 4-32 | Courtesy of The Maiman Company | | 6-2 | Courtesy of Custom Lamination Inc. |
| 4-33 | Courtesy of HEWI, Inc. | | 6-3 | Courtesy of Ligne Roset USA; Designer: Peter Maly, 1995 |
| 4-34 | Courtesy of HEWI, Inc. | | | |
| 4-35 | Courtesy of The Chamberlain Group, Inc. | | 6-4 | Courtesy of Joerns Healthcare Inc. |
| 5-1 | From *Interior Finish Materials for Health Care Facilities,* 1988. Courtesy of Charles C. Thomas, Publisher, Springfield, Illinois. | | 6-5 | Courtesy of Universal Furniture, Alexander Julian, Home Colours |
| | | | 6-6 | Courtesy of Benicia Foundry |
| 5-2 | From *Interior Finish Materials for Health Care Facilities,* 1988. Courtesy of Charles C. Thomas, Publisher, Springfield, Illinois. | | 6-7 | Courtesy of Baker Furniture, Grand Rapids, MI |
| | | | 6-8 | Courtesy of Thomasville Furniture Industries |
| 5-3 | Reproduced by permission from the 1984 Uniform Federal Accessibility Standards by the Publications Division, U.S. General Services Administration. | | 6-9 | Courtesy of Closetmaid |
| | | | 6-10 | Courtesy of HKS Architects; Photography: Peter Malinowski, Insite Architectural Photography |
| 5-4 | Carpet by Philadelphia Carpets, a division of Shaw Industries, Inc. | | 6-11 | Courtesy of Workstations, Inc. |
| 5-5 | From *Interior Finish Materials for Health Care Facilities,* 1988. Courtesy of Charles C. Thomas, Publisher, Springfield, Illinois. | | 6-12 | Courtesy of Goelst Corporation; Photography: Steve Hogben Photography, Atlanta, GA |
| | | | 6-13 | Courtesy of Kimball Office Group |
| 5-6 | Photo by Bonar Floors | | 6-14 | Courtesy of Robern, Inc. |
| 5-7 | Courtesy of Collins & Aikman Floorcoverings, Inc.; Photography: ©Jonathan Hillyer Photography | | 6-15 | Courtesy of Garcia Imports |
| | | | 6-16 | Courtesy of Ligne Roset USA; Designer: Peter Maly, 1991 |
| 5-8 | Courtesy of RT&E for DuPont Flooring Systems | | 6-17 | Reproduced with permission from American National Standards for Buildings and Facilities Providing Accessibility and Usability for Physically Handicapped People A117.1-1986, copyright 1986 by the American National Standards Institute. |
| 5-9 | Reproduced with permission from American National Standards for Buildings and Facilities Providing Accessibility and Usability for Physically Handicapped People A117.1-1986, copyright 1986 by the American National Standards Institute. | | | |
| | | | 6-18 | Courtesy of Evan Terry Associates, P.C. |
| 5-10 | Courtesy of Mercer Products Inc. | | 6-19 | Courtesy of Sekisui House, Ltd. |
| 5-11 | ©Collins & Aikman Floorcoverings, Inc. Powerbond® | | 6-20 | Reproduced with permission from American National Standards for Buildings and Facilities Providing Accessibility and Usability for Physically Handicapped People A117.1-1986, copyright 1986 by the American National Standards Institute. |
| 5-12 | Interior Design: Antonio F. Torrice, ASID, Living and Learning Environments; Photography: Mike Spinelli Photography | | | |
| 5-13 | Courtesy of The Timeless Series acrylic/wood plank by PermaGrain Products, Inc., installed at The Boston Store, Brookfield, Wis. | | 6-21 | Courtesy of Sico North America Inc. |
| | | | 6-22 | Courtesy of Lumex, a division of Lumex, Inc. |
| | | | 6-23 | Courtesy of McGuire |
| 5-14 | From *Interior Finish Materials for Health Care Facilities,* 1988. Courtesy of Charles C. Thomas, Publisher, Springfield, Illinois. | | 6-24 | Courtesy of KI |
| | | | 6-25 | Courtesy of Evan Terry Associates, P.C. |
| 5-15 | From *Interior Finish Materials for Health Care Facilities,* 1988. Courtesy of Charles C. Thomas, Publisher, Springfield, Illinois. | | 6-26 | Reprinted by permission from Bettyann Boetticher Raschko, *Housing Interiors for the Disabled and Elderly.* New York: Van Nostrand Reinhold, copyright 1982. |
| 5-16 | Photo courtesy of Roppe Corporation | | | |
| 5-17 | Courtesy of Fritz Industries; Photography: | | 6-27 | Courtesy of Kids' Studio |

| | | | |
|---|---|---|---|
| 6-28 | Courtesy of Metropolitan Furniture Corp.; Design: Brian Kane | | New York, NY |
| 6-29 | Courtesy of SIS human factor technolo gies, inc. | 7-5 | Photo courtesy of The Lighthouse, Inc., New York, NY |
| 6-30 | Courtesy of Ligne Roset USA; Designer: Pagnon Pelhaitre, 1995 | 7-6 | Photo courtesy of The Lighthouse, Inc., New York, NY |
| 6-31 | Courtesy of McGuire | 7-7 | Courtesy of Egan |
| 6-32 | Courtesy of Thonet Industries, Inc. | 7-8 | Courtesy of Infogrip, Inc. |
| 6-33 | Courtesy of Silvain Joly for Haworth, Inc.; Photography: Bill Sharpe | 7-9 | Courtesy of Haworth, Inc. |
| 6-34 | Courtesy of Cy Mann Designs, Ltd. | 7-10 | Courtesy of Lernout & Hauspie |
| 6-35 | Courtesy of Baker Furniture, Grand Rapids, MI | 7-11 | Courtesy of C.C.T. |
| 6-36 | Courtesy of McGuire | 7-12 | Courtesy of Alva Access Group, Inc. |
| 6-37 | Courtesy of Howe Furniture Corp.; Photo courtesy of Tom Wedell | 7-13 | Courtesy of JBliss Imaging Systems |
| 6-38 | Courtesy of The MoMA Design Store; Designer: Enzo Mari | 7-14 | Reproduced with permission from American National Standards for Buildings and Facilities Providing Accessibility and Usability for Physically Handicapped People A117.1-1986, copyright 1986 by the American National Standards Institute. |
| 6-39 | Courtesy of Palazzetti, Inc. | | |
| 6-40 | Courtesy of Workstations, Inc. | | |
| 6-41 | Courtesy of the Center for Rehabilitation Technology, Georgia Institute of Technology | 7-15 | Reproduced by permission from the 1984 Uniform Federal Accessibility Standards by the Publications Division, U.S. General Services Administration. |
| 6-42 | James Terkeurst—Photographer; Photo courtesy of Herman Miller, Inc. | 7-16 | Photo of members of the Bay Area Breakers and Golden Spokes wheelchair basketball teams courtesy of Haws Drinking Faucet Company |
| 6-43 | Courtesy of Metropolitan Furniture Corp.; Design: Metro Design Group | | |
| 6-44 | Courtesy of SIS human factor technolo- gies, inc. | 7-17 | Courtesy of Evan Terry Associates, P.C. |
| 6-45 | Courtesy of DuPont Corian® | 7-18 | Reproduced by permission from the 1984 Uniform Federal Accessibility Standards by the Publications Division, U.S. General Services Administration. |
| 6-46 | Courtesy of ADD Specialized Seating Technology | | |
| 6-47 | Courtesy of ADD Specialized Seating Technology | 7-19 | Reprinted with permission of AT&T. |
| 6-48 | Courtesy of ADD Specialized Seating Technology | 7-20 | Used by permission of Philips Consumer Communications. |
| 6-49 | Courtesy of KI | 7-21 | Courtesy of Zygo Industries |
| 6-50 | Courtesy of Loewenstein | 7-22 | Courtesy of Ameriphone, Inc. |
| 6-51 | Courtesy of Loewenstein | 7-23 | Used by permission of Philips Consumer Communications. |
| 6-52 | From Interior Finish Materials for Health Care Facilities, 1988. Courtesy of Charles C. Thomas, Publisher, Springfield, Illinois. | 7-24 | Used by permission of Philips Consumer Communications. |
| | | 7-25 | Courtesy of Harris Communications, Inc. |
| 6-53 | Courtesy of ADD Specialized Seating Technology | 7-26 | Used by permission of Philips Consumer Communications. |
| 6-54 | Courtesy of United Chair | 7-27 | Courtesy of Ultratec |
| 6-55 | Courtesy of Jack Cartwright, Inc. | 7-28 | Courtesy of Audex Assistive Listening Systems |
| 6-56 | Courtesy of Thonet Industries, Inc. | | |
| 6-57 | Courtesy of Thonet Industries, Inc. | 7-29 | Courtesy of RT&E DuPont Flooring Systems |
| 6-58 | Courtesy of Bernhardt Furniture Company | | |
| 6-59 | Courtesy of The Charles Stewart Company | 7-30 | Courtesy of Walker Equipment |
| 6-60 | Courtesy of Ligne Roset USA; Designer: Pascal Mourge, 1996 | 7-31 | Courtesy of J. Piercey Studios, Inc. |
| | | 7-32 | Courtesy of Fleetwood |
| 6-61 | Courtesy of Thonet Industries, Inc. | 7-33 | Reprinted by permission from Wolfgang F.E. Preiser, Jacqueline C. Vischer, and Edward T. White, Designing Intervention, New York: Van Nostrand Reinhold, copy- right 1991. |
| 7-1 | Courtesy of Nutone, Inc. | | |
| 7-2 | Courtesy of Harris Communications, Inc. | | |
| 7-3 | Photo courtesy of The Lighthouse, Inc., New York, NY | | |
| | | 7-34 | Courtesy of Carolina Mirror Company |
| 7-4 | Photo courtesy of The Lighthouse, Inc., | 7-35 | Reproduced with permission from American |

| | |
|---|---|
| 8-60 | Courtesy of Jenn-Air |
| 8-61 | Courtesy of Jenn-Air |
| 8-62 | Courtesy of Sub-Zero Freezer Co., Inc. |
| 8-63 | Courtesy of Sub-Zero Freezer Co., Inc. |
| 8-63 | Courtesy of In-Sink Erator |
| 8-64 | Courtesy of Jenn-Air |
| 8-65 | Courtesy of Wm. Ohs Showrooms, Inc.; Designers: Kelly Dunphy and Linda McLean, CKD; Photography: Michael Stillman |
| 8-66 | Courtesy of The Center for Universal Design |
| 8-67 | Reproduced by permission from Barrier Free Environments, Inc., for the U.S. Department of Housing and Urban Development Office of Policy Development and Research. |
| 8-69 | Courtesy of Rutt Custom Cabinetry |
| 8-70 | Courtesy of Maxi-Aids |
| 8-71 | Courtesy of Maxi-Aids |
| 8-72 | Photo courtesy of Smart Design Inc.; Design: Scott Henderson |
| 8-73 | Courtesy of OXO International |
| 8-74 | Photo courtesy of Smart Design Inc.; Design: Tucker Viemeister |
| 8-75 | Courtesy of Maddak Inc. |
| 8-76 | Courtesy of Maddak Inc. |
| 8-77 | Courtesy of Maddak Inc. |
| 9-1 | JCDecaux Universally Accessible Automatic Public Toilet |
| 9-2 | Reproduced by permission from Barrier Free Environments, Inc., for the U.S. Department of Housing and Urban Development Office of Policy Development and Research. |
| 9-3 | Courtesy of Health Resources Development, Inc. |
| 9-4 | Courtesy of HEWI Inc. |
| 9-5 | Courtesy of Evan Terry Associates, P.C. |
| 9-6 | Courtesy of Evan Terry Associates, P.C. |
| 9-7 | Courtesy of Tub-Master, LC |
| 9-8 | Courtesy of Aqua Glass Corporation |
| 9-9 | Courtesy of HEWI INC. |
| 9-10 | Reproduced by permission from the 1984 Uniform Federal Accessibility Standards by the Publications Division, U.S. General Services Administration. |
| 9-11 | Courtesy of Sekisui House, Ltd. |
| 9-12 | Courtesy of DuPont Corian® |
| 9-13 | Reproduced with permission from American National Standards for Buildings and Facilities Providing Accessibility and Usability for Physically Handicapped People A117.1-1986, copyright 1986 by the American National Standards Institute. |
| 9-14 | Courtesy of HEWI INC. |
| 9-15 | Courtesy of Kohler Co. |

| | |
|---|---|
| 9-16 | Courtesy of Kohler Co. |
| 9-17 | Courtesy of Symmons Industries, Inc. |
| 9-18 | Courtesy of Gemini Bath and Kitchen Products |
| 9-19 | Reproduced with permission from American National Standards for Buildings and Facilities Providing Accessibility and Usability for Physically Handicapped People A117.1-1986, copyright 1986 by the American National Standards Institute. |
| 9-20 | Courtesy of DuPont Corian® |
| 9-21 | Courtesy of Better Living Products International Inc. |
| 9-22 | Courtesy of Lyons Industries |
| 9-23 | Reproduced with permission from American National Standards for Buildings and Facilities Providing Accessibility and Usability for Physically Handicapped People A117.1-1986, copyright 1986 by the American National Standards Institute. |
| 9-24 | Courtesy of Century Products Co., Inc.: Robert D. Wise, VP of Research & Development, and Kathleen Campisano, Product Manager—Bath Items; Anderson Design, Inc.: Thomas V. McLinden Industrial Designer/Principal and W. Daniel Haberstich, Industrial Designer; Photography: Stephen Ciuccoli, Ciuccoli Photo Illustrator, Milford, CT |
| 9-25 | Courtesy of American Standard |
| 9-26 | Courtesy of Kohler Co. |
| 9-27 | Courtesy of International Cushioned Products Inc. |
| 9-28 | Courtesy of Kohler Co. |
| 9-29 | Courtesy of Mark Salter and Robert Stanzione of Cashman Photo |
| 9-30 | Courtesy of Aqua Glass Corporation |
| 9-31 | Copy of Kohler Co. |
| 9-32 | Courtesy of Knickerbocker Partition Corp. |
| 9-33 | Courtesy of Evan Terry Associates, P.C. |
| 9-34 | Courtesy of Evan Terry Associates, P.C. |
| 9-35 | Courtesy of Susan Behar, ASID, Universal Design; Photography: George Cott |
| 9-36 | Courtesy of Kohler Co. |
| 9-37 | Reproduced with permission from American National Standards for Buildings and Facilities Providing Accessibility and Usability for Physically Handicapped People A117.1-1986, copyright 1986 by the American National Standards Institute. |
| 9-38 | Courtesy of TOTO USA |
| 9-39 | Courtesy of Eljer Plumbingware, Inc. (bowl) and Olsonite Corp. (seat). |
| 9-40 | Courtesy of Kohler Co. |
| 9-41 | Courtesy of Otto Bock Rehab |
| 9-42 | Courtesy of TOTO USA |
| 9-43 | Courtesy of JCDecaux USA |

| | |
|---|---|
| 9-44 | Courtesy of Kohler Co. |
| 9-45 | Courtesy of Kohler Co. |
| 9-46 | Americans with Disabilities Act Standards for Accessible Design (ADAAG) |
| 9-47 | Courtesy of Barclay Products Limited |
| 9-48 | Courtesy of DuPont Corian® |
| 9-49 | Courtesy of Kohler Co. |
| 9-50 | Courtesy of Sloan Valve |
| 9-51 | Courtesy of Sloan Valve |
| 9-52 | Courtesy of DuPont Corian® |
| 9-53 | Courtesy of DuPont Corian® |
| 9-54 | Bath Slide 'n Stack  System by Rubbermaid |
| 9-55 | Reprinted by permission from Barrier Free Environments. |
| 9-56 | Courtesy of Sunrise Medical Guardian |
| 9-57 | Courtesy of HEWI Inc. |
| 9-58 | Courtesy of Aqua Glass Corporation |
| 9-59 | Courtesy of Sekisui House, Ltd. |
| 9-60 | Reproduced with permission from American National Standards for Buildings and Facilities Providing Accessibility and Usability for Physically Handicapped People A117.1-1986, copyright 1986 by the American National Standards Institute. |
| 9-61 | Courtesy of HEWI Inc. |
| 9-62 | Reproduced with permission from American National Standards for Buildings and Facilities Providing Accessibility and Usability for Physically Handicapped People A117.1-1986, copyright 1986 by the American National Standards Institute. |
| 9-63 | Courtesy of Otto Bock Rehab |
| 9-64 | Courtesy of Bobrick Washroom Equipment Inc. |
| 9-65 | Courtesy of HEWI Inc. |
| 9-66 | Courtesy of Hafele America Co. |
| 9-67 | Courtesy of ASKO Inc. |
| 10-1 | Courtesy of DuPont Corian® |
| 10-2 | Courtesy of Guynes Design Inc. |
| 10-3 | Courtesy of Guynes Design Inc. |
| 10-4 | Courtesy of Guynes Design Inc. |
| 10-5 | Courtesy of Cluster Seating Systems. |
| 10-6 | Courtesy of Pamela Pflueger & Associates |
| 10-7 | Courtesy of Pamela Pflueger & Associates |
| 10-8 | Courtesy of Pamela Pflueger & Associates |
| 10-9 | Courtesy of Evan Terry Associates, P.C. |
| 10-10 | Courtesy of Moore Iacofano Goltsman, Inc.; Photography: © Laurie Black |
| 10-11 | Courtesy of Moore Iacofano Goltsman, Inc.; Photography: MIG, Inc. |
| 10-12 | Courtesy of Moore Iacofano Goltsman, Inc.; Photography: © Laurie Black |
| 10-13 | Courtesy of Shepley Bulfinch Richardson and Abbott (SBRA); Photography: © Peter Aaron/Esto |
| 10-14 | Courtesy of Shepley Bulfinch Richardson and Abbott (SBRA) and Looney Ricks Kiss (LRK) |
| 10-15 | Courtesy of Shepley Bulfinch Richardson and Abbott (SBRA) and Gartner, Burdick, Bauer-Nilsen (GBBN); Photography: © Jeff Goldberg/Esto |
| 10-16 | Courtesy of Mark Salter and Robert Stanzione of Cashman Photo |
| 10-17 | Courtesy of Mark Salter and Robert Stanzione of Cashman Photo |
| 10-18 | Courtesy of Evan Terry Associates, P.C. |
| 10-19 | Courtesy of Elsafe, Inc. |
| 10-20 | Courtesy of UD&C |
| 10-21 | Courtesy of Anmahian Winton Associates, Boston, MA, architects; Michael Powell, Salem, MA, photographer |
| 10-22 | Courtesy of Anmahian Winton Associates, Boston, MA, architects; Michael Powell, Salem, MA, photographer |
| 10-23 | Courtesy of Anmahian Winton Associates, Boston, MA, architects; Michael Powell, Salem, MA, photographer |
| 10-24 | Courtesy of Anmahian Winton Associates, Boston, MA, architects; Michael Powell, Salem, MA, photographer |
| 10-25 | Courtesy of Anmahian Winton Associates, Boston, MA, architects; Michael Powell, Salem, MA, photographer |
| 10-26 | Courtesy of Anmahian Winton Associates, Boston, MA, architects; Michael Powell, Salem, MA, photographer |
| 10-27 | Courtesy of Anmahian Winton Associates, Boston, MA, architects; Michael Powell, Salem, MA, photographer |
| 10-28 | Courtesy of NAHB, National Research Center; Illustration: Adaptable Fire Safe House |
| 10-29 | Courtesy of T.L. Shield & Associates, Inc. |
| 10-30 | Courtesy of Harris Communications, Inc. |
| 10-31 | Courtesy of Lux Steel Contract |
| 10-32 | Courtesy of Capstone Products, Inc. |
| 10-33 | Courtesy of Evan Terry Associates, P.C. |
| 10-34 | Courtesy of HOK Sport |
| 10-35 | Courtesy of Coco Raynes of Coco Raynes Associates, Inc., Boston, MA (Designer), and Claude Gilbert, Chargée de Mission, Ministère de la Culture—Direction des Musées de France, and Jacqueline Spriet, Présidente; Fédération des Amis des Musées de la Région Nord-Pas-de Calais, France (Clients); Photography: Coco Raynes |
| 10-36 | Courtesy of Coco Raynes of Coco Raynes Associates, Inc., Boston, MA (Designer), and Claude Gilbert, Chargée de Mission, Ministère de la Culture—Direction des Musées de France, and Jacqueline Spriet, Présidente, Fédération des Amis des |

Access Industries
4001 East 138 Street
Grandview, MO 64030
816-763-3100

ADD Specialized Seating
Technology
6500 South Avalon Boulevard
Los Angeles, CA 90003-1934
213-752-0101

Accessible Designs
94 North Columbus Road
Athens, OH 45701
614-593-5240

Aiphone Corporation
1700 130th Avenue NE
Bellevue, WA 98009
425-455-0510

Alva Access Group, Inc.
5801 Christie Avenue, Suite 475
Emeryville, CA 94608
510-923-6280

American Olean Tile Company
1000 Cannon Avenue
Lansdale, PA 19446-0271
215-393-2705

American Standard
One Centennial Avenue
Piscataway, NJ 08855
908-980-3000

Ameriphone Inc.
12082 Western Avenue
Garden Grove, CA 92841
800-874-3005

Amerock Corporation
4000 Auburn Street
Rockford, IL 61101
800-435-6959

Andersen Windows, Inc.
100 Fourth Avenue North
Bayport, MN 55003-1096
612-430-5928

Aqua Glass Corporation
PO Box 412, Industrial Park
Adamsville, TN 38310
901-632-0911

Asko, Inc.
1161 Executive Drive West
Richardson, TX 75081
800-367-2444

A-Solution, Inc.
1332 Lobo Place NE
Albuquerque, NM 87106
505-256-0115

Audex Assistive Listening
System
710 Standard Street
Longview, TX 75604
800-237-0716

AVSI
17059 El Cajon Avenue
Yorba Linda, CA 92886
714-524-4488

Baker Furniture
1661 Monroe Avenue NW
Grand Rapids, MI 49505
616-361-7321

Banner Scapes
7106 Mapleridge
Houston, TX 77081
800-344-3524

Barclay Products Limited
4000 Porett Drive
Gurnee, IL 60031
847-244-1234

Benicia Foundry
2995 Bayshore Road
Benicia, CA 94510
800-346-4645

Bernhardt Furniture Company
PO Box 740
Lenoir, NC 28645
704-758-9811

Better Living Products
International, Inc.
150 Norfinch Drive Toronto,
Ontario, Canada M3N 1X9
519-685-1501

Bobrick Washroom
Equipment, Inc.
11611 Hart Street
North Hollywood, CA 91605
818-764-1000

Bonar Floors, Inc.
961 Busse Road
Elk Grove Village, IL 60007
800-852-8292

Brown Jordan
9860 Gidley Street
El Monte, CA 91734
626-443-8971

C/S Group
3 Werner Way
Lebanon, NJ 08833
800-233-8493

Capstone Products, Inc.
203 Flagship Drive
Lutz, FL 33549
813-948-0107

Carolina Mirror Company
201 Elkin Highway
North Wilkesboro, NC 28659
910-838-2151

Center for Rehabilitation
Technology Georgia Institute
of Technology
Atlanta, GA 30332-0130
404-894-2000

Century Products, Inc.
9600 Valley View Road
Macedonia, OH 44056
216-468-2000

The Chamberlain Group, Inc.
845 Larch Avenue
Elmhurst, IL 60126
630-279-3600

The Charles Stewart Company
PO Box 5400
Hickory, NC 28603
704-322-9464

Chicago Botanic Garden
1000 Lake Cook Road
Glencoe, IL 60022
847-835-5440

Closet Maid
650 SW 27th Avenue
Ocala, FL 34471
352-401-6000

Cluster Seating Systems
1000 Philips Knob
Burnsville, NC 28714
704-682-3985

Coco Raynes Associates, Inc.
569 Boylston Street
Boston, MA 02116
617-536-1499

Collins & Aikman
Floorcovering, Inc.
311 Smith Industrial Boulevard
Dalton, GA 30720
706-259-2042

Constantine
2050 Eastchester Road
Bronx, NY 10461
718-792-1600

Custom Laminations, Inc.
932 Market St.
Paterson, NJ 07509-2066
973-279-9332

Dacor
950 South Raymond
Pasadena, CA 91109
800-793-0093

The Dorma Group
Dorma Drive
Reamstown, PA 17567-0411
717-336-3881

Dor-O-Matic
7350 West Wilson Avenue
Harwood Heights, IL 60656
502-339-8891

Du Seung Trading Co.
3190 Northeast Expressway
Suite 240
Atlanta, GA
800-274-7267

DuPont Corian®
Barley Mill Plaza
Price Mill Building
PO Box 80012
Wilmington, DE 19880-0012
800-426-7426

DuPont Flooring Systems
One Town Park Commons
Suite 400
125 Town Park Drive
Kennesaw, GA 30144
770-420-7700

Dwyer Products Corp.
418 North Calumet Avenue
Michigan City, IN 46360
219-874-5236

Egan Visual International
300 Hanlan Road
Woodbridge, Ontario, Canada
L4L 3P6
905-851-2826

Eljer Plumbingware, Inc.
14801 Quorum Drive
Dallas, TX 75240-7584
800-423-5537

Elkay Manufacturing Company
2222 Camden Court
Oak Brook, IL 60523
630-574-8484

Elsafe, Inc.
4303 Vineland Road
Suite F15
Orlando, FL 32811
407-423-7233

Eurotex
165 West Ontario Street
Philadelphia, PA 19140
800-523-0731
215-739-8844

EVAC+CHAIR Corporation
17 East 67th Street
New York, NY 10021
212-734-6222

Fieldstone Cabinetry
600 East 48th Street N
Sioux Falls, SD 57104
605-335-8600

Fleetwood
PO Box 1259
Holland, MI 49422-1259
616-396-5346

Fritz Industries
500 Sam Houston Road
Mesquite, TX 75149-2789
800-955-1323

Fyrnetics, Inc.
1055 Stevenson Court
Suite 102W
Roselle, IL 60172
800-654-7665

Gaggenau USA Corp.
425 University Avenue
Norwood, MA 02062
781-255-1766

Garcia Imports
P.O. Box 5066
Redwood City, CA 94063
650-367-9600

GE Appliances
Appliance Park
Louisville, KY 40225
502-452-3071

Gemini Bath and Kitchen
Products
PO Box 43398
Tucson, AZ 85733
520-770-0667

Genon Wallcoverings
Three University Plaza
Suite 200
Hackensack, NJ 07601
201-489-0100

Goelst Corporation
915 Bridge Street
Winston-Salem, NC 27104
910-917-0001

Hafele America Co.
3901 Cheyenne Drive,
Archdale, NC 27263
336-889-2322

Harris Communications, Inc.
15159 Technology Drive
Eden Prairie, MN 55344-2277
612-906-9144

Haworth, Inc.
One Haworth Center
Holland, MI 49423
800-344-2600

Haws Drinking Faucet
Company
PO Box 1999
Berkeley, CA 94710-1499
510-525-5801

Herman Miller, Inc.
Zeeland, MI 49464
616-654-8909

Hewi, Inc.
2851 Old Tree Drive
Lancaster, PA 17603
717-293-1313

Holtkötter International, Inc.
155 Hardman Avenue S
St. Paul, MN 55075
612-552-8776

The Hon Company
200 Oak Street
Muscatine, IA 52761
319-264-7080

Honeywell, Inc.
1985 Douglas Drive
Golden Valley, MN 55422
612-954-4574

Horton Automatics
4242 Baldwin Boulevard
Corpus Christi, TX 78405-3399
800-531-3111

Howe Furniture Corp.
12 Cambridge Drive
Trumbull, CT 06611-0386
800-888-4693

Hunter Douglas Window
Fashions
2 Park Way
Upper Saddle River, NJ 07458
800-444-8844

Infogrip, Inc.
1141 East Main Street
Ventura, CA 93001
805-652-0770

In-Sink-Erator
Division of Emerson Electric Co.
4700 21st Street
Racine, WI 53406-5093
414-554-5432

International Cushioned
Products, Inc.
8360 Bridgeport Road #202
Richmond, British Columbia,
Canada V6X 3C7
604-244-7638

The Ironmonger, Inc.
122 West Illinois Street
Chicago, IL 60610-4506
312-527-4800

J. Piercey Studios, Inc.
1714 Acme Street
Orlando, FL 32805
407-841-7594

J.C. Penney Co., Inc.
PO Box 10001
Dallas, TX 75301
972-431-1000

Jack Cartwright, Inc.
PO Box 2798
High Point, NC 27261
910-889-9400

JBliss Imaging Systems
650 Saratoga Avenue
San Jose, CA 95129
408-246-5783

JCDecaux USA
212-604-9160

Jenn-Air
403 West 4th Street N
Newton, IA 50208
800-JENN-AIR

Joerns Healthcare, Inc.
5001 Joerns Drive
Stevens Point, WI 54481
800-826-0270

Johnsonite
16910 Munn Road
Chagrin Falls, OH 44023
800-899-8916

Julius Blum, Inc.
Stanley, NC 28164
800-438-6788

Kimball Office Group
1155 West 12th Avenue
Jasper, IN 47549
800-482-1616

Kindred Industries
1000 Kindred Road
Midland, Ontario, Canada
800-456-5586

King Products, Inc.
195 The West Mall
Suite 915
Etobicoke, Ontario, Canada
M9C 5KI
416-620-1230

KitchenAid
2000 M-63 North MD #4302
Benton Harbor, MI 49022
616-923-5000

Knickerbocker Partition Corp.
193 Hanse Avenue
Freeport, NY 11520
516-546-0550

Kohler Co.
444 Highland Drive
Kohler, WI 53044
920-457-4441

KraftMaid Cabinetry, Inc.
PO Box 1055
Middlefield, OH 44062
800-571-1990 (consumer);
440-632-5333 (trade)

Krueger International
1330 Bellevue Street
Green Bay, WI 54308-8100
920-468-8100

Lee Rowan
900 South Highway Drive
Fenton, MO 63026
800-325-6150

Lernout & Hauspie
20 Mall Road
Burlington, MA 01803
617-238-0960

Leviton Manufacturing Co.
59-25 Little Neck Parkway
Little Neck, NY 11362-2591
800-323-8920

Lifespec Cabinet Systems, Inc.
100 Lifespec Drive
Oxford, MS 38655
601-234-0330

The Lighthouse, Inc.
111 East 59th Street
New York, NY 10022-1202
212-821-9556

Ligne Roset USA
200 Lexington Avenue
Suite 601
New York, NY 10016
212-685-2238

Loewenstein
1801 North Andrews Extension
Pompano Beach, FL 33061-6369
954-960-1100

Lumex
100 Spence Street
Bay Shore, NY 11706-2290
800-645-5272

Lutron Electronics Co., Inc.
7200 Suter Road
Coopersburg, PA 18036-1299
610-282-3800

Lux Steel Contract
P.O. Box 1085
Elkart, IN 46515-1085219-295-0229

Lyons Industries, Inc.
30000 M-62 West
Dowagiac, MI 49047
616-782-3404

Maddak, Inc.
6 Industrial Road
Pequannock, NJ 07440-1992
973-628-7600

The Maiman Company
3839 East Mustard Way
Springfield, MO 65803
800-641-4320
417-862-0681

Mat Factory, Inc.
760 West 16th Street
Building E
Costa Mesa, CA 92627
800-628-7626

Maxi Aids, Inc.
PO Box 3209
Farmingdale, NY 11735
516-752-0521

Maytag
403 West 4th Street
Newton, IA 50208
888-4MAYTAG

McGuire
1201 Bryant Street
San Francisco, CA 94103
415-626-1414

Metropolitan Furniture Corp.
1635 Rollins Road
Burlingame, CA 94010-2301
650-697-7900

The MoMA Design Store
44 West 53rd Street
New York, NY 10019
800-793-3167

Nichols Design Associates, Inc.
2016 Mt. Vernon Avenue
Suite 200
Alexandria, VA 22301
703-519-2198 tty

Nutone, Inc.
Madison and Red Bank Roads
Cincinnati, OH 45227
800-543-8687

Olsonite Corp.
25 Dart Road
Newnan, GA 30265
770-253-3930

Otto Bock Rehab
3000 Xenium Lane North
Minneapolis, MN 55441
800-328-4058

OXO International
230 Fifth Ave #1100
New York, NY 10001
212-213-0707

Palazzetti, Inc.
10-40 45th Avenue
Long Island City, NY 11101
718-937-1199

Pella Corp.
102 Main Street
Pella, IA 50219-2147
515-628-1000

Phillips Consumer
Communications
5 Wood Hollow Road 3H10
Parsippany, NJ 07054
888-582-3688

Pinecrest
2118 Blaisdell Avenue
Minneapolis, MN 55404
800-443-5357

Research Products Corp.
1015 East Washington Avenue
Madison, WI 53701-1467
608-257-8801
800-334-6011

Rev-A-Shelf, Inc.
2409 Plantside Drive
Louisville, KY 40299
502-499-5835

Robern, Inc.
7 Wood Avenue
Bristol, PA 19007
215-826-9800

Roppe Corporation
1602 N. Union Street
Fostoria, OH 44830-1158
800-537-9527

Rubbermaid, Inc.
1147 Akron Road
Wooster, OH 44691-6000
800-643-3490

Rutt Custom Cabinetry
1564 Main Street
Box 129
Goodville, PA 17528
800-240-7888

Senior Technologies
1620 North 20th
Lincoln, NE 68503
402-475-4002

Shaw Industries, Inc.
1000 South Harris Street
Dalton, GA 30722
706-275-1755

SICO North America, Inc.
7525 Cahill Road
Minneapolis, MN 55439
800-328-6138

SIS human factor
technologies, inc.
55C Harvey Road
Londonderry, NH 03053
603-432-4495

Sloan Valve Company
10500 Seymour Avenue
Franklin Park, IL 60131
847-671-4300

Smart Design, Inc.
137 Varick Street
8th Floor
New York, NY 10013
212-807-8150

Sub-Zero Freezer Co., Inc.
4717 Hammersley Road
Madison, WI 53711
800-222-7820

Summitville Tiles, Inc.
PO Box 73
Summitville, OH 43962
330-223-1511

Sunrise Medical
7477 East Dry Creek Parkway
Longmont, CO 80503
888-333-2572

Superior Millwork Ltd.
2502 Thayer Avenue
Saskatoon, Saskatchewan,
Canada 57L 5Y2
306-373-8588

Symmons Industries, Inc.
31 Brooks Drive
Braintree, MA 02184
800-SYMMONS

T.L. Shield & Associates, Inc.
PO Box 6845
Thousand Oaks, CA 91359-6845
818-509-8228

Talking Signs, Inc.
812 North Boulevard
Baton Rouge, LA 70802
504-344-2812

Tempo Industries, Inc.
2002A South Grand Avenue
Santa Ana, CA 92705
714-662-4860

Thomasville Furniture Industries
PO Box 339
Thomasville, NC 27360
910-472-4000

Thonet Industries, Inc.
403 Meacham Road
Statesville, NC 28677
704-878-2222

Tielsa
IZ-NO-Sud, Strasse 3,
Obj. 41, A-2355
Wiener Neudorf, Austria
02236161 5 25

TOTO USA
1155 Southern Road
Morrow, GA 30260
770-282-8686

Truth Hardware
700 West Bridge Street
Owatonna, MN 55060
800-866-7884

Tub-Master, LC
413 Virginia Drive
Orlando, FL 32803
407-898-2881

Ultratec
450 Science Drive
Madison, WI 53711
800-482-2424

United Chair Company
114 Churchill Avenue
Leeds, AL 35094
205-699-5181

Universal Furniture
2226 Uwharrie Road
High Point, NC 27263
910-861-7200

Visible Interactive
1000 Sansome Street
Suite 375
San Francisco, CA 94111
415-433-7781

Walker Equipment
4009 Cloud Springs Road
Ringgold, GA 30736
800-HANDSET (426-3738)

Whirlpool Corp.
2000 M-63
Benton Harbor, MI 49022
800-446-0724

White Home Products
PO Box 2656
Union, NJ 07803
800-200-9272

Winona Manufacturing, Inc.
24 Laird Street
Winona, MN 55987
507-454-3511

Wm. Ohs Showrooms, Inc.
115 Madison Street
Denver, CO 80206
303-321-3232

Workstations, Inc.
11 Silver Street
South Hadley, MA 01075
413-535-3340

York Wallcoverings Inc.
750 Linden Avenue
York, PA 17404
717-846-4456

Zygo Industries
PO Box 1008
Portland, OR 97207-1008
503-684-6006

Anderson Design, Inc.
175 New Britain Avenue
Plainville, CT 06062
860-747-0707

Anmahian Winton Associates
192 South Street
Boston, MA 02111
617-426-3639

Arthur M. Sackler Gallery
Smithsonian Institution, 1050
Independence Avenue SW
Washington, DC 20560
202-357-4880

BFE Architecture, P.A.
410 Oberlin Road
Suite 400
Raleigh, NC 27605
919-839-6380

Carolyn Latteier
1641 Hastings Avenue W
Port Townsend, WA 98368
360-385-0058

Coco Raynes Associates, Inc.
569 Boylston Street
Boston, MA 02116
617-536-5777

Dana K. Stockwell
U.S. Army Corps of Engineers
John H. Kerr Reservoir
1930 Mays Chapel Road
Boydton, VA 23917-9725
804-738-6143

Evan Terry Associates, P.C.
One Perimeter Park South,
Suite 200
Birmingham, AL 35243
205-972-9101

Gail Finkel, M. Architecture
205-270 Roslyn Road
Winnipeg, Manitoba, Canada R3L 0H3
204-453-1294

Guynes Design, Inc.
305 West Granada
Phoenix, AZ 85003
800-264-0390

Hilderman Thomas Frank Cram, Landscape
Architecture
500-115 Bannatyne Avenue E
Winnipeg, Manitoba, Canada R3B 0R3
204-944-9907

HKS Architects
700 North Pearl Street
Suite 1100
Dallas, TX 75201
214-969-5599

HOK Sport
323 West 8th Street
Suite 700
Kansas City, MO 64105
816-221-1576

Jack Bowersox, AIA,
O'Keefe Architects
2424 Curlew Road
Palm Harbor, FL 34683
813-781-5885

Kids' Studio
8342 West 4th Street
Los Angeles, CA 90048
213-655-4028

Moore Iacofano Goltsman (MIG)
800 Hearst Avenue Berkeley, CA 94710
510-845-7549

National Air and Space Museum
Smithsonian Institution, 1050
Independence Avenue SW
Washington, DC 20560
202-357-1552

Nichols Design Associates, Inc.
2016 Mt. Vernon Avenue
Suite 200
Alexandria, VA 22301
703-519-2198
voice/tty/fax

*For current information, see www.evanterry.com.

One Particular Harbor
c/o Frank Colgan
75 Fonthill Park
Rochester, NY 14618-1034
716-271-1577

Pamela Pflueger & Associates
3800 North Central Avenue
Suite 1120
Phoenix, AZ 85012
602-266-4785

Polshek & Partners Architects
320 West 13th Street
New York, NY 10014
212-807-7171

Richard Gibbs
1300 Federal Boulevard
Carteret, NJ 08831
732-249-3339

Sekisui House, Ltd.
Tower East, Umeda Sky Building
1-88, Oyodonaka 1-Chome
Kita-ku, Osaka, Japan 531
011 81 6-440-3268

Shepley Bulfinch Richardson and Abbott (SBRA)
40 Broad Street Boston, MA
617-423-1700

Smith Carter Architects and Engineers 1601 Buffalo
Place
Winnipeg, Manitoba, Canada R3T 3K7
204-477-1260

Susan Behar, ASID
1732 Hickory Gate Drive N
Dunedin, FL 33528
813-784-0261

The Center for Universal Design
North Carolina State University
School of Design
PO Box 8613
Raleigh, NC 27695-8613
919-515-3082

Universal Designers & Consultants, Inc.
6 Grant Avenue
Takoma Park, MD 20912-4324
301-270-2470

Whitehouse & Company
18 East 16th Street
New York, NY 10003
212-206-1080

# INDEX